ML.
p 190
cref

The Benchley Roundup

A Selection by

NATHANIEL
BENCHLEY

of his favorites

Drawings by

GLUYAS
WILLIAMS

HARPER & BROTHERS   *PUBLISHERS*   NEW YORK

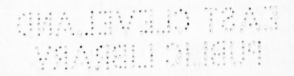

Library of Congress catalog card number: 54-8937

Contents

Foreword ix

"Take the Witness!" 1

How to Get Things Done 5

The Social Life of the Newt 11

Football Rules or Whatever They Are 16

The Tortures of Week-End Visiting 20

From Nine to Five 26

Shakespeare Explained 33

Christmas Afternoon 36

Family Life in America 41

Do Insects Think? 44

The Stranger Within Our Gates 46

Opera Synopses 51

Malignant Mirrors 57

How to Understand International Finance 59

Kiddie-Kar Travel 61

Uncle Edith's Ghost Story 67

French for Americans 71

Is This the Missing Link? 76

The Mystery of the Poisoned Kipper 79

"Ask That Man" 83

Editha's Christmas Burglar 87

What Does It Mean? 92

A Talk to Young Men 94

Paul Revere's Ride 98

Throwing Back the European Offensive 103

More Songs for Meller 108

Compiling an American Tragedy 111

v

Inter-office Memo   114
Fascinating Crimes   121
Back to the Game   124
The Typical New Yorker   130
Carnival Week in Sunny Las Los   138
Another Uncle Edith Christmas Story   143
If These Old Walls Could Talk!   149
Happy Childhood Tales   152
The Sunday Menace   155
Can We Believe Our Eyes?   160
The King's English: Not Murder but Suicide   164
"One Minute, Please!"   169
Looking Shakespeare Over   174
How I Create   178
First—Catch Your Criminal   183
The Noon Telephone Operator   187
Fall In!   190
"Could You Tell Me . . . ?"   194
The Wreck of the Sunday Paper   198
What—No Budapest?   201
Mind's Eye Trouble   204
How to Understand Music   210
The King and the Old Man   214
The Real Public Enemies   217
Matinees—Wednesdays and Saturdays   222
The Chinese Situation   227
Saturday's Smells   230
Route Nationale 14   233
Naming Our Flowers   239
Johnny-on-the-Spot   241
Down with Pigeons   244
Contributors to This Issue   249
No Pullmans, Please!   251
Mysteries from the Sky   253
Isn't It Remarkable?   255

Do Dreams Go by Opposites?	257
News from Home	259
The Children's Hour	262
Back to Mozart	264
Spy Scares	266
Artist's Model Succumbs!	268
Ladies Wild	270
Cocktail Hour	275
Why We Laugh—or Do We?	277
Weather Records	281
Home Made Jokes	283
Men of Harlech!	285
Summer Shirtings	289
Word Torture	292
"I Know of It"	294
The Card	296
How Long Can You Live?	299
My Face	301
Easy Tests	305
Encore	307
Hey, Waiter!	309
Sporting Life in America	314
Why I Am Pale	319
Whoa!	322
The Menace of Buttered Toast	323
Do I Hear Twenty Thousand?	326

Foreword

ONE time, during the recent war, an Air Force sergeant accosted Robert Benchley in a bar and, with little or no preamble, said, "I might as well tell you that I don't like your work." Benchley replied that he had moments of doubt himself, and the sergeant then explained that he had hitched a ride from Africa to Italy on a cargo plane, and that the only available sleeping space had been on bags that were full of overseas editions of Benchley's books. By the time they passed Sicily, the man said, he was so stiff and sore that he hoped never to hear the name Benchley again. "Try it yourself sometime," he concluded. "That stuff isn't funny when you have to sleep on it."

In somewhat the same way, I would suggest that *The Benchley Roundup* be read piecemeal rather than in one lump—picked up and put down as though you were waiting for a telephone call, or for guests to arrive—because, after all, the pieces had their original appeal as separate entities. In making my selection from about a thousand previously published pieces, I read in fits and starts over a long period of time.

Many people have tried to analyze Robert Benchley's particular form of humor, and I would be the last one to add my tiny voice to that of the throng, because I don't think it can be analyzed. It is sometimes mad, sometimes penetrating, and sometimes based on nothing more than word associations, and the only generalization that can be made with any degree of certainty is that it is different— or, if you will, unique.

So let's just leave it that the humorous pieces collected here, written between 1915 and 1945, are those which seem to stand up best over the years. There were some that were much admired when they first appeared, but were based on premises that now seem a little soft; others were glorious in part but evaporated when taken as a whole; and all these have been left out in an attempt to select the most durable. Another compiler might have picked an entirely different group, but that would have been his worry. These are the ones that I like best, and beyond that there isn't much more I ought to say.

—NATHANIEL BENCHLEY

The Benchley Roundup

"Take the Witness!"

NEWSPAPER accounts of trial cross-examinations always bring out the cleverest in me. They induce day dreams in which I am the witness on the stand, and if you don't know some of my imaginary comebacks to an imaginary cross-examiner (Doe vs. Benchley: 482-U.S.-367-398), you have missed some of the most stimulating reading in the history of American jurisprudence.

These little reveries usually take place shortly after I have read the transcript of a trial, while I am on a long taxi ride or seated at a desk with plenty of other work to do. I like them best when I have work to do, as they deplete me mentally so that I am forced to go and lie down after a particularly sharp verbal rally. The knowledge that I have completely floored my adversary, and the imaginary congratulations of my friends (also imaginary), seem more worthwhile than any amount of fiddling work done.

During these cross-questionings I am always very calm. Calm in a nice way, that is—never cocky. However frantic my inquisitor may wax (and you should see his face at times—it's purple!), I just sit there, burning him up with each answer, winning the admiration of the courtroom, and, at times, even a smile from the judge himself. At the end of my examination, the judge is crazy about me.

Just what the trial is about, I never get quite clear in my mind. Sometimes the subject changes in the middle of the questioning, to allow for the insertion of an especially good crack on my part. I don't think that I am ever actually the defendant, although I don't know why I should feel that I am immune from trial by a jury of my peers—if such exist.

I am usually testifying in behalf of a friend, or perhaps as just an

1

impersonal witness for someone whom I do not know, who, naturally, later becomes my friend for life. It is Justice that I am after—
Justice and a few well-spotted laughs.

Let us whip right into the middle of my cross-examination, as I
naturally wouldn't want to pull my stuff until I had been insulted by
the lawyer, and you can't really get insulted simply by having your
name and address asked. I am absolutely fair about these things.
If the lawyer will treat me right, I'll treat him right. He has got

I just sit there, burning him up with each answer

to start it. For a decent cross-examiner, there is no more tractable
witness in the world than I am.

Advancing toward me, with a sneer on his face, he points a finger
at me. (I have sometimes thought of pointing my finger back at
him, but have discarded that as being too fresh. I don't have to resort
to clowning.)

Q—You think you're pretty funny, don't you? (*I have evidently
just made some mildly humorous comeback, nothing smart-
alecky, but good enough to make him look silly.*)

A—I have never given the matter much thought.

Q—Oh, you haven't given the matter much thought, eh? Well, you seem to be treating this examination as if it were a minstrel show.

A (*very quietly and nicely*)—I have merely been taking my cue from your questions. (*You will notice that all this presupposes quite a barrage of silly questions on his part, and pat answers on mine, omitted here because I haven't thought them up. At any rate, it is evident that I have already got him on the run before this reverie begins.*)

Q—Perhaps you would rather that I conducted this inquiry in baby talk?

A—If it will make it any easier for you. (*Pandemonium, which the Court feels that it has to quell, although enjoying it obviously as much as the spectators.*)

Q (*furious*)—I see. Well, here is a question that I think will be simple to elicit an honest answer: Just how did you happen to know that it was eleven-fifteen when you saw the defendant?

A—Because I looked at my watch.

Q—And just why did you look at your watch at this particular time?

A—To see what time it was.

Q—Are you accustomed to looking at your watch often?

A—That is one of the uses to which I often put my watch.

Q—I see. Now, it couldn't, by any chance, have been ten-fifteen instead of eleven-fifteen when you looked at your watch this time, could it?

A—Yes, sir. It could.

Q—Oh, it *could* have been ten-fifteen?

A—Yes, sir—if I had been in Chicago. (*Not very good, really. I'll work up something better. I move to have that answer stricken from the record.*)

When I feel myself lowering my standards by answering like that, I usually give myself a rest, and, unless something else awfully good pops into my head, I adjourn the court until next day. I can always convene it again when I hit my stride.

If possible, however, I like to drag it out until I have really given my antagonist a big final wallop which practically curls him up on the floor (I may think of one before this goes to press), and, wiping his forehead, he mutters, "Take the witness!"

As I step down from the stand, fresh as a daisy, there is a round of applause which the Court makes no attempt to silence. In fact, I have known certain judges to wink pleasantly at me as I take my seat. Judges are only human, after all.

My only fear is that, if I ever really am called upon to testify in court, I won't be asked the right questions. That *would* be a pretty kettle of fish!

How to Get Things Done

A GREAT many people have come up to me and asked me how I manage to get so much work done and still keep looking so dissipated. My answer is "Don't you wish you knew?" and a pretty good answer it is, too, when you consider that nine times out of ten I didn't hear the original question.

But the fact remains that hundreds of thousands of people throughout the country are wondering how I have time to do all my painting, engineering, writing and philanthropic work when, according to the rotogravure sections and society notes I spend all my time riding to hounds, going to fancy-dress balls disguised as Louis XIV or spelling out GREETINGS TO CALIFORNIA in formation with three thousand Los Angeles school children. "All work and all play," they say.

The secret of my incredible energy and efficiency in getting work done is a simple one. I have based it very deliberately on a well-known psychological principle and have refined it so that it is now almost *too* refined. I shall have to begin coarsening it up again pretty soon.

The psychological principle is this: anyone can do any amount of work, provided it isn't the work he is *supposed* to be doing at that moment.

Let us see how this works out in practice. Let us say that I have five things which have to be done before the end of the week: (1) a basketful of letters to be answered, some of them dating from October, 1928, (2) some bookshelves to be put up and arranged with books (3) a hair-cut to get (4) a pile of scientific magazines to go through and clip (I am collecting all references to tropical

fish that I can find, with the idea of some day buying myself one)
and (5) an article to write for this paper.

Now. With these five tasks staring me in the face on Monday
morning, it is little wonder that I go right back to bed as soon as
I have had breakfast, in order to store up health and strength for
the almost superhuman expenditure of energy that is to come.
Mens sana in corpore sano is my motto, and, not even to be funny,
am I going to make believe that I don't know what the Latin means.
I feel that the least that I can do is to treat my body right when it
has to supply fuel for an insatiable mind like mine.

As I lie in bed on Monday morning storing up strength, I make
out a schedule. "What do I have to do first?" I ask myself. Well,
those letters really should be answered and the pile of scientific
magazines should be clipped. And here is where my secret process
comes in. Instead of putting them first on the list of things which
have to be done, I put them last. I practice a little deception on
myself and say, "First you must write that article for the newspaper." I even say this out loud (being careful that nobody hears
me, otherwise they would *keep* me in bed) and try to fool myself
into really believing that I must do the article that day and that
the other things can wait. I sometimes go so far in this self-deception as to make out a list in pencil, with "No. 1. Newspaper article"
underlined in red. (The underlining in red is rather difficult, as
there is never a red pencil on the table beside the bed, unless I
have taken one to bed with me on Sunday night.)

Then, when everything is lined up, I bound out of bed and have
lunch. I find that a good, heavy lunch, with some sort of glutinous
dessert, is good preparation for the day's work as it keeps one from
getting nervous and excitable. We workers must keep cool and
calm, otherwise we would just throw away our time in jumping
about and fidgeting.

I then seat myself at my desk with my typewriter before me, and
sharpen five pencils. (The sharp pencils are for poking holes in
the desk-blotter, and a pencil has to be pretty sharp to do that. I
find that I can't get more than six holes out of one pencil.) Follow-

I push back my chair and start clipping

ing this I say to myself (again out loud, if it is practical), "Now, old man! Get at this article!"

Gradually the scheme begins to work. My eye catches the pile of magazines, which I have artfully placed on a nearby table beforehand. I write my name and address at the top of the sheet of paper in the typewriter and then sink back. The magazines being within reach (also part of the plot) I look to see if anyone is watching me and get one off the top of the pile. Hello, what's this! In the very first one is an article by Dr. William Beebe, illustrated by horrifying photographs! Pushing my chair away from my desk, I am soon hard at work clipping.

One of the interesting things about the *Argyopelius*, or "Silver Hatchet" fish, I find, is that it has eyes in its wrists. I would have been sufficiently surprised just to find out that a fish had wrists, but to learn that it has eyes in them is a discovery so astounding that I am hardly able to cut out the picture. What a lot one learns simply by thumbing through the illustrated weeklies! It is hard work, though, and many a weaker spirit would give it up half-done, but when there is something else of "more importance" to be finished (you see, I still keep up the deception, letting myself go on thinking that the newspaper article is of more importance) no work is too hard or too onerous to keep one busy.

Thus, before the afternoon is half over, I have gone through the scientific magazines and have a neat pile of clippings (including one of a Viper Fish which I wish you could see. You would die laughing). Then it is back to the grind of the newspaper article.

This time I get as far as the title, which I write down with considerable satisfaction until I find that I have misspelled one word terribly, so that the whole sheet of paper has to come out and a fresh one be inserted. As I am doing this, my eye catches the basket of letters.

Now, if there is one thing that I hate to do (and there is, you may be sure) it is to write letters. But somehow, with the magazine article before me waiting to be done, I am seized with an epistolary fervor that amounts to a craving, and I slyly sneak the first of the unanswered letters out of the basket. I figure out in my mind that I will get more into the swing of writing the article if I practice a little on a few letters. This first one, anyway, I really must answer. True, it is from a friend in Antwerp asking me to look him up when I am in Europe in the summer of 1929, so he can't actually be watching the incoming boats for an answer, but I owe something to politeness after all. So instead of putting a fresh sheet of copy-paper into the typewriter, I slip in one of my handsome bits of personal stationery and dash off a note to my friend in Antwerp. Then, being well in the letter-writing mood, I clean up the entire batch. I feel a little guilty about the article, but the pile of freshly stamped envelopes and the neat bundle of clippings on tropical fish do much to salve my conscience. Tomorrow I will do the article, and no fooling this time, either.

When tomorrow comes I am up with one of the older and more sluggish larks. A fresh sheet of copy-paper in the machine, and my name and address neatly printed at the top, and all before eleven A.M.! "A human dynamo" is the name I think up for myself. I have decided to write something about snake-charming and am already more than satisfied with the title "These Snake-Charming People." But, in order to write about snake-charming, one has to know a little about its history, and where should one go to find history but to a book? Maybe in that pile of books in the corner is one on snake-charming! Nobody could point the finger of scorn at me if I went over to those books for the avowed purpose of re-search work for the matter at hand. No writer could be supposed to carry all that information in his head.

So, with a perfectly clear conscience, I leave my desk for a few minutes and begin glancing over the titles of the books. Of course, it is difficult to find any book, much less one on snake-charming, in a pile which has been standing in the corner for weeks. What really is needed is for them to be on a shelf where their titles will be visible at a glance. And there is the shelf, standing beside the pile of books! It seems almost like a divine command written in the sky: "If you want to finish that article, first put up the shelf and arrange the books on it!" Nothing could be clearer or more logical.

In order to put up the shelf, the laws of physics have decreed that there must be nails, a hammer and some sort of brackets to hold it up on the wall. You can't just wet a shelf with your tongue and stick it up. And, as there are no nails or brackets in the house (or, if there are, they are probably hidden somewhere) the next thing to do is put on my hat and go out to buy them. Much as it disturbs me to put off the actual start of the article, I feel that I am doing only what is in the line of duty to put on my hat and go out to buy nails and brackets. And, as I put on my hat, I realize to my chagrin that I need a hair-cut badly. I can kill two birds with one stone, or at least with two, and stop in at the barber's on the way back. I will feel all the more like writing after a turn in the fresh air. Any doctor would tell me that.

So in a few hours I return, spick and span and smelling of lilac, bearing nails, brackets, the evening papers and some crackers and peanut butter. Then it's ho! for a quick snack and a glance through the evening papers (there might be something in them which would alter what I was going to write about snake-charming) and in no time at all the shelf is up, slightly crooked but up, and the books are arranged in a neat row in alphabetical order and all ready for almost instantaneous reference. There does not happen to be one on snake-charming among them, but there is a very interesting one containing some Hogarth prints and one which will bear even closer inspection dealing with the growth of the Motion Picture, illustrated with "stills" from famous productions. A really remarkable industry, the motion pictures. I might want to write an article on it sometime. Not today, probably, for it is six o'clock and there is still the one on snake-charming to finish up first. To-morrow morning sharp! Yes, *sir!*

And so, you see, in two days I have done four of the things I had to do, simply by making believe that it was the fifth that I *must* do. And the next day, I fix up something else, like taking down the bookshelf and putting it somewhere else, that I *have* to do, and then I get the fifth one done.

The only trouble is that, at this rate, I will soon run out of things to do, and will be forced to get at that newspaper article the first thing Monday morning.

The Social Life of the Newt

IT IS not generally known that the newt, although one of the smallest of our North American animals, has an extremely happy home life. It is just one of those facts which never get bruited about.

I first became interested in the social phenomena of newt life early in the spring of 1913, shortly after I had finished my researches in sexual differentiation among ameba. Since that time I have practically lived among newts, jotting down observations, making lan-

Since that time I have practically lived among the newts

tern-slides, watching them in their work and in their play (and you may rest assured that the little rogues have their play—as who does not?) until, from much lying in a research posture on my stomach, over the inclosure in which they were confined, I found myself developing what I feared might be rudimentary creepers. And so, late this autumn, I stood erect and walked into my house, where I immediately set about the compilation of the notes I had made.

So much for the non-technical introduction. The remainder of this article bids fair to be pretty scientific.

In studying the more intimate phases of newt life, one is chiefly impressed with the methods by means of which the males force their attentions upon the females, with matrimony as an object. For the newt is, after all, only a newt, and has his weaknesses just as any of the rest of us. And I, for one, would not have it different. There is little enough fun in the world as it is.

The peculiar thing about a newt's courtship is its restraint. It is carried on, at all times, with a minimum distance of fifty paces (newt measure) between the male and the female. Some of the bolder males may now and then attempt to overstep the bounds of good sportsmanship and crowd in to forty-five paces, but such tactics are frowned upon by the Rules Committee. To the eye of an uninitiated observer, the pair might be dancing a few of the more open figures of the minuet.

The means employed by the males to draw the attention and win the affection of those of the opposite sex (females) are varied and extremely strategic. Until the valuable researches by Strudle-hoff in 1887 (in his *"Entwickelungsmechanik"*) no one had been able to ascertain just what it was that the male newt did to make the female see anything in him worth throwing herself away on. It had been observed that the most personally unattractive newt could advance to within fifty paces of a female of his acquaintance and, by some *coup d'œil*, bring her to a point where she would, in no uncertain terms, indicate her willingness to go through with the marriage ceremony at an early date.

It was Strudlehoff who discovered, after watching several thousand courting newts under a magnifying lens (questionable taste on his part, without doubt, but all is fair in pathological love) that the male, during the courting season (the season opens on the tenth of March and extends through the following February, leaving about ten days for general overhauling and redecorating), gives forth a strange, phosphorescent glow from the center of his highly colored dorsal crest, somewhat similar in effect to the flash of a diamond scarf-pin in a red necktie. This glow, according to Strudle-hoff, so fascinates the female with its air of elegance and indication of wealth, that she immediately falls a victim to its lure.

But the little creature, true to her sex-instinct, does not at once give evidence that her morale has been shattered. She affects a coyness and lack of interest, by hitching herself sideways along the bottom of the aquarium, with her head turned over her right shoulder away from the swain. A trained ear might even detect her whistling in an indifferent manner.

The male, in the meantime, is flashing his gleamer frantically two blocks away and is performing all sorts of attractive feats, calculated to bring the lady newt to terms. I have seen a male, in the stress of his handicap courtship, stand on his forefeet, gesticulating in amorous fashion with his hind feet in the air. Franz Ingehalt, in his *Über Weltschmerz des Newt*, recounts having observed a distinct and deliberate undulation of the body, beginning with the shoulders and ending at the filament of the tail, which might well have been the origin of what is known today in scientific circles as "the shimmy." The object seems to be the same, except that in the case of the newt, it is the male who is the active agent.

In order to test the power of observation in the male during these maneuvers, I carefully removed the female, for whose benefit he was undulating, and put in her place, in slow succession, another (but less charming) female, a paper-weight of bronze shaped like a newt, and, finally, a common rubber eraser. From the distance at which the courtship was being carried on, the male (who was, it must be admitted, a bit near-sighted congenitally) was unable to detect the change in personnel, and continued, even in the presence of the rubber eraser, to gyrate and undulate in a most conscientious manner, still under the impression that he was making a conquest.

At last, worn out by his exertions, and disgusted at the meagerness of the reaction on the eraser, he gave a low cry of rage and despair and staggered to a nearby pan containing barley-water, from which he proceeded to drink himself into a gross stupor.

Thus, little creature, did your romance end, and who shall say that its ending was one whit less tragic than that of Camille? Not I, for one. . . . In fact, the two cases are not at all analogous.

And now that we have seen how wonderfully Nature works in the fulfilment of her laws, even among her tiniest creatures, let us study for a minute a cross-section of the community life of the newt. It is a life full of all kinds of exciting adventure, from weaving nests to crawling about in the sun and catching insect larvæ and crustaceans. The newt's day is practically never done, largely because the insect larvæ multiply three million times as fast as the newt can possibly catch and eat them. And it takes the closest kind of community teamwork in the newt colony to get things anywhere near cleaned up by nightfall.

It is early morning, and the workers are just appearing hurrying to the old log which is to be the scene of their labors. What a scampering! What a bustle! Ah, little scamperers! Ah, little bustlers! How lucky you are, and how wise! You work long hours, without pay, for the sheer love of working. An ideal existence, I'll tell the scientific world.

Over here on the right of the log are the Master Draggers. Of all the newt workers, they are the most futile, which is high praise indeed. Come, let us look closer and see what it is that they are doing.

The one in the lead is dragging a bit of gurry out from the water and up over the edge into the sunlight. Following him in single file, come the rest of the Master Draggers. They are not dragging anything, but are sort of helping the leader by crowding against him and eating little pieces out of the filament of his tail.

And now they have reached the top. The leader, by dint of much leg-work, has succeeded in dragging his prize to the ridge of the log.

The little workers, reaching the goal with their precious freight, are now giving it over to the Master Pushers, who have been waiting for them in the sun all this while. The Master Pushers' work is soon accomplished, for it consists simply in pushing the piece of gurry over the other side of the log until it falls with a splash into the water, where it is lost.

This part of their day's task finished, the tiny toilers rest, clustered together in a group, waving their heads about from side to side, as who should say, "There—that's done!" And so it *is* done, my little Master Draggers and my little Master Pushers, and *well* done, too. Would that my own work were as clean-cut and as satisfying.

And so it goes. Day in and day out, the busy army of newts go on making the world a better place in which to live. They have their little trials and tragedies, it is true, but they also have their fun, as any one can tell by looking at a logful of sleeping newts on a hot summer day.

And, after all, what more has life to offer?

Football Rules or Whatever They Are

HOW many of my little readers remember the day when a perfectly ordinary citizen could watch a football game and know what was going on? Rather than wait for an answer to this question, which would have to be obtained by a post-card ballot and might take months, I will make a stab at the answer and venture to say that it is only the older boys who remember. For during the last ten years the Football Rules Committee has seen to it that no one who understood the game the year before should understand it this year. The motto of the Rules Committee seems to have been: "New rules and new rooters each year."

In the old days, when they changed the rules maybe once every ten years, watching football was something of a pastime. You took your seat in the stands and, provided you knew anything at all about the game, you followed the plays as they were executed and knew at least which side had the ball and what their general line of attack was. Oftentimes you knew enough about the game to yell suggestions to the quarterback or to tell the man next to you where the boys would have done well to try rushing on the third down. (If you did do this, however, you are not alive today—not if the man next you was I.)

It wasn't so bad when they began tampering with the number of downs to go to ten yards in. It was confusing at first, but they let you alone and didn't try to rattle you by changing it again the next year, and before long you got to liking the four downs to ten yards better than the old way. I sometimes wonder how we ever got along with the old way, but I suppose it was all right for that period, what with gas lights and everything. But I certainly should resent any move to go back to the old number of downs, although, for all I know now, they *have* gone back to them. The spectator would never know.

For after the war the Rules Committee began to get jittery. They acted as if they thought somebody was following them. First they would put on a beard, then they would take it off and walk on their hands, then they would duck around a corner and then appear walking very tall. They changed rules every season as if they were trying to work up a new game out of football and make it into something they didn't quite know about. They made illegal all the old plays that used to be the essence of the game and sat up nights trying to think up new things to put in their places. It has got so now that the Rules Committee itself is about the only body of men who know enough about the game to play it, and they haven't anybody to play it with.

The freshman teams, or better the prep-school teams, who learn the game for the first time each year, have the drop on veterans, for they don't have to forget anything that they learned the year before. A senior, who has been taught all his life to pick up a fumble and run with it, suddenly finds that he can't do this, but must, when an opponent drops the ball, place his right hand to his mouth and call out "Co-e-e-e!" until a substitute quarter runs out from the side lines and shoots the ball with a revolver. This naturally confuses the senior. What it does to the spectators in the stands can be judged by the way they instinctively jump up and yell "Fumble!" only to sink back a second later and go back to reading the program.

All that the spectator gets out of a game now is the fresh air, the comical articles in his program, the sight of twenty-two young men rushing about in mysterious formations, and whatever he brought along in his flask. The murmur which you hear running through the stands after each play is caused by people asking other people what the idea of that was and other people trying to explain.

The thing to do is to change the rules for good and all this winter and then let us take a couple of years to learn them. It is this dribbling along, a couple of changes this year and a couple more next, which is driving us old boys crazy. I would suggest the following outline of rule revisions for the year 1931 along the lines of the changes to date, this revision to stand for ten years or until the game has been discontinued entirely.

Early Season Rules

(September 22 to October 6)

1. Only the quarterback shall be allowed to carry the ball and he shall run only when there is nobody after him. At other times he shall walk, dribbling the ball as in basket ball. He must keep whistling at all times.

2. A touchdown shall be considered made when the quarterback has placed the ball on the 55-yard line, with each team lined up on its own goal line. As soon as the quarterback shall have made a touchdown thus, he shall call out "Come out, come out, wherever you are, or else I'll catch you standing still!" At this signal both teams shall run very fast and try to get to the opposite goal line without being tagged. A penalty of 10 points shall be accorded to the team making the touchdown.

3. A fumble shall count four points for the side making it, except in the following instances: (1) when made by a right guard (2) when made by a man in a white head guard (3) when made by a player who shall have first signalled to the referee indicating that he is about to fumble (4) when made by a professor who has got onto the field by mistake and can't find his way out.

Mid-Season Rules

(October 13 to November 3)

1. Only a left tackle shall be allowed to carry the ball, and he shall not weigh more than 190 pounds (with the ball). He need not whistle.

2. A touchdown shall be considered made when the left tackle shall have tossed the ball into a basket held on the 30-yard side

line by an assistant manager, who shall run to the coach with it and say: "Look! A ball in the basket!" A touchdown thus made shall count seven points, providing nine rahs are given.

3. When the ball is fumbled, nobody shall pay any attention to it at all, but another ball shall be brought out and put into play on the 10-yard line. If the old ball rolls into a pocket (there shall be four pockets dug into the field 20 yards apart on the side-lines) it counts 10 if it be in a 20-pocket, 20 if in a 10-pocket and 100 if in either of the booby-pockets.

Late-Season Rules

(November 10 to November 30)

1. Nobody at all shall be allowed to touch the ball with his hands, but it shall be kicked along with the right side of the ankle of the right foot. Any player may kick it but he must run to the referee and hold up two fingers, saying "Kick, sir?" The referee shall answer "Please do."

2. There shall be no touchdowns, as such, and no scoring, as such. The side winning the game shall be the one which can prove that it has had the most exercise. After all, the game should be played for the game's sake, not to score points.

3. All spectators shall be blindfolded and made to sit with their backs to the field so that none shall peek. This will do away with overemphasis on football in college life and prevent the game from becoming a gigantic spectacle. It will also do away with graduate-domination. It may even do away with the graduates. The money hitherto furnished by the graduates can be made up by the sale of banners and arm bands to residents of the town in which the game is played.

With these new rules definitely in force, so that the spectators will know what to expect each year, they can make their own plans for Saturday afternoons during October and November.

And probably, at that, the stands will be crowded.

The Tortures of Week-End Visiting

THE present labor situation shows to what a pretty pass things may come because of a lack of understanding between the parties involved. I bring in the present labor situation just to give a touch of timeliness to this thing. Had I been writing for the Christmas number, I should have begun as follows: "The indiscriminate giving of Christmas presents shows to what a pretty pass things may come because of a lack of understanding between the parties involved."

The idea to be driven home is that things may come to a pretty pass by the parties involved in an affair of any kind if they do not come to an understanding before commencing operations.

I hope I have made my point clear. Especially is this true, (watch out carefully now, as the whole nub of the article will be coming along in just a minute), especially is this true in the relations between host and guest on week-end visits. (There, you have it! In fact, the title to this whole thing might very well be "The Need for a Clearer Definition of Relations between Host and Guest on Week-end Visits," and not be at all overstating it, at that.)

The logic of this will be apparent to anyone who has ever been a host or a guest at a week-end party, a classification embracing practically all Caucasians over eleven years of age who can put powder on the nose or tie a bow tie. Who has not wished that his host would come out frankly at the beginning of the visit and state, in no uncertain terms, the rules and preferences of the household in such matters as the breakfast hour? And who has not sounded his guest to find out what he likes in the regulation of his diet and *modus vivendi* (mode of living)? Collective bargaining on the part of labor unions and capital makes it possible for employers to know just what the workers think on matters of common interest. Is collective bargaining between host and guest so impossible, then?

Take, for example, the matter of arising in the morning. Of course, where there is a large house-party the problem is a simple one, for you can always hear the others pattering about and brushing their teeth. You can regulate your own arising by the number of people who seem to be astir. But if you are the only guest, there is apt to be a frightful misunderstanding.

"At what time is breakfast?" you ask.

"Oh, any old time on Sundays," replies the hostess with a generous gesture. "Sleep as late as you like. This is 'Liberty Hall.'"

The sentiment in this attitude is perfectly bully, but there is nothing that you can really take hold of in it. It satisfies at the time, but in the morning there is a vagueness about it that is simply terrifying.

Let us say that you awake at eight. You listen and hear no one stirring. Then, over on the cool pillow again until eight-twenty. Again up on the elbow, with head cocked on one side. There is a creak in the direction of the stairs. They may all be up and going down to breakfast! It is but the work of a moment to bound out of bed and listen at the door. Perhaps open it modestly and peer out. Deathlike silence, broken only, as the phrase goes, by the ticking of the hall clock, and not a soul in sight. Probably they are late sleepers. Maybe eleven o'clock is their Sunday rising hour. Some people *are* like that.

Shut the door and sit on the edge of the bed. More sleep is out of the question. Let's take a look at the pictures in the guest room, just to pass the time. Here's one of Lorna Doone. How d'e do, Lorna? Here's a group—taken in 1902—showing your host in evening clothes, holding a mandolin. Probably a member of his college musical club. Rather unkempt-looking bunch, you *must* say. Well, how about this one? An etching, showing suspicious-looking barges on what is probably the Thames. Fair enough, at that.

Back to the door and listen again. Tick-tock-tick-tock. Probably, if you started your tub, you'd wake the whole house. Let's sit down on the edge of the bed again.

Hello, here are some books on the table. *Fifty Famous Sonnets*, illustrated by Maxfield Parrish. Never touch a sonnet before breakfast. *My Experiences in the Alps*, by a woman mountain-climber who has written on the fly leaf "To my good friends the Elbridges, in memory of many happy days together at Chamounix. October, 1907." That settles *that*. *Essay on Compensation* in limp leather, by R. W. Emerson, published by Houghton, Mifflin & Co. Oh, very well! You suppose they thought that would be over your head, did they? Well, we'll just show them! We'll read it just for spite. Opening, to the red ribbon:

"Of the like nature is that expectation of change which instantly follows the suspension of our voluntary activity. The terror of cloudless noon—"

By the way, it must be nearly noon now! Ten minutes past nine, only! Well, the only thing to do is get dressed and go out and walk about the grounds. Eliminate the tub as too noisy. And so, very cautiously, almost clandestinely, you proceed to dress.

And now, just to reverse the process, suppose you are the host. You have arisen at eight and listened at the guest's door. No sound. Tiptoe back and get dressed, talking in whispers to your wife (the hostess) and cramming flannel bears into the infant's mouth to keep him from disturbing the sleeper.

"Bill looked tired last night. Better let him sleep a little longer," you suggest. And so, downstairs on your hands and knees, and look over the Sunday papers. Then a bracing walk on the porch, resulting in a terrific appetite.

A glance at the watch shows nine o'clock. Sunday breakfast is usually at eight-thirty. The warm aroma of coffee creeps in from the kitchen and, somewhere, *someone* is baking muffins. This is awful! You suppose it feels something like this to be caught on an ice floe without any food and so starve to death. Only there you can't smell coffee and muffins. You sneak into the dining room and steal one of the property oranges from the sideboard, but little Edgar sees you and sets up such a howl that you have to give it to him. The hostess suggests that your friend may have the sleeping sickness.

Weakened by hunger, you hotly resent this, and one word leads to another.

"Oh, very well, I'll go up and rout him out," you snarl.

Upstairs again, and poise, in listening attitude, just in front of the guest's door. Slowly the door opens, inch by inch, and, finally his head is edged cautiously out toward yours.

"Hello, Bill," you say flatly, "what are you getting up this time of the morning for? Thought I told you to sleep late."

"Morning, Ed," he says, equally flatly, "hope I haven't kept you all waiting." Then you both lie and eat breakfast.

Such a misunderstanding is apt to go to almost any length. I once knew of a man on a week-end visit who spent an entire Sunday in his room, listening at his door to see if the family were astir, while, in the meantime, the family were, one by one, tiptoeing to his door to see if they could detect any signs of life from him.

Each thought the other needed rest.

Along about three in the afternoon the family threw all hospitality aside and ate breakfast, deadening the sound of the cutlery as much as possible, little dreaming that their guest was looking through the "A Prayer for Each Day" calendar for the ninth time and seriously considering letting himself down from the window on a sheet and making for the next train. Shortly after dark persistent rumors got abroad that he had done away with himself, and everyone went up and sniffed for gas. It was only when the maid, who was not in on the secret, bolted into the room to turn down his bed for the night, that she found him tiptoeing about, packing and unpacking his bag and listening eagerly at the wall. (Now don't ask how it happened that the maid didn't know that his bed hadn't been made that morning. What difference does it make, anyway? It is such questions as *that* that blight any attempt at individual writing in this country.)

Don't think, just because I have taken all this space to deal with the rising-hour problem that there are no other points to be made. Oh, not at all. There is, for instance, the question of exercise. After dinner the host says to himself, "Something must be done. I wonder if he likes to walk." Aloud, he says, "Well, Bill, how about a little hike in the country?"

A hike in the country being the last thing in the world that Bill wants, he says, "Right-o! Anything you say." And so, although walking is a tremendous trial to the host, who has weak ankles, he bundles up with a great show of heartiness and grabs his stick as if this were the one thing he lived for.

After about a mile of hobbling along the country road the host says, hopefully, "Don't let me tire you out, old man. Any time you want to turn back, just say the word."

The guest, thinking longingly of the fireside, scoffs at the idea of turning back, insisting that if there is one thing in all the world that he likes better than walking it is running. So on they jog, hippity-hop, hippity-hop, each wishing that it would rain so that they could turn about and go home.

Here again the thing may go to almost tragic lengths. Suppose neither has the courage to suggest the return move. They might walk on into Canada, or they might become exhausted and have to be taken into a roadhouse and eat a "$2 old-fashioned Southern dinner of fried chicken and waffles." The imagination revolts at a further contemplation of the possibilities of this lack of co-operation between guest and host.

I once visited a man who had an outdoor swimming pool on his estate. (Consider that as very casually said.) It was in April, long before Spring had really understood what was expected of her. My first night there my host said, "Are you a morning plunger?"

Thinking that he referred to a tub plunge in a warm bathroom, I glowed and said, "You bet."

"I'll call for you at seven in the morning, then," he said, "and we'll go out to the pool."

It was evidently his morning custom and I wasn't going to have it said of me that a middle-aged man could outdo me in virility. So, at seven in the morning, in a dense fog (with now and then a slash of cold rain), we picked our way out to the pool and staged a vivid Siberian moving-picture scene, showing naked peasants bathing in the Nevsky. My visit lasted five days, and I afterward learned, from one to whom my host had confided, that it was the worst five days he had ever gone through, and that he has chronic joint trouble as a result of those plunges. "But I couldn't be outdone by a mere stripling," he said, "and the boy certainly enjoyed it."

All of this might have been avoided by the posting of a sign in a conspicuous place in my bedroom, reading as follows: "Personally, I dislike swimming in the pool at this time of the year. Guests wishing to do so may obtain towels at the desk." How very simple and practical!

The sign system is the only solution I can offer. It is crude and brutal, but it admits of no misunderstanding. A sign in each guest room, giving the hours of meals, political and religious preferences of the family, general views on exercise, etc., etc., with a blank for the guest to fill out, stating his own views on these subjects, would make it possible to visit (or entertain) with a sense of security thus far unknown upon our planet.

From Nine to Five

ONE of the necessary qualifications of an efficient businessman in these days of industrial literature seems to be the ability to write, in clear and idiomatic English, a thousand-word story on how efficient he is and how he got that way. A glance through any one of our more racy commercial magazines will serve nicely to illustrate my point, for it was after glancing through one of them only five minutes ago that the point suggested itself to me.

"What Is Making Our Business Grow"; "My $10,000 System of Carbon-Copy Hunting"; "Making the Turnover Turn In"; "If I Can Make My Pencil Sharpenings Work, Why Can't You?" "Getting Sales Out of Sahara," etc., are some of the intriguing titles which catch the eye of the student of world affairs as he thumbs over the business magazines on the newsstands before buying his newspaper. It seems as if the entire business world were devoting its working hours to the creation of a school of introspective literature.

But the trouble with these writers is that they are all successful. There is too much sameness to their stuff. They have their little troubles at first, it is true, such as lack of co-ordination in the central typing department, or congestion of office boys in the room where the water cooler is situated; but sooner or later you may be perfectly sure that Right will triumph and that the young salesman will bring in the order that puts the firm back on its feet again. They seem to have no imagination, these writers of business confessions. What the art needs is some Strindberg of Commerce to put down on paper the sordid facts of Life as they really are, and to show, in bitter words of cynical realism, that ink erasers are not always segregated or vouchers always all that they should be, and that, behind the happy exterior of many a mahogany railing, all is not so gosh-darned right with the world after all.

Now, without setting myself up as a Strindberg, I would like to start the ball rolling toward a more realistic school of business literature by setting down in my rough, impulsive way a few of the items in the account of "How We Make Our Business Lose $100,000 a Year."

All that I ask in the way of equipment is an illustration showing a square-jawed, clean-cut American businessman sitting at a desk and shaking his finger at another man, very obviously the head of the sales department because it says so under the picture, who is standing with his thumbs in the armholes of his waistcoat, gnawing at a big, black cigar, and looking out through the window at the smoke-stacks of the works. With this picture as a starter, and a chart or two, I can build up a very decent business story around them.

In the first place let me say that what we have done in our business any firm can do in theirs. It is not that we have any extraordinary talents along organization lines. We simply have taken the lessons learned in everyday trading, have tabulated them, and filed them in triplicate. Then we have forgotten them.

I can best give an idea of the secret of our mediocrity as a business organization by outlining a typical day in our offices. I do this in no spirit of boasting, but simply to show these thousands of sys-tematized businessmen who are devoting themselves to literature that somewhere in all this miasma of success there shines a ray of inefficiency, giving promise of the day that is to come.

The first part of the morning in our establishment is devoted to the mail. This starts the day off right, for it gives everyone some-thing to do, which is, I have found, a big factor in keeping the place looking busy.

Personally I am not what is known as a "snappy" dictator. It makes me nervous to have a stenographer sitting there waiting for me to say something so that she can pounce on it and tear it into hiero-glyphics. I feel that, mentally, she is checking me up with other men who have dictated to her, and that I am being placed in Class

5a, along with the licensed pilots and mental defectives, and the more I think of it the more incoherent I become. If exact and detailed notes were to be preserved of one of my dictated letters, mental processes, and all, they might read something like this:

"Good morning, Miss Kettle. . . . Take a letter, please . . . to the Nipco Drop Forge and Tool Company, Schenectady . . . S-c-h-e-c —er—well, Schenectady; you know how to spell that, I guess, Miss Kettle, ha! ha! . . . Nipco Drop Forge and Tool Company, Schenectady, New York. . . . Gentlemen—er (business of touching finger tips and looking at the ceiling meditatively)—Your favor of the 17th inst. at hand, and in reply would state that—er (I should have thought this letter out before beginning to dictate and decided just what it *is* that we desire to state in reply)—and in reply would state that—er . . . our Mr. Mellish reports that—er . . . where is that letter from Mr. Mellish, Miss Kettle? . . . The one about the castings. . . . Oh, never mind, I guess I can remember what he said. . . . Let's see, where were we? . . . Oh, yes, that our Mr. Mellish reports that he shaw the sipment—I mean *saw* the *shipment*—what's the matter with me? (this girl must think that I'm a perfect fool) . . . that he shaw the sipment in question on the platform of the station at Miller's Falls, and that it—er . . . ah . . . ooom . . . (I'll have this girl asleep in her chair in a minute. I'll bet that she goes and tells the other girls that she has just taken a letter from a man with the mind of an eight-year-old boy). . . . We could, therefore, comma . . . what's the matter? . . . Oh, I didn't finish that other sentence, I guess. . . . Let's see, how did it go? . . . Oh, yes . . . and that I, or rather *it*, was in good shape . . . er, cross that out, please (this girl is simply wasting her time here. I could spell this out with alphabet blocks quicker and let her copy it) . . . and that it was in excellent shape at that shape—er . . . or rather, at that *time* . . . er . . . period. New paragraph.

"We are, comma, therefore, comma, unable to . . . hello, Mr. Watterly, be right with you in half a second. . . . I'll finish this later, Miss Kettle . . . thank you."

When the mail is disposed of we have what is known as Memorandum Hour. During this period everyone sends memoranda to everyone else. If you happen to have nothing in particular about which to dictate a memorandum, you dictate a memorandum to someone, saying that you have nothing to suggest or report. This gives a stimulating exchange of ideas, and also helps to use up the blue memorandum blanks which have been printed at some expense for just that purpose.

As an example of how this system works, I will give a typical instance of its procedure. My partner, let us say, comes in and sits down at the desk opposite me. I observe that his scarfpin is working its way out from his tie. I call a stenographer and say: "Take a memo to Mr. MacFurdle, please. *In re* Loosened Scarfpin. You are losing your scarfpin."

As soon as she has typed this it is given to Mr. MacFurdle's secretary, and a carbon copy is put in the files. Mr. MacFurdle, on receiving my memo, adjusts his scarfpin and calls his secretary.

"A memo to Mr. Benchley, please. *In re* Tightened Scarfpin. Thank you. I have given the matter my attention."

As soon as I have received a copy of this typewritten reply to my memorandum we nod pleasantly to each other and go on with our work. In all, not more than half an hour has been consumed, and we have a complete record of the negotiations in our files in case any question should ever arise concerning them. In case *no* question should ever arise, we still have the complete record. So we can't lose—unless you want to call that half hour a loss.

It is then almost lunchtime. A quick glance at a pile of carbons of mill reports which have but little significance to me owing to the fact that the figures are illegible (it being a fifth-string carbon); a rapid survey of the matter submitted for my O.K., most of which I dislike to take the responsibility for and therefore pass on to Mr. Houghtelling for his O.K.; a short tussle in the washroom with the liquid-soap container which contains no liquid soap, and a thorough drying of the hands on my handkerchief, the paper towels having given out early in the morning, and I am ready to go to lunch with a man from the Eureka Novelty Company who wants to sell us a central paste-supply system (whereby all the office paste is kept in one large vat in the storeroom, individual brushfuls being taken out only on requisitions O.K.'d by the head of the department).

Both being practical businessmen, we spend only two hours at lunch. And, both being practical businessmen, we know all the subtleties of selling. It is a well-known fact that personality plays a big role in the so-called "selling game" (one of a series of American games, among which are "the newspaper game," "the advertising game," "the cloak-and-suit game," "the ladies' mackintosh and over-shoe game," "the seedless-raisin-and-dried-fruit game," etc.), and so Mr. Ganz of the Eureka Novelty Company spends the first hour and three-quarters developing his "personality appeal." All through the tomato bisque aux croutons and the roast prime ribs of beef, dish gravy, he puts into practice the principles enunciated in books on Selling, by means of which the subject at hand is deferred in a subtle manner until the salesman has had a chance to impress his prospect with his geniality and his smile (an attractive smile has been known to sell a carload of 1897-style derbies, according to au-thorities on The Smile in Selling), his knowledge of baseball, his rich fund of stories, and his general aversion to getting down to the disagreeable reason for his call.

The only trouble with this system is that I have done the same thing myself so many times that I know just what his next line is going to be, and can figure out pretty accurately at each stage of his conversation just when he is going to shift to one position nearer the thing he has to sell. I know that he has not the slightest interest in my entertainment other than the sale of a Eureka Central Paste-Supply System, and he knows that I know it, and so we spend an hour and three-quarters fooling the waiter into thinking that we are engaged in disinterested camaraderie.

For fifteen minutes we talk business, and I agree to take the matter up with the directors at the next meeting, holding the mental reservation that a central paste-supply system will be installed in our plant only over my dead body.

This takes us until two-thirty, and I have to hurry back to a conference. We have two kinds of "conference." One is that to which the office boy refers when he tells the applicant for a job that Mr. Blevitch is "in conference." This means that Mr. Blevitch is in good health and reading the paper, but otherwise unoccupied. The other kind of "conference" is bona fide in so far as it implies that three or four men are talking together in one room, and don't want to be disturbed.

This conference is on, let us say, the subject of Window Cards for display advertising: shall they be triangular or diamond shaped?

There are four of us present, and we all begin by biting off the ends of four cigars. Watterly has a pile of samples of window cards of various shapes, which he hangs, with a great deal of trouble, on the wall, and which are not referred to again. He also has a few ideas on Window Card Psychology.

"It seems to me," he leads off, "that we have here a very important question. On it may depend the success of our Middle Western sales. The problem as I see it is this: what will be the reaction on the retina of the eye of a prospective customer made by the sight of a diamond-shaped card hanging in a window? It is a well-known fact in applied psychology that when you take the average man into a darkened room, loosen his collar, and shout "Diamonds!" at him suddenly, his mental reaction is one in which the ideas of Wealth, Value, Richness, etc., predominate. Now, it stands to reason that the visual reaction from seeing a diamond-shaped card in the window will . . ."

"Excuse me a moment, George," says MacFurdle, who has absorbed some pointers on Distribution from a book entitled *The World Salesman*, "I don't think that it is so important to get after the psychology of the thing first as it is to outline thoroughly the Theory of Zone Apportionment on which we are going to work. If we could make up a chart, showing in red ink the types of retail stores and in green ink the types of jobber establishments, in this district, then we could get at the window display from that angle and tackle the psychology later, if at all. Now, on such a chart I would try to show the zones of Purchasing Power, and from these could be deduced . . ."

"Just a minute, Harry," Inglesby interrupts, "let me butt in for half a second. That chart system is all very well when you are selling goods with which the public is already familiar through association with other brands, but with ours it is different. We have got to estimate the Consumer Demand first in terms of dollar-and-a-quarter units, and build our selling organization up around that. Now, if I know anything about human nature at all—and I think I do, after being in the malleable-iron game for fifteen years—the people in this section of the country represent an entirely different trade current than . . ."

At this point I offer a few remarks on one of my pet hobbies, the influence of the Gulf Stream on Regional Commerce, and then we all say again the same things that we said before, after which we say them again, the pitch of the conversation growing higher at each repetition of views and the room becoming more and more filled with cigar smoke. Our final decision is to have a conference to-morrow afternoon, before which each one is to "think the matter over and report his reactions."

This brings the day to a close. There has been nothing remarkable in it, as the reader will be the first one to admit. And yet it shows the secret of whatever we have not accomplished in the past year in our business.

And it also shows why we practical businessmen have so little sympathy with a visionary, impractical arrangement like this League of Nations. President Wilson was all right in his way, but he was too academic. What we practical men in America want is deeds, not words.

Shakespeare Explained

CARRYING ON THE SYSTEM OF FOOTNOTES
TO A SILLY EXTREME

PERICLES

ACT II. SCENE 3

Enter first Lady-in-Waiting (Flourish,[1] Hautboys[2] and[3] torches[4])
First Lady-in-Waiting—What[5] ho![6] Where[7] is[8] the[9] music?[10]

NOTES

1. *Flourish:* The stage direction here is obscure. Clarke claims it should read "flarish," thus changing the meaning of the passage to "flarish" (that is, the King's), but most authorities have agreed that it should remain "flourish," supplying the predicate which is to be flourished. There was at this time a custom in the countryside of England to flourish a mop as a signal to the passing vender of berries, signifying that in that particular household there was a consumer-demand for berries, and this may have been meant in this instance. That Shakespeare was cognizant of this custom of flourishing the mop for berries is shown in a similar passage in the second part of King Henry IV, where he has the Third Page enter and say, "Flourish." Cf. also Hamlet, IV, 7:4.

2. *Hautboys*, from the French *haut*, meaning "high" and the Eng. *boys*, meaning "boys." The word here is doubtless used in the sense of "high boys," indicating either that Shakespeare intended to convey the idea of spiritual distress on the part of the First Lady-in-Waiting or that he did not. Of this Rolfe says: "Here we have one of the chief indications of Shakespeare's knowledge of human nature, his remarkable insight into the petty foibles of this work-a-day

33

Might be one of the hautboys bearing a box of
"trognies" for the actors to suck

world." Cf. T. N. 4:6, "Mine eye hath play'd the painter, and hath stell'd thy beauty's form in table of my heart."

3. *and.* A favorite conjunctive of Shakespeare's in referring to the need for a more adequate navy for England. Tauchnitz claims that it should be pronounced "und," stressing the anti-penult. This interpretation, however, has found disfavor among most commentators because of its limited significance. We find the same conjunctive in A. W. T. E. W. 6:7, "Steel-boned, unyielding *and* uncomplying virtue," and here there can be no doubt that Shakespeare meant that if the King should consent to the marriage of his daughter the excuse of Stephano, offered in Act 2, would carry no weight.

4. *Torches.* The interpolation of some foolish player and never the work of Shakespeare (Warb.). The critics of the last century have disputed whether or not this has been misspelled in the original, and should read "trochies" or "troches." This might well be since the introduction of tobacco into England at this time had wrought havoc with the speaking voices of the players, and we might well

imagine that at the entrance of the First Lady-in-Waiting there might be perhaps one of the hautboys mentioned in the preceding passage bearing a box of "troches" or "trognies" for the actors to suck. Of this entrance Clarke remarks: "The noble mixture of spirited firmness and womanly modesty, fine sense and true humility, clear sagacity and absence of conceit, passionate warmth and sensitive delicacy, generous love and self-diffidence with which Shakespeare has endowed this First Lady-in-Waiting renders her in our eyes one of the most admirable of his female characters." Cf. M. S. N. D. 8:9, "That solder'st close impossibilities and mak'st them kiss."

5. *What*—What.

6. *Ho!* In conjunction with the preceding word doubtless means "What ho!" changed by Clarke to "what hoo!" In the original MS. it reads "What hi!" but this has been accredited to the tendency of the time to write "What hi" when "what ho" was meant. Techner alone maintains that it should read "What humpf!" Cf. Ham. 5:0, "High-ho!"

7. *Where.* The reading of the folio, retained by Johnson, the Cambridge editors and others, but it is not impossible that Shakespeare wrote "why," as Pope and others give it. This would make the passage read "Why the music?" instead of "Where is the music?" and would be a much more probable interpretation in view of the music of that time. Cf. George Ade. Fable No. 15, "Why the gunnysack?"

8. *is*—is not. That is, would not be.

9. *the.* Cf. Ham. 4:6. M. S. N. D. 3:5. A. W. T. E. W. 2:6. T. N. 1:3 and Macbeth 3:1, "that knits up *the* raveled sleeves of care."

10. *music.* Explained by Malone as "the art of making music" or "music that is made." If it has but one of these meanings we are inclined to think it is the first; and this seems to be favored by what precedes, "*the* music!" Cf. M. of V. 4:2, "The man that hath no music in himself."

The meaning of the whole passage seems to be that the First Lady-in-Waiting has entered, concomitant with a flourish, hautboys and torches and says, "What ho! Where is the music?"

Christmas Afternoon

WHAT an afternoon! Mr. Gummidge said that, in his estimation, there never had *been* such an afternoon since the world began, a sentiment which was heartily endorsed by Mrs. Gummidge and all the little Gummidges, not to mention the relatives who had come over from Jersey for the day.

In the first place, there was the *ennui*. And such *ennui* as it was! A heavy, overpowering *ennui*, such as results from a participation in eight courses of steaming, gravied food, topping off with salted nuts which the little old spinster Gummidge from Oak Hill said she never knew when to stop eating—and true enough she didn't—a dragging, devitalizing *ennui*, which left its victims strewn about the living room in various attitudes of prostration suggestive of those of the petrified occupants in a newly unearthed Pompeiian dwelling; an *ennui* which carried with it a retinue of yawns, snarls and thinly veiled insults, and which ended in ruptures in the clan spirit serious enough to last throughout the glad new year.

Then there were the toys! Three and a quarter dozen toys to be divided among seven children. Surely enough, you or I might say, to satisfy the little tots. But that would be because we didn't know the tots. In came Baby Lester Gummidge, Lillian's boy, dragging an electric grain-elevator which happened to be the only toy in the entire collection that appealed to little Norman, five-year-old son of Luther, who lived in Rahway. In came curly-headed Effie in frantic and throaty disputation with Arthur, Jr., over the possession of an articulated zebra. In came Everett, bearing a mechanical negro which would no longer dance, owing to a previous

What an afternoon!

forcible feeding by the baby of a marshmallow into its only available aperture. In came Fonlansbee, teeth buried in the hand of little Ormond, who bore a popular but battered remnant of what had once been the proud false bosom of a hussar's uniform. In they all came, one after another, some crying, some snapping, some pulling, some pushing—all appealing to their respective parents for aid in their intramural warfare.

And the cigar smoke! Mrs. Gummidge said that she didn't mind the smoke from a good cigarette, but would they mind if she opened the windows for just a minute in order to clear the room of the heavy aroma of used cigars? Mr. Gummidge stoutly maintained that they were good cigars. His brother, George Gummidge, said that he, likewise, would say that they were. At which colloquial sally both Gummidge brothers laughed testily, thereby breaking the laughter record for the afternoon.

Aunt Libbie, who lived with George, remarked from the dark corner of the room that it seemed just like Sunday to her. An amendment was offered to this statement by the cousin, who was in the insurance business, stating that it was worse than Sunday. Murmurings indicative of as hearty agreement with this sentiment as their lethargy would allow came from the other members of the family circle, causing Mr. Gummidge to suggest a walk in the air to settle their dinner.

And then arose such a chorus of protestations as has seldom been heard. It was too cloudy to walk. It was too raw. It looked like snow. It looked like rain. Luther Gummidge said that he must be starting along home soon, anyway, bringing forth the acid query from Mrs. Gummidge as to whether or not he was bored. Lillian said that she felt a cold coming on, and added that something they had had for dinner must have been undercooked. And so it went, back and forth, forth and back, up and down, and in and out, until Mr. Gummidge's suggestion of a walk in the air was reduced to a tattered impossibility and the entire company glowed with ill-feeling.

In the meantime, we must not forget the children. No one else could. Aunt Libbie said that she didn't think there was anything like children to make a Christmas; to which Uncle Ray, the one with the Masonic fob, said, "No, thank God!" Although Christmas is supposed to be the season of good cheer, you (or I, for that matter) couldn't have told, from listening to the little ones, but what it was the children's Armageddon season, when Nature had decreed that only the fittest should survive, in order that the race might be carried on by the strongest, the most predatory and those possessing the best protective coloring. Although there were constant admonitions to Fonlansbee to "Let Ormond have that whistle now; it's his," and to Arthur, Jr., not to be selfish, but to "give the kiddie-car to Effie; she's smaller than you are," the net result was always that Fonlansbee kept the whistle and Arthur, Jr., rode in permanent, albeit disputed, possession of the kiddie-car. Oh, that we mortals should set ourselves up against the inscrutable workings of Nature!

Hallo! A great deal of commotion! That was Uncle George stumbling over the electric train which had early in the afternoon ceased to function and which had been left directly across the threshold. A great deal of crying! That was Arthur, Jr., bewailing the destruction of his already useless train, about which he had forgotten until the present moment. A great deal of recrimination! That was Arthur, Sr., and George fixing it up. And finally a great crashing! That was Baby Lester pulling over the tree on top of himself, necessitating the bringing to bear of all of Uncle Ray's knowledge of forestry to extricate him from the wreckage.

And finally Mrs. Gummidge passed the Christmas candy around. Mr. Gummidge afterward admitted that this was a tactical error on the part of his spouse. I no more believe that Mrs. Gummidge thought they wanted that Christmas candy than I believe that she thought they wanted the cold turkey which she later suggested. My opinion is that she wanted to drive them home. At any rate, that is what she succeeded in doing. Such cries as there were of "Ugh! Don't let me see another thing to eat!" and "Take it away!" Then came hurried scramblings in the coat-closet for overshoes. There were the rasping sounds made by cross parents when putting wraps on children. There were insincere exhortations to "come and see us soon" and to "get together for lunch some time." And, finally, there were slammings of doors and the silence of utter exhaustion, while Mrs. Gummidge went about picking up stray sheets of wrapping paper.

And, as Tiny Tim might say in speaking of Christmas afternoon as an institution, "God help us, every one."

Family Life in America

PART 1

The naturalistic literature of this country has reached such a state that no family of characters is considered true to life which does not include at least two hypochondriacs, one sadist, and one old man who spills food down the front of his vest. If this school progresses, the following is what we may expect in our national literature in a year or so.

THE living room in the Twillys' house was so damp that thick, soppy moss grew all over the walls. It dripped on the picture of Grandfather Twilly that hung over the melodeon, making streaks down the dirty glass like sweat on the old man's face. It was a mean face. Grandfather Twilly had been a mean man and had little spots of soup on the lapel of his coat. All his children were mean and had soup spots on their clothes.

Grandma Twilly sat in the rocker over by the window, and as she rocked the chair snapped. It sounded like Grandma Twilly's knees snapping as they did whenever she stooped over to pull the wings off a fly. She was a mean old thing. Her knuckles were grimy and she chewed crumbs that she found in the bottom of her reticule. You would have hated her. She hated herself. But most of all she hated Grandfather Twilly.

"I certainly hope you're frying good," she muttered as she looked up at his picture.

"Hasn't the undertaker come yet, Ma?" asked young Mrs. Wilbur Twilly petulantly. She was boiling water on the oil-heater and every now and again would spill a little of the steaming liquid on the baby

41

who was playing on the floor. She hated the baby because it looked like her father. The hot water raised little white blisters on the baby's red neck and Mabel Twilly felt short, sharp twinges of pleasure at the sight. It was the only pleasure she had had for four months.

"Why don't you kill yourself, Ma?" she continued. "You're only in the way here and you know it. It's just because you're a mean old woman and want to make trouble for us that you hang on."

Grandma Twilly shot a dirty look at her daughter-in-law. She had always hated her. Stringy hair, Mabel had. Dank, stringy hair. Grandma Twilly thought how it would look hanging at an Indian's belt. But all that she did was to place her tongue against her two front teeth and make a noise like the bathroom faucet.

Wilbur Twilly was reading the paper by the oil lamp. Wilbur had watery blue eyes and cigar ashes all over his knees. The third and fourth buttons of his vest were undone. It was too hideous.

He was conscious of his family seated in chairs about him. His mother, chewing crumbs. His wife Mabel, with her stringy hair, reading. His sister Bernice, with projecting front teeth, who sat thinking of the man who came every day to take away the waste paper. Bernice was wondering how long it would be before her family would discover that she had been married to this man for three years.

How Wilbur hated them all. It didn't seem as if he could stand it any longer. He wanted to scream and stick pins into every one of them and then rush out and see the girl who worked in his office snapping rubber bands all day. He hated her too, but she wore side-combs.

PART 2

The street was covered with slimy mud. It oozed out from under Bernice's rubbers in unpleasant bubbles until it seemed to her as if she must kill herself. Hot air coming out from a steam laundry. Hot, stifling air. Bernice didn't work in the laundry but she wished that she did so that the hot air would kill her. She wanted to be stifled.

She needed torture to be happy. She also needed a good swift clout on the side of the face.

A drunken man lurched out from a doorway and flung his arms about her. It was only her husband. She loved her husband. She loved him so much that, as she pushed him away and into the gutter, she stuck her little finger into his eye. She also untied his necktie. It was a bow necktie, with white, dirty spots on it and it was wet with gin. It didn't seem as if Bernice could stand it any longer. All the repressions of nineteen sordid years behind protruding teeth surged through her untidy soul. She wanted love. But it was not her husband that she loved so fiercely. It was old Grandfather Twilly. And he was too dead.

PART 3

In the dining room of the Twillys' house everything was very quiet. Even the vinegar cruet which was covered with fly specks. Grandma Twilly lay with her head in the baked potatoes, poisoned by Mabel, who, in her turn, had been poisoned by her husband and sprawled in an odd posture over the china closet. Wilbur and his sister Bernice had just finished choking each other to death and between them completely covered the carpet in that corner of the room where the worn spot showed the bare boards beneath, like ribs on a chicken carcass.

Only the baby survived. She had a mean face and had great spillings of Imperial Granum down her bib. As she looked about her at her family, a great hate surged through her tiny body and her eyes snapped viciously. She wanted to get down from her high-chair and show them all how much she hated them.

Bernice's husband, the man who came after the waste paper, staggered into the room. The tips were off both his shoe-lacings. The baby experienced a voluptuous sense of futility at the sight of the tipless lacings and leered suggestively at her uncle-in-law.

"We must get the roof fixed," said the man, very quietly. "It lets the sun in."

Do Insects Think?

IN A recent book entitled *The Psychic Life of Insects,* Professor Bouvier says that we must be careful not to credit the little winged fellows with intelligence when they behave in what seems like an intelligent manner. They may be only reacting. I would like to confront the Professor with an instance of reasoning power on the part of an insect which can not be explained away in any such manner.

During the summer of 1899, while I was at work on my treatise *Do Larvae Laugh?* we kept a female wasp at our cottage in the Adirondacks. It really was more like a child of our own than a wasp, except that it *looked* more like a wasp than a child of our own. That was one of the ways we told the difference.

It was still a young wasp when we got it (thirteen or fourteen years old) and for some time we could not get it to eat or drink, it was so shy. Since it was a female, we decided to call it Miriam, but soon the children's nickname for it—"Pudge"—became a fixture, and "Pudge" it was from that time on.

One evening I had been working late in my laboratory fooling round with some gin and other chemicals, and in leaving the room I tripped over a nine of diamonds which someone had left lying on the floor and knocked over my card catalogue containing the names and addresses of all the larvae worth knowing in North America. The cards went everywhere.

I was too tired to stop to pick them up that night, and went sobbing to bed, just as mad as I could be. As I went, however, I noticed the wasp flying about in circles over the scattered cards. "Maybe Pudge will pick them up," I said half-laughingly to myself, never thinking for one moment that such would be the case.

When I came down the next morning Pudge was still asleep over in her box, evidently tired out. And well she might have been. For there on the floor lay the cards scattered all about just as I had left them the night before. The faithful little insect had buzzed about all night trying to come to some decision about picking them up and arranging them in the catalogue box, and then, figuring out for herself that, as she knew practically nothing about larvae of any sort except wasp-larvae, she would probably make more of a mess of rearranging them than as if she left them on the floor for me to fix. It was just too much for her to tackle, and, discouraged, she went over and lay down in her box, where she cried herself to sleep.

If this is not an answer to Professor Bouvier's statement that insects have no reasoning power, I do not know what is.

The Stranger Within Our Gates

ONE OF the problems of child education which is not generally included in books on the subject is the Visiting Schoolmate. By this is meant the little friend whom your child brings home for the holidays. What is to be done with him, the Law reading as it does?

He is usually brought home because his own home is in Nevada, and if he went way out there for Christmas he would no sooner get there than he would have to turn right around and come back—an ideal arrangement on the face of it. But there is something in the idea of a child away from home at Christmas-time that tears at the heart-strings, and little George is received into the bosom of your family with open arms and a slight catch in the throat. Poor little nipper! He must call up his parents by telephone on Christmas Day; they will miss him so. (It later turns out that even when George's parents lived in Philadelphia he spent his vacations with friends, his parents being no fools.)

For the first day George is a model of politeness. "George is a nice boy," you say to your son. "I wish you knew more like him." "George seems to be a very manly little chap for fourteen," your wife says after the boys have gone to bed. "I hope that Bill is impressed." Bill, as a matter of fact, does seem to have caught some of little George's gentility and reserve, and the hope for his future, which had been practically abandoned, is revived again under his schoolmate's influence.

The first indication that George's stay is not going to be a blessing comes at the table, when, with confidence born of one day's association, he announces flatly that he does not eat potatoes, lamb or peas, the main course of the meal consisting of potatoes, lamb and peas. "Perhaps you would like an egg, George?" you suggest. "I hate eggs," says George, looking out the window while he waits for you to hit on something that he does like.

"I'm afraid you aren't going to get much to eat tonight, then, George," you say. "What is there for dessert?"

"A nice bread pudding with raisins," says your wife.

George, at the mention of bread pudding, gives what is known as "the bird," a revolting sound made with the tongue and lower lip. "I can't eat raisins anyway," he adds, to be polite. "They make me come out in a rash."

"Ah-h! The old raisin-rash," you say. "Well, we'll keep you away from raisins, I guess. And just what is it that you can eat, George? You can tell me. I am your friend."

Under cross-examination it turns out that George can eat beets if they are cooked just right, a rare species of eggplant grown only in Nevada, and all the ice cream in the world. He will also cram down a bit of cake now and then for manners' sake.

All this would not be so bad if it were not for the fact that, coincidentally with refusing the lamb, George criticizes your carving of it. "My father carves lamb across the grain instead of the way you do," he says, a little crossly.

"Very interesting," is your comment.

"My father says that only old ladies carve straight down like that," he goes on.

"Well, well," you say pleasantly between your teeth, "That makes me out sort of an old lady, doesn't it?".

"Yes, sir," says George.

"Perhaps you have a different kind of lamb in Nevada," you suggest, hacking off a large chunk. (You have never carved so badly.) "A kind that feeds on your special kind of eggplant."

"We don't have lamb very often," says George. "Mostly squab and duck."

"You stick to squab and duck, George," you say, "and it will be just dandy for that rash of yours. Here take this and like it!" And you toss him a piece of lamb which oddly enough is later found to have disappeared from his plate.

It also turns out later that George's father can build sailboats, make a monoplane that will really fly, repair a broken buzzer and imitate birds, none of which you can do and none of which you have ever tried to do, having given it to be understood that they *couldn't* be done. You begin to hate George's father almost as much as you do George.

The presents turn out to be things he already has,
only his are better

"I suppose your father writes articles for the magazines, too, doesn't he, George?" you ask sarcastically.

"Sure," says George with disdain. "He does that Sundays—Sunday afternoons."

This just about cleans up George so far as you are concerned, but there are still ten more days of vacation. And during these ten days your son Bill is induced by George to experiment with electricity to the extent of blowing out all the fuses in the house and burning the cigarette lighter out of the sedan; he is also inspired to call the cook a German spy who broils babies, to insult several of the neighbors' little girls to the point of tears and reprisals, and to refuse spinach. You know that Bill didn't think of these things himself, as he never could have had the imagination.

On Christmas Day all the little presents that you got for George turn out to be things that he already has, only his are better. He incites Bill to revolt over the question of where the tracks to the electric train are to be placed (George maintaining that in his home they run through his father's bathroom, which is the only sensible place for tracks to run). He breaks several of little Barbara's more fragile presents and says that she broke them herself by not knowing how to work them. And the day ends with George running a high temperature and coming down with mumps, necessitating a quarantine and enforced residence in your house for a month.

This is just a brief summary of the Visiting Schoolmate problem. Granted that every child should have a home to go to at Christmas, could there not be some sort of State subsidy designed to bring their own homes on to such children as are unable to go home themselves? On such a day each home should be a sanctuary, where only members of the tribe can gather and overeat and quarrel. Outsiders just complicate matters, especially when outsiders cannot be spanked.

Opera Synopses

SOME SAMPLE OUTLINES OF GRAND OPERA PLOTS
FOR HOME STUDY

I

DIE MEISTER-GENOSSENSCHAFT

SCENE: *The Forests of Germany.*
TIME: *Antiquity.*

CAST

STRUDEL, *God of Rain* ....Basso
SCHMALZ, *God of Slight Drizzle* ....Tenor
IMMERGLÜCK, *Goddess of the Six Primary Colors* ....Soprano
LUDWIG DAS EIWEISS, *the Knight of the Iron Duck* ....Baritone
THE WOODPECKER ....Soprano

ARGUMENT

The basis of "Die Meister-Genossenschaft" is an old legend of Germany which tells how the Whale got his Stomach.

ACT 1

The Rhine at Low Tide Just Below Weldschnoffen.—Immerglück has grown weary of always sitting on the same rock with the same fishes swimming by every day, and sends for Schwül to suggest something to do. Schwül asks her how she would like to have pass before her all the wonders of the world fashioned by the hand of man. She says, rotten. He then suggests that Ringblattz, son of Pflucht, be made to appear before her and fight a mortal combat

51

with the Iron Duck. This pleases Immerglück and she summons
to her the four dwarfs: Hot Water, Cold Water, Cool, and Cloudy.
She bids them bring Ringblattz to her. They refuse, because Pflucht
has at one time rescued them from being buried alive by acorns,
and, in a rage, Immerglück strikes them all dead with a thunderbolt.

ACT 2

A Mountain Pass.—Repenting of her deed, Immerglück has sought
advice of the giants, Offen and Besitz, and they tell her that she
must procure the magic zither which confers upon its owner the
power to go to sleep while apparently carrying on a conversation.
This magic zither has been hidden for three hundred centuries in
an old bureau drawer, guarded by the Iron Duck, and, although
many have attempted to rescue it, all have died of a strange ailment
just as success was within their grasp.

But Immerglück calls to her side Dampfboot, the tinsmith of the
gods, and bids him make for her a tarnhelm or invisible cap which
will enable her to talk to people without their understanding a word
she says. For a dollar and a half extra Dampfboot throws in a magic
ring which renders its wearer insensible. Thus armed, Immerglück
starts out for Walhalla, humming to herself.

ACT 3

The Forest Before the Iron Duck's Bureau Drawer.—Merglitz,
who has up till this time held his peace, now descends from a balloon and demands the release of Betty. It has been the will of
Wotan that Merglitz and Betty should meet on earth and hate each
other like poison, but Zweiback, the druggist of the gods, has diso-
beyed and concocted a love-potion which has rendered the young
couple very unpleasant company. Wotan, enraged, destroys them
with a protracted heat spell.

Encouraged by this sudden turn of affairs, Immerglück comes to
earth in a boat drawn by four white Holsteins, and, seated alone
on a rock, remembers aloud to herself the days when she was a
girl. Pilgrims from Augenblick, on their way to worship at the
shrine of Schmürr, hear the sound of reminiscence coming from the

rock and stop in their march to sing a hymn of praise for the drying-up of the crops. They do not recognize Immerglück, as she has her hair done differently, and think that she is a beggar girl selling pencils.

In the meantime, Ragel, the papercutter of the gods, has fashioned himself a sword on the forge of Schmalz, and has called the weapon "Assistance-in-Emergency." Armed with "Assistance-in-Emergency" he comes to earth, determined to slay the Iron Duck and carry off the beautiful Irma.

But Frimsel overhears the plan and has a drink brewed which is given to Ragel in a golden goblet and which, when drunk, makes him forget his past and causes him to believe that he is Schnorr, the God of Fun. While laboring under this spell, Ragel has a funeral pyre built on the summit of a high mountain and, after lighting it, climbs on top of it with a mandolin which he plays until he is consumed.

Immerglück never marries.

II

IL MINNESTRONE

(Peasant Love)

Scene: *Venice and Old Point Comfort.*
Time: *Early 16th Century.*

Cast

Alfonso, *Duke of Minnestrone*		Baritone
Partola, *a Peasant Girl*		Soprano
Cleanso		Tenor
Turino	*Young Noblemen of Venice.*	Tenor
Bombo		Basso
Ludovico	*Assassins in the Service of*	Basso
Astolfo	*Cafeteria Rusticana*	Methodist
	Townspeople, Cabbies and Sparrows	

Argument

"Il Minnestrone" is an allegory of the two sides of a man's nature (good and bad), ending at last in an awfully comical mess with everyone dead.

Act 1

A Public Square, Ferrara.—During a peasant festival held to celebrate the sixth consecutive day of rain, Rudolpho, a young nobleman, sees Lilliano, daughter of the village bell-ringer, dancing along throwing artificial roses at herself. He asks of his secretary who the young woman is, and his secretary, in order to confuse Rudolpho and thereby win the hand of his ward, tells him that it is his (Rudolpho's) own mother, disguised for the festival. Rudolpho is astounded. He orders her arrest.

Act 2

Banquet Hall in Gorgio's Palace.—Lilliano has not forgotten Breda, her old nurse, in spite of her troubles, and determines to avenge herself for the many insults she received in her youth by poisoning her (Breda). She therefore invites the old nurse to a banquet and poisons her. Presently a knock is heard. It is Ugolfo. He has come to carry away the body of Michelo and to leave an extra quart of pasteurized. Lilliano tells him that she no longer loves him, at which he goes away, dragging his feet sulkily.

Act 3

In Front of Emilo's House.—Still thinking of the old man's curse, Borsa has an interview with Cleanso, believing him to be the Duke's wife. He tells him things can't go on as they are, and Cleanso stabs him. Just at this moment Betty comes rushing in from school and falls in a faint. Her worst fears have been realized. She has been insulted by Sigmundo, and presently dies of old age. In a fury, Ugolfo rushes out to kill Sigmundo and, as he does so, the dying Rosenblatt rises on one elbow and curses his mother.

III

LUCY DE LIMA

SCENE: *Wales.*
TIME: *1700 (Greenwich).*

CAST

WILLIAM WONT, *Lord of Glennnn* ....Basso
LUCY WAGSTAFF, *his daughter* ....Soprano
BERTRAM, *her lover* ....Tenor
LORD ROGER, *friend of Bertram* ....Soprano
IRMA, *attendant to Lucy* ....Basso
    Friends, Retainers, and Members of the local Lodge of Elks.

ARGUMENT

"Lucy de Lima," is founded on the well-known story by Boccaccio of the same name and address.

ACT 1

Gypsy Camp Near Waterbury.—The gypsies, led by Edith, go singing through the camp on the way to the fair. Following them comes Despard, the gypsy leader, carrying Ethel, whom he has just kidnapped from her father, who had previously just kidnapped her from her mother. Despard places Ethel on the ground and tells Mona, the old hag, to watch over her. Mona nurses a secret grudge against Despard for having once cut off her leg, and decides to change Ethel for Nettie, another kidnapped child. Ethel pleads with Mona to let her stay with Despard, for she has fallen in love with him on the ride over. But Mona is obdurate.

ACT 2

The Fair.—A crowd of sightseers and villagers is present. Roger appears, looking for Laura. He can not find her. Laura appears, looking for Roger. She can not find him. The gypsy queen approaches

Roger and thrusts into his hand the locket stolen from Lord Brym.
Roger looks at it and is frozen with astonishment, for it contains the
portrait of his mother when she was in high school. He then realizes
that Laura must be his sister, and starts out to find her.

Act 3

Hall in the Castle.—Lucy is seen surrounded by every luxury, but
her heart is sad. She has just been shown a forged letter from
Stewart saying that he no longer loves her, and she remembers her
old free life in the mountains and longs for another romp with
Ravensbane and Wolfshead, her old pair of rompers. The guests
begin to assemble for the wedding, each bringing a roast ox. They
chide Lucy for not having her dress changed. Just at this moment
the gypsy band bursts in and Cleon tells the wedding party that
Elsie and not Edith is the child who was stolen from the summer-
house, showing the blood-stained derby as proof. At this, Lord
Brym repents and gives his blessing on the pair, while the fishermen
and their wives celebrate in the courtyard.

Malignant Mirrors

AS A rule, I try not to look into mirrors any more than is absolutely necessary. Things are depressing enough as they are without my going out of my way to make myself miserable.

But every once in a while it is unavoidable. There are certain mirrors in town with which I am brought face to face on occasion and there is nothing to do but make the best of it. I have come to classify them according to the harshness with which they fling the truth into my face.

I am unquestionably at my worst in the mirror before which I try on hats. I may have been going along all winter thinking of other things, dwelling on what people tell me is really a splendid spiritual side to my nature, thinking of myself as rather a fine sort of person, not dashing perhaps, but one from whose countenance shines a great light of honesty and courage which is even more to be desired than physical beauty. I rather imagine that little children on the street and grizzled Supreme Court justices out for a walk turn as I pass and say, "A fine face. Plain, but fine."

Then I go in to buy a hat. The mirror in the hat store is triplicate, so that you see yourself not only head-on but from each side. The appearance that I present to myself in this mirror is that of three police-department photographs showing all possible approaches to the face of Harry DuChamps, alias Harry Duval, alias Harry Duffy, wanted in Rochester for the murder of Nettie Lubitch, age 5. All that is missing is the longitudinal scar across the right cheek.

I have never seen a meaner face than mine is in the hat-store mirror. I could stand its not being handsome. I could even stand looking weak in an attractive, man-about-town sort of way. But in the right-hand mirror there confronts me a hang-dog face, the face of a yellow craven, while at the left leers an even more repulsive type, sensual and cruel.

Furthermore, even though I have had a haircut that very day, there is an unkempt fringe showing over my collar in back and the collar itself, (a Wimpet, 14½, which looked so well on the young man in the car-card) seems to be something that would be worn by a Maine guide when he goes into Portland for the day. My suit needs pressing and there is a general air of its having been given to me, with ten dollars, by the State on my departure from Sing Sing the day before.

But for an unfavorable full-length view, nothing can compare with the one that I get of myself as I pass the shoe store on the corner. They have a mirror in the window, so set that it catches the reflection of people as they step up on the curb. When there are other forms in the picture it is not always easy to identify yourself at first, especially at a distance, and every morning on my way to work, unless I deliberately avert my face, I am mortified to discover that the unpleasant-looking man, with the rather effeminate, swinging gait, whom I see mincing along the crowd, is none other than myself.

The only good mirror in the list is the one in the elevator of my clothing store. There is a subdued light in the car, a sort of golden glow which softens and idealizes, and the mirror shows only a two-thirds length, making it impossible to see how badly the cuffs on my trousers bag over the tops of my shoes. Here I become myself again. I have even thought that I might be handsome if I paid as much attention to my looks as some men do. In this mirror, my clothes look (for the last time) as similar clothes look on well-dressed men. A hat which is in every respect perfect when seen here, immediately becomes a senatorial sombrero when I step out into the street, but for the brief space of time while I am in that elevator, I am the *distingué*, clean-cut, splendid figure of a man that the original blueprints called for. I wonder if it takes much experience to run an elevator, for if it doesn't, I would like to make my life work running that car with the magic mirror.

How to Understand
International Finance

IT IS high time that someone came out with a clear statement of the international financial situation. For weeks and weeks officials have been rushing about holding conferences and councils and having their pictures taken going up and down the steps of buildings. Then, after each conference, the newspapers have printed a lot of figures showing the latest returns on how much Germany owes the bank. And none of it means anything.

Now there is a certain principle which has to be followed in all financial discussions involving sums over one hundred dollars. There is probably not more than one hundred dollars in actual cash in circulation today. That is, if you were to call in all the bills and silver and gold in the country at noon tomorrow and pile them up on the table, you would find that you had just about one hundred dollars, with perhaps several Canadian pennies and a few peppermint life-savers. All the rest of the money you hear about doesn't exist. It is conversation money. When you hear of a transaction involving $50,000,000 it means that one firm wrote "50,000,000" on a piece of paper and gave it to another firm, and the other firm took it home and said, "Look, Momma, I got $50,000,000!" But when Momma asked for a dollar and a quarter out of it to pay the man who washed the windows, the answer probably was that the firm hadn't got more than seventy cents in cash.

This is the principle of finance. So long as you can pronounce any number above a thousand, you have got that much money. You can't work this scheme with the shoe-store man or the restaurant owner, but it goes big on Wall St. or in international financial circles.

This much understood, we see that when the Allies demand 132,-000,000,000 gold marks from Germany they know very well that nobody in Germany has ever seen 132,000,000,000 gold marks and never will. A more surprised and disappointed lot of boys you couldn't ask to see than the Supreme Financial Council would be if Germany were actually to send them a money order for the full amount demanded.

What they mean is that, taken all in all, Germany owes the world 132,000,000,000 gold marks plus carfare. This includes everything, breakage, meals sent to room, good will, everything. Now, it is understood that if they really meant this, Germany couldn't even draw cards; so the principle on which the thing is figured out is as follows: (Watch this closely; there is a trick in it).

You put down a lot of figures, like this. Any figures will do, so long as you can't read them quickly:

132,000,000,000 gold marks

$33,000,000,000 on a current value basis

$21,000,000,000 on reparation account plus 12½% yearly tax on German exports

11,000,000,000 gold fish

$1.35 amusement tax

866,000 miles. Diameter of the sun

2,000,000,000

27,000,000,000

31,000,000,000

Then you add them together and subtract the number you first thought of. This leaves 11. And the card you hold in your hand is the seven of diamonds. Am I right?

Kiddie-Kar Travel

IN AMERICA there are two classes of travel—first class, and with children. Traveling with children corresponds roughly to traveling third class in Bulgaria. They tell me there is nothing lower in the world than third-class Bulgarian travel.

The actual physical discomfort of traveling with the Kiddies is not so great, although you do emerge from it looking as if you had just moved the piano upstairs single-handed. It is the mental wear-and-tear that tells and for a sensitive man there is only one thing worse, and that is a church wedding in which he is playing the leading comedy rôle.

There are several branches of the ordeal of Going on Choo-Choo, and it is difficult to tell which is the roughest. Those who have taken a very small baby on a train maintain that this ranks as pleasure along with having a nerve killed. On the other hand, those whose wee companions are in the romping stage, simply laugh at the claims of the first group. Sometimes you will find a man who has both an infant *and* a romper with him. Such a citizen should receive a salute of twenty-one guns every time he enters the city and should be allowed to wear the insignia of the Pater Dolorosa, giving him the right to solicit alms on the cathedral steps.

There is much to be said for those who maintain that rather should the race be allowed to die out than that babies should be taken from place to place along our national arteries of traffic. On the other hand, there *are* moments when babies are asleep. (Oh, yes, there are. There *must* be.) But it is practically a straight run of ten or a dozen hours for your child of four. You may have a little trouble in getting the infant to doze off, especially, as the train newsboy waits crouching in the vestibule until he sees signs of slumber on the

61

You start with the pronounced ill-will of the rest of the occupants

child's face and then rushes in to yell, "Copy of *Life*, out today!" right by its pink, shell-like ear. But after it *is* asleep, your troubles are over except for wondering how you can shift your ossifying arm to a new position without disturbing its precious burden.

If the child is of an age which denies the existence of sleep, however, preferring to run up and down the aisle of the car rather than sit in its chair (at least a baby can't get out of its chair unless it falls out and even then it can't go far), then every minute of the trip is full of fun. On the whole, having traveled with children of all the popular ages, I would be inclined to award the Hair Shirt to the man who successfully completes the ride with a boy of, let us say, three.

In the first place, you start with the pronounced ill-will of two-thirds of the rest of the occupants of the car. You see them as they come in, before the train starts, glancing at you and yours with little or no attempt to conceal the fact that they wish they had waited for the four o'clock. Across from you is perhaps a large man who, in his home town, has a reputation for eating little children. He wears a heavy gold watch chain and wants to read through a lot of reports on the trip. He is just about as glad to be opposite a small boy as he would be if it were a hurdy-gurdy.

In back of you is a lady in a black silk dress who doesn't like the porter. Ladies in black silk dresses always seem to board the train with an aversion to the porter. The fact that the porter has to be in the same car with her makes her fussy to start with, and when she discovers that in front of her is a child of three who is already eating (you simply have to give him a lemon drop to keep him quiet at least until the train starts) she decides that the best thing to do is simply to ignore him and not give him the slightest encouragement to become friendly. The child therefore picks her out immediately to be his buddy.

For a time after things get to going all you have to do is answer questions about the scenery. This is only what you must expect when you have children, and it happens no matter where you are. You can always say that you don't know who lives in that house or what that cow is doing. Sometimes you don't even have to look up when you say that you don't know. This part is comparatively easy.

It is when the migratory fit comes on that you will be put to the test. Suddenly you look and find the boy staggering down the aisle, peering into the faces of people as he passes them. "Here! Come back here, Roger!" you cry, lurching after him and landing across the knees of the young lady two seats down. Roger takes this as a signal for a game and starts to run, screaming with laughter. After four steps he falls and starts to cry.

On being carried kicking back to his seat, he is told that he mustn't run down the aisle again. This strikes even Roger as funny, because it is such a flat thing to say. Of course he is going to run down the aisle again and he knows it as well as you do. In the meantime, however, he is perfectly willing to spend a little time with the lady in the black silk dress.

"Here, Roger," you say, "don't bother the lady."

"Hello, little boy," the lady says, nervously, and tries to go back to her book. The interview is over as far as she is concerned. Roger, however, thinks that it would be just dandy to get up in her lap. This has to be stopped, and Roger has to be whispered to.

He then announces that it is about time that he went to the washroom. You march down the car, steering him by the shoulders and both lurching together as the train takes the curves and attracting wide attention to your very obvious excursion. Several kindly people smile knowingly at you as you pass and try to pat the boy on the head, but their advances are repelled, it being a rule of all children to look with disfavor on any attentions from strangers. The only people they want to play with are those who hate children.

On reaching the washroom you discover that the porter had just locked it and taken the key with him, simply to be nasty. This raises quite a problem. You explain the situation as well as possible, which turns out to be not well enough. There is every indication of loud crying and perhaps worse. You call attention to the Burrows Rustless Screen sign which you are just passing and stand in the passageway by the drinking cups, feverishly trying to find things in the landscape as it whirls by which will serve to take the mind off the tragedy of the moment. You become so engrossed in this important task that it is some time before you discover that you are completely blocking the passageway and the progress of some fifteen people who want to get off at Utica. There is nothing for you to do but head the procession and get off first.

Once out in the open, the pride and prop of your old age decides that the thing to do is pay the engineer a visit, and starts off up the platform at a terrific rate. This amuses the onlookers and gives you a little exercise after being cramped up in that old car all the morning. The imminent danger of the train's starting without you only adds to the fun. At that, there might be worse things than being left in Utica. One of them is getting back on the train again to face the old gentleman with the large watch chain.

The final phase of the ordeal, however, is still in store for you

*Before you discover that you are completely blocking
the passageway*

when you make your way (and Roger's way) into the diner. Here
the plunging march down the aisle of the car is multiplied by six
(the diner is never any nearer than six cars and usually is part of
another train). On the way, Roger sees a box of animal crackers
belonging to a little girl and commandeers it. The little girl, putting
up a fight, is promptly pushed over, starting what promises to be
a free-for-all fight between the two families. Lurching along after
the apologies have been made, it is just a series of unwarranted attacks by Roger on sleeping travelers and equally unwarranted
evasions by Roger of the kindly advances of very nice people who
love children.

In the diner, it turns out that the nearest thing they have suited
to Roger's customary diet is veal cutlets, and you hardly think that

his mother would approve of those. Everything else has peppers or sardines in it. A curry of lamb across the way strikes the boy's fancy and he demands some of that. On being told that he has not the slightest chance in the world of getting it but how would he like a little crackers-and-milk, he becomes quite upset and threatens to throw a fork at the Episcopal clergyman sitting opposite. Pieces of toast are waved alluringly in front of him and he is asked to consider the advantages of preserved figs and cream, but it is curry of lamb or he gets off the train. He doesn't act like this at home. In fact, he is noted for his tractability. There seems to be something about the train that brings out all the worst that is in him, all the hidden traits that he has inherited from his mother's side of the family. There is nothing else to do but say firmly, "Very well, then, Roger. We'll go back *without* any nice dinner," and carry him protesting from the diner, apologizing to the head steward for the scene and considering dropping him overboard as you pass through each vestibule.

In fact, I had a cousin once who had to take three of his little ones on an all-day trip from Philadelphia to Boston. It was the hottest day of the year and my cousin had on a woolen suit. By the time he reached Hartford, people in the car noticed that he had only two children with him. At Worcester he had only one. No one knew what had become of the others and no one asked. It seemed better not to ask. He reached Boston alone and never explained what had become of the tiny tots. Anyone who has ever traveled with tiny tots of his own, however, can guess.

Uncle Edith's Ghost Story

"TELL US a ghost story, Uncle Edith," cried all the children late Christmas afternoon when everyone was cross and sweaty.

"Very well, then," said Uncle Edith, "it isn't much of a ghost story, but you will take it—and like it," he added, cheerfully. "And if I hear any whispering while it is going on, I will seize the luckless offender and baste him one.

"Well, to begin, my father was a poor woodchopper, and we lived in a charcoal-burner's hut in the middle of a large, dark forest."

"That is the beginning of a fairy story, you big sap," cried little Dolly, a fat, disagreeable child who never should have been born, "and what we wanted was a *ghost* story."

"To be sure," cried Uncle Edith, "what a stupid old woopid I was. The ghost story begins as follows:

"It was late in November when my friend Warrington came up to me in the club one night and said, 'Craige, old man, I want you to come down to my place in Whoopshire for the week-end. There is greffle shooting to be done and grouse no end. What do you say?'

"I had been working hard that week, and the prospect pleased. And so it was that the 3:40 out of Charing Cross found Warrington and me on our way into Whoopshire, loaded down with guns, plenty of flints, and two of the most beautiful snootfuls ever accumulated in Merrie England.

"It was getting dark when we reached Breeming Downs, where Warrington's place was, and as we drove up the shadowy path to the door, I felt Warrington's hand on my arm.

" 'Cut that out!' I ordered, peremptorily. 'What is this I'm getting into?'

" 'Sh-h-h!' he replied, and his grip tightened. With one sock I knocked him clean across the seat. There are some things which I simply will not stand for.

"He gathered himself together and spoke. 'I'm sorry,' he said. 'I was a bit unnerved. You see, there is a shadow against the pane in the guest room window.'

" 'Well, what of it?' I asked. It was my turn to look astonished.

"Warrington lowered his voice. 'Whenever there is a shadow against the windowpane as I drive up with a guest, that guest is found dead in bed the next morning—dead from fright,' he added, significantly.

"I looked up at the window toward which he was pointing. There, silhouetted against the glass, was the shadow of a gigantic man. I say, 'a man,' but it was more the figure of a large weasel except for a fringe of dark-red clappers that it wore suspended from its beak."

"How do you know they were dark red," asked little Tom-Tit, "if it was the shadow you saw?"

"You shut your face," replied Uncle Edith. "I could hardly control my astonishment at the sight of this thing, it was so astonishing. 'That is in my room?' I asked Warrington.

" 'Yes,' he replied, 'I am afraid that it is.'

"I said nothing, but got out of the automobile and collected my bags. 'Come on,' I announced cheerfully, 'I'm going up and beard Mr. Ghost in his den.'

"So up the dark, winding stairway we went into the resounding corridors of the old seventeenth-century house, pausing only when we came to the door which Warrington indicated as being the door to my room. I knocked.

"There was a piercing scream from within as we pushed the door open. But when we entered, we found the room empty. We searched high and low, but could find no sign of the man with the shadow. Neither could we discover the source of the terrible scream, although the echo of it was still ringing in our ears.

" 'I guess it was nothing,' said Warrington, cheerfully. 'Perhaps the wind in the trees,' he added.

" 'But the shadow on the pane?' I asked.

"He pointed to a fancily carved piece of guest soap on the wash-stand. 'The light was behind that,' he said, 'and from outside it looked like a man.'

" 'To be sure,' I said, but I could see that Warrington was as white as a sheet.

" 'Is there anything that you need?' he asked. 'Breakfast is at nine—if you're lucky,' he added, jokingly.

" 'I think that I have everything,' I said. 'I will do a little reading before going to sleep, and perhaps count my laundry. . . . But stay,' I called him back, 'you might leave that revolver which I see sticking out of your hip pocket. I may need it more than you will.'

"He slapped me on the back and handed me the revolver as I had asked. 'Don't blow into the barrel,' he giggled, nervously.

" 'How many people have died of fright in this room?' I asked, turning over the leaves of a copy of *Town and Country*.

" 'Seven,' he replied. 'Four men and three women.'

" 'When was the last one here?'

" 'Last night,' he said.

" 'I wonder if I might have a glass of hot water with my break-fast,' I said. 'It warms your stomach.'

" 'Doesn't it though?' he agreed, and was gone.

"Very carefully I unpacked my bag and got into bed. I placed the revolver on the table by my pillow. Then I began reading.

"Suddenly the door to the closet at the farther end of the room opened slowly. It was in the shadows and so I could not make out whether there was a figure or not. But nothing appeared. The door shut again, however, and I could hear footfalls coming across the soft carpet toward my bed. A chair which lay between me and the closet was upset as if by an unseen hand, and simultaneously, the window was slammed shut and the shade pulled down. I looked, and there, against the shade, as if thrown from the *outside*, was the same shadow that we had seen as we came up the drive that afternoon."

"I have to go to the bathroom," said little Roger, aged six, at this point.

"Well, go ahead," said Uncle Edith. "You know where it is."

"I don't want to go alone," whined Roger.

"Go with Roger, Arthur," commanded Uncle Edith, "and bring me a glass of water when you come back."

"And whatever was this horrible thing that was in your room, Uncle Edith?" asked the rest of the children in unison when Roger and Arthur had left the room.

"I can't tell you that," replied Uncle Edith, "for I packed my bag and got the 9:40 back to town."

"That is the lousiest ghost story I have ever heard," said Peterkin. And they all agreed with him.

French for Americans

A HANDY COMPENDIUM FOR VISITORS TO PARIS

THE following lessons and exercises are designed for the exclusive use of Americans traveling in France. They are based on the needs and behavior of Americans, as figured from the needs and behavior of 14,000 Americans last summer. We wish to acknowledge our indebtedness to American Express Co., 11 Rue Scribe, for some of our material.

THE FRENCH LANGUAGE

1. *Pronunciation*

Vowels	Pronounced
a	ong
e	ong
i	ong
o	ong
u	ong

2. *Accents*

The French language has three accents, the acute *e*, the grave *e*, and the circumflex *e*, all of which are omitted.

3. *Phrases most in demand by Americans*

English	French
Haven't you got any griddle-cakes?	*N'avez-vous pas des griddle-cakes?*
What kind of a dump is this, anyhow?	*Quelle espèce de dump is this, anyhow?*
Do you call that coffee?	*Appelez-vous cela coffee?*
Where can I get a copy of the N. Y. Times?	*Où est le N. Y. Times?*
What's the matter? Don't you understand English?	*What's the matter? Don't you understand English?*

3. *Phrases most in demand by Americans* (*Continued*)

English	French
Of all the godam countries I ever saw.	*De tous les pays godams que j'ai vu.*
Hey there, driver, go slow!	*Hey there, chauffeur, allez lentement!*
Where's Sister?	*Où est Sister?*
How do I get to the Louvre from here?	*Où est le Louvre?*
Two hundred francs? In your hat.	*Deux cents francs? Dans votre chapeau.*
Where's Brother?	*Où est Brother?*
I haven't seen a good-looking woman yet.	*Je n'ai pas vu une belle femme jusqu'à présent.*
Where can I get laundry done by six tonight?	*Où est le laundry?*
Here is where we used to come when I was here during the War.	*Ici est où nous used to come quand j'étais ici pendant la guerre.*
Say, this is real beer all right!	*Say, ceci est de la bière vrai!*
Oh boy!	*O boy!*
Two weeks from tomorrow we sail for home.	*Deux semaines from tomorrow nous sail for home.*
Then when we land I'll go straight to Childs and get a cup of coffee and a glass of ice-water.	*Sogleich wir zu hause sind, geh ich zum Childs und eine tasse kaffee und ein glass eiswasser kaufen.*
Very well.	*Très bien.*
Leave it in my room.	*Très bien.*
Good night!	*Très bien.*
Where did Father go to?	*Où est Papa?*

PLACES IN PARIS FOR AMERICANS TO VISIT

The Lobby of the Ritz

This is one of the most interesting places in Paris for the American tourist, for it is there that he meets a great many people from America. If he will stand by the potted palms in the corner he will surely find someone whom he knows before long and can enter into a conversation on how things are going at home.

The American Express Co., 11 Rue Scribe

Here again the American traveler will find surcease from the irritating French quality of most of the rest of Paris. If he comes here for his mail, he will hear the latest news of the baseball leagues, how the bathing is on the Maine Coast, what the chances are for the Big Fight in September at the Polo Grounds, and whom Nora Bayes has married in August. There will be none of this unintelligible *French* jabber with which Paris has become so infested of late years. He will hear language spoken as it should be spoken, whether he come from Massachusetts or Iowa.

WHERE TO EAT IN PARIS

Hartford Lunch

There has been a Hartford Lunch opened at 115 Rue Lord Byron where the American epicure can get fried-egg sandwiches, Boston baked beans, coffee rings, and crullers almost as good as those he can get at home. The place is run by Martin Keefe, formerly of the Hartford Lunch in Fall River, Massachusetts, and is a mecca for those tourists who want good food well cooked.

United States Drug Store

At the corner of Rue Bonsard and the Boulevard de Parteuille there is an excellent American drug store where are served frosted chocolates, ice-cream sodas, Coca-Cola, and pimento cheese sandwiches. A special feature which will recall the beloved homeland to Americans is the buying of soda checks *before* ordering.

FRENCH CURRENCY

Here is something which is likely to give the American traveler no little trouble. In view of the fluctuating value of the franc, the following table should be memorized in order to insure against mistakes:

Day of Week	American value of Franc
Monday	5 cents
Tuesday	5.1 cents
Wednesday	4.9 cents
Thursday	1 lb. chestnuts
Friday	2½ yds. linoleum
Saturday	What-have-you

The proper procedure for Americans in making purchases is as follows:

1. Ascertain the value of the franc.
2. Make the purchase of whatever it is you want.
3. Ask *"Combien?"* (How much?)
4. Say *"Trop cher."* (What the hell!)
5. Try to understand the answer.
6. Pay the asking price and leave the shop swearing in English, American or other mother tongue.

SIDE TRIPS FROM PARIS

There are many fascinating trips which may be made by the American sojourning in Paris which will relieve him of the tedium of his stay.

TRIP A.—Take the train at Paris for Havre and from there go by steamer to New York. The State of Maine Express leaves New York (Grand Central Station) at 7:30 P.M. and in the morning the traveler finds himself in Portland, Maine, from which many delightful excursions may be made up and down the rock-ribbed Atlantic coast.

TRIP B.—Entrain at Paris for Cherbourg, where there are frequent sailings westward. By the payment of a slight *pourboire* the ship's captain will put her in at the island of Nantucket, a quaint whaling center of olden times. Here you may roam among the moors and swim to your heart's content, unconscious of the fact that you are within a six-day run of the great city of Paris.

Ordinal Numbers and their Pronunciation

Numbers	Pronounced
1st. *le premier*	leh premyai
2nd. *le second*	leh zeggong
3rd. *le troisième*	leh trouazzeame
4th. *le quatrième*	leh kattreame
8th. *le huitième*	leh wheeteeame

Oh, well, you won't have occasion to use these much, anyway. Never mind them.

Other Words You Will Have Little Use For

Vernisser—to varnish, glaze.

Nuque—nape (of the neck).

Egriser—to grind diamonds.

Dromer—to make one's neck stiff from working at a sewing machine.

Rossignol—nightingale, picklock.

Ganache—lower jaw of a horse.

Serin—canary bird.

Pardon—I beg your pardon.

Is This the Missing Link?

BONE FRAGMENTS DISCOVERED IN WEEMIX
AND THE PROBLEMS THEY PRESENT

SCIENTISTS are partially agog at the recent discovery in a gravel pit at Rudney Downs, Weemix, Filtshire, England, of certain scraps of skull bone which give every indication of having belonged to a sub-man of the Second Interglacial period. He has already been named (it was a boy, and a bouncing one at that) *Homo Weemixensis*, or Peter Pan.

The discovery was made by an old scientist named Harry, who was digging around in the gravel pit trying to find a caramel he had lost. He first came upon a bone fragment about the size of a new buffalo nickel, and, thinking nothing of it, called the police. A few weeks later, in quite another part of Rudney Downs (Rudney Downs has two parts, Rudney and Downs, contracted to Rudney Downs), another bone fragment was discovered which quite obviously belonged to the first, as it was marked "B" to correspond with the mark "A" on the original find. The two pieces, when placed together, spelled "MOTHER."

It is estimated that this sub-man lived approximately 100,000 years ago, before there were any streetcars. People went from place to place then in stagecoaches, and a letter written in London on a Tuesday might take three or four days by courier to reach Plymouth. So you see, we have things much easier today than *Homo Weemixensis* had, for all his bone fragments.

Fellows from the University of London (jolly good fellows, you may be sure) have worked night and day on the reconstruction of this precursor of the human race, and have found out that the brain capacity of his skull was somewhere between that of the old *Pithecanthropus* and man. You would laugh if you knew how small that was. Old *Pithecanthropus* (the one discovered in Java, not one of the Hartford *Pithecanthropi*) is supposed to have had a brain capacity just a little larger than a canary's. A good big canary, though. This would mean that if you yelled "Hi!" very suddenly in *Pithecanthropus*' face he would just laugh good-naturedly.

Now the newly discovered sub-man was brighter than that. Dr. William Evett, in charge of the work of excavation and reconstruction, says of him:

"It is quite probable that we have here the link between the Second Interglacial and the Pleiocene. This ape-man, from what we have been able to deduce, must have been about four feet seven inches high, with a broad nose and a scar running diagonally across his cheek, when last seen wore a dark blue serge suit and spoke with a slight Weemix accent. There is every reason to believe that he was with a woman named Mortimer, or Wadleigh."

Sir Robert Womm, however, does not agree with Dr. Evett that *Homo Weemixensis* walked with a slight limp.

"Although I bow to Dr. Evett's eminence in the field of ethnological research," writes Sir Robert, "I can not feel that a man who would leave his wife as Dr. Evett did is a fit person to instruct our young."

Certain it is that trophies of the hunt were buried with the ape-man by his associates, for in the same gravel pit in which the bone fragments were found were later discovered a colored top, with the string still attached to it, and an old glove.

A description of the probable appearance of the *Weemix* jaw is given us by Lord Duncaman, who took the two fragments home with him that night and shined them up a little.

"The jaw is imperfect in front, but has the broad, flat symphysis of the ape-jaw. It has marks showing a lateral movement of the tubercles of the molars which would indicate that its owner either smoked a pipe or else stored nuts away for the winter in his mouth.

On this hypothesis we are able to base our conclusion that *Homo Weemixensis* was nobody's fool."

It is hoped that the researches which are still going on will disclose some explanation of the fact that the material of these bony fragments seems to be similar in taste and texture to the material of which laundry soap is now made.

The Mystery of the Poisoned Kipper

WHO sent the poisoned kipper to Major General Hannafield of the Royal Welch Lavaliers? That is the problem which is distorting Scotland Yard at the present moment, for the solution lies evidently in the breast of Major General Hannafield himself. And Major General Hannafield is dead. (At any rate, he doesn't answer his telephone.)

Following are the details, such as they are. You may take them or leave them. If you leave them, please leave them in the coat room downstairs and say that Martin will call for them.

One Saturday night about three weeks ago, after a dinner given by the Royal Welch Lavaliers for the Royal Platinum Watch, Major General Hannafield returned home just in time for a late breakfast which he really didn't want. In fact, when his wife said, rather icily, "I suppose you've had your breakfast," the Maj. Gen. replied, "I'll thank you not to mention breakfast, *or* lunch, *or* dinner, until such time as I give you the signal." Mrs. Hannafield thereupon packed her bags and left for her mother's in New Zealand.

Along about eleven-thirty in the morning, however, the Maj. Gen. extricated himself from the hatrack where he had gone to sleep, and decided that something rather drastic had to be done about his mouth. He thought of getting a new mouth; but as it was Sunday all the mouth shops were closed, and he had no chance of sending into London for anything. He thought of water, great tidal waves of water, but even that didn't seem to be exactly adequate. So naturally his mind turned next to kippered herring. "Send a thief to catch a thief," is an old saying but a good one, and applies especially to Sunday-morning mouths.

So he rang for his man, and nobody answered.

The Maj. Gen. then went to the window and called out to the gardener, who was wrestling with a dahlia, and suggested that he let those dahlias alone and see about getting a kipper, and what's more a very salty kipper, immediately. This the gardener did.

On receiving the kipper, the Maj. Gen., according to witnesses, devoured it with avidity, paper and all, and then hung himself back up on the hatrack. This was the last that was seen of Major General Hannafield alive, although perhaps "alive" is too strong a word. Perhaps "breathing" would be better.

Mrs. Hannafield, being on her way to New Zealand, has been absolved of any connection with the crime (if causing the Maj. Gen.'s death can be called a crime, as he was quite an offensive old gentleman). The gardener, from his cell in the Old Bailey, claims that he bought the kipper from a fish stall in the High Street, and the fish vender in the High Street claims that he bought the kipper from the gardener.

According to the officials of Scotland Yard, there are two possible solutions to the crime, neither of them probable: revenge, or inadvertent poisoning of the kipper in preparation. Both have been discarded, along with the remainder of the kipper.

Revenge as a motive is not plausible, as the only people who could possibly seek revenge on the Maj. Gen. were killed by him a long time ago. The Maj. Gen. was notoriously hot-tempered, and, when opposed, was accustomed to settling his neck very low in his collar and rushing all the blood available to his temples. In such states as this he usually said, "Gad, sir!" and lashed out with an old Indian weapon which he always carried, killing his offender. He was always acquitted, on account of his war record.

It is quite possible that some relatives of one of the Maj. Gen.'s victims might have tracked him from the Punjab or the Kit-Kat Club to his "diggings" in Diggings Street, but he usually was pretty careful to kill only people who were orphans or unmarried.

There was some thought at first that the Maj. Gen. might have at one time stolen the eye of an idol in India and brought it back to England, and that some zealot had followed him across the world and wreaked vengeance on him. A study of the records, however, shows that the Maj. Gen. once tried to steal an emerald eye out of an Indian idol, but that the idol succeeded in getting the Maj. Gen.'s eye instead, and that the Maj. Gen. came back to England wearing a glass eye—which accounted for his rather baffling mannerism of looking over a person's shoulder while that person was talking to him.

Now as for the inadvertent poisoning of a kipper in the process of being cured. Herring are caught off the coast of Normandy (they are also caught practically everywhere, but Normandy makes a better story), brought to shore by Norman fishermen dressed up as Norman fishermen, and carried almost immediately to the kipperers.

The herring kipperers are all under State control and are examined by government agents both before and after kippering. They are subjected to the most rigid mental tests, and have to give satisfactory answers to such questions as "Do you believe in poisoning herring?" and "Which of the following statements is true? (a) William the Norman was really a Swede; (b) herring placed in the handkerchief drawer, give the handkerchiefs that *je ne sais quoi;* (c) honesty is the best policy."

If the kipperers are able to answer these questions, and can, in addition, chin themselves twelve times, they are allowed to proceed with their work. Otherwise they are sent to the French Chamber of Deputies, or Devil's Island, for ten years. So you can see that there is not much chance for a herring kipperer to go wrong, and practically no chance for Major General Hannafield to have been poisoned by mistake.

This leaves really nothing for Scotland Yard to work on, except an empty stomach. The motive of revenge being out, and accidental poisoning being out, the only possible solution remaining is that Major General Hannafield was in no state to digest a kippered herring and practically committed suicide by eating it. This theory they are working on, and at the coroner's inquest (which ought to come along any day now) the whole matter will be threshed out.

An examination of the Maj. Gen.'s vital organs has disclosed nothing except a possible solution of the whereabouts of the collier Cyclops, which was lost during the Great War.

Here the matter stands, or rather *there*. (It was here a minute ago.) Mrs. Hannafield may have some suggestions to offer, if she ever will land in New Zealand, but, according to radio dispatches, she is having an awfully good time on the boat and keeps going back and forth without ever getting off when they put into port. She and the ship's doctor have struck up an acquaintance, and you know what that means.

"Ask That Man"

THIS is written for those men who have wives who are constantly insisting on their asking questions of officials.

For years I was troubled with the following complaint: Just as soon as we started out on a trip of any kind, even if it were only to the corner of the street, Doris began forcing me to ask questions of people. If we weren't quite sure of the way: "Why don't you ask that man? He could tell you." If there was any doubt as to the best place to go to get chocolate ice-cream, she would say, "Why don't you ask that boy in uniform? He would be likely to know."

I can't quite define my aversion to asking questions of strangers. From snatches of family battles which I have heard drifting up from railway stations and street corners, I gather that there are a great many men who share my dislike for it, as well as an equal number of women who, like Doris, believe it to be the solution of most of this world's problems. The man's dread is probably that of making himself appear a pest or ridiculously uninformed. The woman's insistence is based probably on experience which has taught her that *any*one, no matter who, knows more about things in general than her husband.

Furthermore, I never know exactly how to begin a request for information. If I preface it with, "I beg your pardon!" the stranger is likely not to hear, especially if he happens to be facing in another direction, for my voice isn't very reliable in crises and sometimes makes no intelligible sound at all until I have been talking for fully a minute. Often I say, "I beg your pardon!" and he turns quickly and says, "What did you say?" Then I have to repeat, "I beg your pardon!" and he asks, quite naturally, "What for?" Then

I gather that there are a great many men who share my dislike for it

My voice isn't very reliable in crises

I am stuck. Here I am, begging a perfect stranger's pardon, and for no apparent reason under the sun. The wonder is that I am not knocked down oftener.

It was to avoid going through life under this pressure that I evolved the little scheme detailed herewith. It cost me several thousand dollars, but Doris is through with asking questions of outsiders.

We had started on a little trip to Boston. I could have found out where the Boston train was in a few minutes had I been left to my-self. But Doris never relies on the signs. Someone must be asked, too, just to make sure. Confronted once by a buckboard literally swathed in banners which screamed in red letters, "This bus goes to the State Fair Grounds," I had to go up to the driver (who had on his cap a flag reading "To the State Fair Grounds") and ask him if this bus surely went to the State Fair Grounds. He didn't even answer me.

So when Doris said, "Go and ask that man where the Boston

train leaves from," I gritted my teeth and decided that the time had come. Simulating conversation with him, I really asked him nothing, and returned to Doris, saying, "Come on. He says it goes from Track 10."

Eight months later we returned home. The train that left on Track 10 was the Chicago Limited, which I had taken deliberately. In Chicago I again falsified what "the man" told me, and instead of getting on the train back to New York we went to Little Rock, Arkansas. Every time I had to ask where the best hotel was, I made up information which brought us out into the suburbs, cold and hungry. Many nights we spent wandering through the fields look-ing for some place that never existed, or else in the worst hotel in town acting on what I said was the advice of "that kind-looking man in uniform."

From Arkansas, we went into Mexico, and once, guided by what I told her had been the directions given me by the man at the news-stand in Vera Cruz, we made a sally into the swamps of Central America, or whatever that first republic is on the way south. After that, Doris began to lose faith in what strange men could tell us. One day, at a little station in Mavicos, I said, "Wait a minute, till I ask that man what is the best way to get back into America," and she said sobbing, "Don't ask anybody. Just do what you think is best." Then I knew that the fight was over. In ten days I had her limp form back in New York and from that day to this she hasn't once suggested that I ask questions of a stranger.

The funny part of it is, I constantly find myself asking them. I guess the humiliation came in being told to ask.

Editha's Christmas Burglar

Caroline

IT WAS the night before Christmas, and ~~Editha~~ was all agog. It was all so exciting, so exciting! From her little bed up in the nursery she could hear Mumsey and Daddy downstairs putting the things on the tree and jamming her stocking full of broken candy and oranges.

"Hush!" Daddy was speaking. "Eva," he was saying to Mumsey, "it seems kind of silly to put this ten-dollar gold piece that ~~Aunt Issac~~ sent to Editha into her stocking. She is too young to know the value of money. It would just be a bauble to her. How about putting it in with the household money for this month? Editha would then get some of the food that was bought with it and we would be ten dollars in."

Dear old Daddy! Always thinking of someone else! Editha wanted to jump out of bed right then and there and run down and throw her arms about his neck, perhaps shutting off his wind.

"You are right, as usual, Hal," said Mumsey. "Give me the gold piece and I will put it in with the house funds."

"In a pig's eye I will give you the gold piece," ~~replied Daddy~~. "You would nest it away somewhere until after Christmas and then go out and buy yourself a muff with it. I know you, you old grafter." And from the sound which followed, Editha knew that Mumsey was kissing Daddy. Did ever a little girl have two such darling parents? And, hugging her Teddy bear close to her, Editha rolled over and went to sleep.

She awoke suddenly with the feeling that someone was downstairs. It was quite dark and the radiolite traveling clock which stood by her bedside said eight o'clock, but, as the radiolite travel-ing clock hadn't been running since Easter, she knew that that couldn't be the right time. She knew that it must be somewhere between three and four in the morning, however, because the blanket had slipped off her bed, and the blanket always slipped off her bed between three and four in the morning.

And now to take up the question of who it was downstairs. At first she thought it might be Daddy. Often Daddy sat up very late working on a case of Scotch and at such times she would hear him downstairs counting to himself. But whoever was there now was being very quiet. It was only when he jammed against the china cabinet or joggled the dinner gong that she could tell that anyone was there at all. It was evidently a stranger.

Of course, it might be that the old folks had been right all along and that there really was a Santa Claus after all, but Editha dis-missed this supposition at once. The old folks had never been right before and what chance was there of their starting in to be right now, at their age? None at all. It couldn't be Santa, the jolly old soul!

It must be a burglar then! Why, to be sure! Burglars always come around on Christmas Eve and little yellow-haired girls always get up and go down in their nighties and convert them. Of course! How silly of Editha not to have thought of it before!

With a bound the child was out on the cold floor, and with another bound was back in bed again. It was too cold to be fooling around without slippers on. Reaching down by the bedside, she pulled in her little fur foot-pieces which Cousin Mabel had left behind by mistake the last time she visited Editha, and drew them on her tiny feet. Then out she got and started on tip-toe for the stairway.

She did hope that he would be a good-looking burglar and easily converted, because it was pretty gosh-darned cold, even with slip-pers on, and she wished to save time.

As she reached the head of the stairs, she could look down into the living room where the shadow of the tree stood out black against the gray light outside. In the doorway leading into the dining room stood a man's figure, silhouetted against the glare of

"Hello, Mr. Man!" she said

an old-fashioned burglar's lantern which was on the floor. He was
rattling silverware. Very quietly, Editha descended the stairs until
she stood quite close to him.

"Hello, Mr. Man!" ~~she said~~.

The burglar looked up quickly and reached for his gun.

"Who the hell do you think you are?" ~~he asked~~.

"I'se Editha," replied the little girl in the sweetest voice she could
summon, which wasn't particularly sweet at that as Editha hadn't
a very pretty voice.

"You's Editha, is youse?" replied the burglar. "Well, come on
down here. Grandpa wants to speak to you."

"Youse is not my Drandpa," said the tot, getting her baby and
tough talk slightly mixed. "Youse is a dreat, bid burglar."

"All right, kiddy," replied ~~the man~~. "Have it your own way. But
come on down. I want ter show yer how yer kin make smoke come
outer yer eyes. It's a Christmas game."

"This guy is as good as converted already," thought Editha to

"A Merry Christmas to all and to all a Good Night!"

herself. "Right away he starts wanting to teach me games. Next he'll be telling me I remind him of his little girl at home."

So with a light heart she came the rest of the way downstairs, and stood facing the burly stranger.

"Sit down, Editha," he said, and gave her a hearty push which sent her down heavily on the floor. "And stay there, or I'll mash you one on that baby nose of yours."

This was not in the schedule as Editha had read it in the books, but it doubtless was this particular burglar's way of having a little fun. He *did* have nice eyes, too.

"Dat's naughty to do," she said, scoldingly.

"Yeah?" said the burglar, and sent her spinning against the wall. "I guess you need attention, kid. You can't be trusted." Whereupon he slapped the little girl. Then he took a piece of rope out of his bag and tied her up good and tight, with a nice bright bandana handkerchief around her mouth, and trussed her up on the chandelier.

"Now hang there," he said, "and make believe you're a Christmas present, and if you open yer yap, I'll set fire to yer."

Then, filling his bag with the silverware and Daddy's imitation sherry, Editha's burglar tip-toed out by the door. As he left, he turned and smiled. "A Merry Christmas to all and to all a Good Night," he whispered, and was gone.

And when Mumsey and Daddy came down in the morning, there was Editha up on the chandelier, sore as a crab. So they took her down and spanked her for getting out of bed without permission.

What Does It Mean?

THERE seems to be no lengths to which humorless people will not go to analyze Humor. It seems to worry them. They can't believe that anything could be funny just on its own hook.

One of the most worried of these Humor analysts is the gentleman who, in a book called *Carroll's Alice* (a reprint of a lecture, as one might guess), has tried to wrench deep meanings out of *Alice in Wonderland*. He certainly picked a good one to wrench on.

According to this savant, the Lion and the Unicorn were really meant by Carroll to represent "the contemporary battle between the traditional classics, plus mathematics, and the new sciences." This is just a starter. Hold your hats!

Reading further, we learn that the Mad Hatter was actually a derivative of the numerous Hatta family mentioned in Sharon Turner's *History of the Anglo-Saxons*. (This space is reserved for any expletive that Alice-lovers may care to burst into. I, personally, have a copy desk and the Post Office Department to think of.)

This leads to the interesting speculation that the Dormouse might have been intended by Carroll as a satirical crack at Father Doremus, the Fifteenth Century monk mentioned in Swarthouth's *Fifteenth Century Monks and Their Relations to Dormice*.

Or might not Alice, herself, have been a figure symbolical of the proposal to construct a tunnel under the English Channel? We can't have Alice just banging around without any significance at all.

Of course, it is true that many present-day situations have parallels in the situations of the Alice books, but I like to believe that this is not because Carroll put sense into his nonsense but because the present-day situations are sheer nonsense in themselves. Why monkey around with Nonsense? It can stand well enough on its own feet.

And why monkey around with any kind of Humor? I recently got a letter from another worried citizen who is, for reasons best known to himself, getting out a book on Humor. He asked just two questions:

"What is Humor? What makes people laugh?"

Boy, if I knew I wouldn't be sitting here, I can tell you!

A Talk to Young Men

TO YOU young men who only recently were graduated from our various institutions of learning (laughter), I would bring a message, a message of warning and yet, at the same time, a message of good cheer. Having been out in the world a whole month, it is high time that you learned something about the Facts of Life, something about how wonderfully Nature takes care of the thousand and one things which go to make up what some people jokingly call our "sex" life. I hardly know how to begin. Perhaps "Dear Harry" would be as good a way as any.

You all have doubtless seen, during your walks in the country, how the butterflies and bees carry pollen from one flower to another? It is very dull and you should be very glad that you are not a bee or a butterfly, for where the fun comes in *that* I can't see. However, they think that they are having a good time, which is all that is necessary, I suppose. Some day a bee is going to get hold of a real book on the subject, and from then on there will be mighty little pollen-toting done or I don't know my bees.

Well, anyway, if you have noticed carefully how the bees carry pollen from one flower to another (and there is no reason why you should have noticed carefully as there is nothing to see), you will have wondered what connection there is between this process and that of animal reproduction. I may as well tell you right now that there is no connection at all, and so your whole morning of bee-stalking has been wasted.

We now come to the animal world. Or rather, first we come to One Hundred and Twenty-fifth Street, but you don't get off there.

The animal world is next, and off you get. And what a sight meets your eyes! My, my! It just seems as if the whole world were topsy-turvy.

The next time you are at your grocer's buying gin, take a look at his eggs. They really are some hen's eggs, but they belong to the grocer now, as he has bought them and is entitled to sell them. So they really *are* his eggs, funny as it may sound to anyone who doesn't know. If you will look at these eggs, you will see that each one is *almost* round, but not *quite*. They are more of an "egg-shape." This may strike you as odd at first, until you learn that this is Nature's way of distinguishing eggs from large golf balls. You see, Mother Nature takes no chances. She used to, but she learned her lesson. And that is a lesson that all of you must learn as well. It is called Old Mother Nature's Lesson, and begins on page 145.

Now, these eggs have not always been like this. That stands to reason. They once had something to do with a hen or they wouldn't be called hen's eggs. If they are called duck's eggs, that means that they had something to do with a duck. Who can tell me what it means if they are called "ostrich's eggs"? . . . That's right.

But the egg is not the only thing that had something to do with a hen. Who knows what else there was? . . . That's right.

Now the rooster is an entirely different sort of bird from the hen. It is very proud and has a red crest on the top of his head. This red crest is put there by Nature so that the hen can see the rooster coming in a crowd and can hop into a taxi or make a previous engagement if she wants to. A favorite dodge of a lot of hens when they see the red crest of the rooster making in their direction across the barnyard is to work up a sick headache. One of the happiest and most contented roosters I ever saw was one who had had his red crest chewed off in a fight with a dog. He also wore sneakers.

But before we take up this phase of the question (for it is a question), let us go back to the fish kingdom. Fish are probably the worst example that you can find; in the first place, because they work under water, and in the second, because they don't know anything. You won't find one fish in a million that has enough sense to come in when it rains. They are just stupid, that's all, and nowhere is their stupidity more evident than in their sex life.

Take, for example, the carp. The carp is one of the least promising of all the fish. He has practically no forehead and brings nothing at all to a conversation. Now the mother carp is swimming around some fine spring day when suddenly she decides that it would be nice to have some children. So she makes out a deposit slip and deposits a couple million eggs on a rock (all this goes on *under* water, mind you, of all places). This done, she adjusts her hat, powders her nose, and swims away, a woman with a past.

It is not until all this is over and done with that papa enters the picture, and then only in an official capacity. Papa's job is very casual. He swims over the couple of million eggs and takes a chance that by sheer force of personality he can induce half a dozen of them to hatch out. The remainder either go to waste or are blacked up to represent caviar.

So you will see that the sex life of a fish is nothing much to brag about. It never would present a problem in a fish community as it does in ours. No committees ever have to be formed to regulate it, and about the only way in which a fish can go wrong is through drink or stealing. This makes a fish's life highly unattractive, you will agree, for, after a time, one would get very tired of drinking and stealing.

We have now covered the various agencies of Nature for populating the earth with the lesser forms of life. We have purposely omitted any reference to the reproduction of those unicellular organisms which reproduce by dividing themselves up into two, four, eight, etc., parts without any outside assistance at all. This method is too silly even to discuss.

We now come to colors. You all know that if you mix yellow with blue you get green. You also get green if you mix cherries and milk. (Just kidding. Don't pay any attention.) The derivation of one color from the mixture of two other colors is not generally considered a sexual phenomenon, but that is because the psychoanalysts haven't got around to it yet. By next season it won't be safe to admit that

you like to paint, or you will be giving yourself away as an inhibited old uncle-lover and debauchee. The only thing that the
sex-psychologists can't read a sexual significance into is trap-shooting, and they are working on that now.

All of which brings us to the point of wondering if it *all* isn't a
gigantic hoax. If the specialists fall down on trap-shooting, they
are going to begin to doubt the whole structure which they have
erected, and before long there is going to be a reaction which will
take the form of an absolute negation of sex. An Austrian scientist
has already come out with the announcement that there is no
such thing as a hundred per cent male or a hundred per cent female.
If this is true, it is really a big step forward. It is going to throw
a lot of people out of work, but think of the money that will be
saved!

And so, young men, my message to you is this: Think the thing
over very carefully and examine the evidence with fair-minded
detachment. And if you decide that, within the next ten years, sex
is going out of style, make your plans accordingly. Why not be
pioneers in the new movement?

Paul Revere's Ride

HOW A MODEST GO-GETTER DID HIS BIT FOR THE
JUNO ACID BATH CORPORATION

FOLLOWING are the salesman's report sheets sent into the home office in New York by Thaddeus Olin, agent for the Juno Acid Bath Corporation. Mr. Olin had the New England territory during the spring of 1775 and these report sheets are dated April 16, 17, 18, and 19, of that year.

> *April 16, 1775.*
> *Boston.*

Called on the following engravers this A.M.: Boston Engraving Co., E. H. Hosstetter, Theodore Platney, Paul Revere, Benjamin B. Ashley and Roger Durgin.

Boston Engraving Co. are all taken care of for their acid.

E. H. Hosstetter took three tins of acid No. 4 on trial and renewed his old order of 7 Queen-Biters.

Theodore Platney has gone out of business since my last trip.

Paul Revere was not in. The man in his shop said that he was busy with some sort of local shindig. Said I might catch him in tomorrow morning.

The Benjamin Ashley people said they were satisfied with their present product and contemplated no change.

Roger Durgin died last March.

Things are pretty quiet in Boston right now.

> *April 17.*

Called on Boston Engraving people again to see if they might not want to try some Daisy No. 3. Mr. Lithgo was interested and said to come in tomorrow when Mr. Lithgo, Senior, would be there.

Paul Revere was not in. He had been in for a few minutes before the shop opened and had left word that he would be up at Sam Adams' in case anyone wanted him. Went up to the Adams place, but the girl there said that Mr. Revere and Mr. Adams had gone over to Mr. Dawes' place on Milk Street. Went to Dawes' place, but the man there said Dawes and Adams and Revere were in conference. There seems to be some sort of parade or something they are getting up, something to do with the opening of the new footbridge to Cambridge, I believe.

Things are pretty quiet here in Boston, except for the trade from the British fleet which is out in the harbour.

Spent the evening looking around in the coffee houses. Everyone here is cribbage-crazy. All they seem to think of is cribbage, cribbage, cribbage.

April 18.

To the Boston Engraving Company and saw Mr. Lithgo, Senior. He seemed interested in the Daisy No. 3 acid and said to drop in again later in the week.

Paul Revere was out. His assistant said that he knew that Mr. Revere was in need of a new batch of acid and had spoken to him about our Vulcan No. 2 and said he might try some. I would have to see Mr. Revere personally, he said, as Mr. Revere makes all purchases himself. He said that he thought I could catch him over at the Dawes' place.

Tried the Dawes' place but they said that he and Mr. Revere had gone over to the livery stable on State Street.

Went to the livery stable but Revere had gone. They said he had engaged a horse for tonight for some sort of entertainment he was taking part in. The hostler said he heard Mr. Revere say to Mr. Dawes that they might as well go up to the North Church and see if everything was all set; so I gather it is a church entertainment.

Followed them up to the North Church, but there was nobody there except the caretaker, who said that he thought I could catch Mr. Revere over at Charlestown late that night. He described him to me so that I would know him and said that he probably would be on horseback. As it seemed to me to be pretty important that we land the Revere order for Vulcan No. 2, I figured out that whatever inconvenience it might cause me to go over to Charlestown or whatever added expense to the firm, would be justified.

Spent the afternoon visiting several printing establishments, but none of them do any engraving.

Things are pretty quiet here in Boston.

Went over to Charlestown after supper and hung around "The Bell in Hand" tavern looking for Mr. Revere. Met a man there who used to live in Peapack, N. J., and we got to talking about what a funny name for a town that was. Another man said that in Massachusetts there was actually a place called Podunk, up near Worcester. We had some very good cheese and talked over names of towns for a while. Then the second man, the one who knew about Podunk, said he had to go as he had a date with a man. After he had left I happened to bring the conversation around to the fact that I was waiting for a Mr. Paul Revere, and the first man told me that I had been talking to him for half an hour and that he had just gone.

I rushed out to the corner, but the man who keeps the watering-trough there said that someone answering Mr. Revere's description had just galloped off on a horse in the direction of Medford. Well, this just made me determined to land that order for Juno Acid Bath Corporation or die in the attempt. So I hired a horse at the Tavern stable and started off toward Medford.

Just before I hit Medford I saw a man standing out in his night-shirt in front of his house looking up the road. I asked him if he had seen anybody who looked like Mr. Revere. He seemed pretty sore and said that some crazy coot had just ridden by and knocked at his door and yelled something that he couldn't understand and that if he caught him he'd break his back. From his description of the horse I gathered that Mr. Revere was the man; so I galloped on.

A lot of people in Medford Town were up and standing in front of their houses, cursing like the one I had just seen. It seems that Mr. Revere had gone along the road-side, knocking on doors and yelling something which nobody understood, and then galloping on again.

"Some goddam drunk," said one of the Medfordites, and they all went back to bed.

I wasn't going to be cheated out of my order now, no matter what happened, and I don't think that Mr. Revere could have been drunk, because while he was with us at "The Bell in Hand," he had only four short ales. He had a lot of cheese, though.

Something seemed to have been the matter with him, however, because in every town that I rode through I found people just going back to bed after having been aroused up out of their sleep by a mysterious rider. I didn't tell them that it was Mr. Revere, or that it was probably some stunt to do with the shindig that he and Mr. Dawes were putting on for the North Church. I figured out that it was a little publicity stunt.

Finally, just as I got into Lexington, I saw my man getting off his horse at a house right alongside the Green. I rushed up and caught him just as he was going in. I introduced myself and told him that I represented the Juno Acid Bath Corporation of New York and asked him if he could give me a few minutes, as I had been following him all the way from Charlestown and had been to his office three days in succession. He said that he was busy right at that minute, but that if I wanted to come along with him upstairs he would talk business on the way. He asked me if I wasn't the man he had been talking to at "The Bell in Hand" and I said yes, and asked him how Podunk was. This got him in good humor and he said that we might as well sit right down then and that he would get someone else to do what he had to do. So he called a man-servant and told him to go right up stairs, wake up Mr. Hancock and Mr. Adams and tell them to get up, and no fooling. "Keep after them, Sambo," he said, "and don't let them roll over and go to sleep again. It's very important."

So we sat down in the living room and I got out our statement of sales for 1774 and showed him that, in face of increased competition, Juno had practically doubled its output. "There must be some reason for an acid outselling its competitors three to one," I said, "and that reason, Mr. Revere, is that a Juno product is a guaranteed product." He asked me about the extra sixpence a tin and I asked him if he would rather pay a sixpence less and get an inferior grade of acid and he said, "No." So I finally landed an order of three dozen tins of Vulcan No. 2 and a dozen jars of Acme Silver Polish, as Mr. Revere is a silversmith, also, on the side.

Took a look around Lexington before I went back to Boston, but didn't see any engraving plants. Lexington is pretty quiet right now.

Respectfully submitted,

THADDEUS OLIN.

Attached.

Expense Voucher

Juno Acid Bath Corp., New York

Thaddeus Olin, Agent.

Hotel in Boston		15s.
Stage fare		30s.
Meals (4 days)		28s.
Entertaining prospects	£3	4s.
Horse rent. Charlestown to Lexington and return	£2	6s.
Total Expense	£9	3s.
To Profit on three dozens tins of Vulcan No. 2 and		18s.
One dozen jars Acme Silver Polish		4s.
	£1	2s.
Net Loss	£8	1s.

Throwing Back the European Offensive

THIS is probably the hardest time of year for those of us who didn't go to Europe last summer. It was bad enough when the others were packing and outlining their trips for you. It was pretty bad when the postcards from Lausanne and Venice began coming in. But now, in the fall, when the travelers are returning with their Marco Polo travelogs, now is when we must be brave and give a cheer for the early frost.

There are several ways to combat this menace of returning travelers. The one that I have found most effective is based on the old football theory that a strong offense is the best defense. I rush them right off their feet, before they can get started.

In carrying out this system, it is well to remember that very few travelers know anything more about the places they have visited than the names of one hotel, two points of interest, and perhaps one street. You can bluff them into insensibility by making up a name and asking them if they saw that when they were in Florence. My whole strategy is based on my ability to make up names. You can do it, too, with practice.

Thus, let us say that I am confronted by Mrs. Reetaly who has just returned from a frantic tour of Spain, southern France, and the Ritz Hotel, Paris. You are inextricably cornered with her at a tea, or beer night, or something. Following is a transcript of the conversation. (Note the gathering power of my offense.)

MRS. R.: Well, we have just returned from Europe, and everything seems so strange here. I simply can't get used to our money.

Mr. B.: I never see enough of it to get used to it myself. (*Just a pleasantry.*)

Mrs. R.: When we were in Madrid, I just gave up trying to figure out the Spanish money. You see, they have *pesetas* and—

Mr. B.: A very easy way to remember Spanish money is to count ten *segradas* to one *mesa*, ten *mesas* to one *rintilla* and twenty *rintillas* to one *peseta*.

A strong offensive is the best defense

Mrs. R.: Oh, you have been to Spain? Did you go to Toledo?

Mr. B.: Well, of course, Toledo is just the beginning. You pushed on to Mastilejo, of course?

Mrs. R.: Why—er—no. We were in quite a hurry to get to Granada and—

Mr. B.: You didn't see Mastilejo? That's too bad. Mastelejo is Toledo multiplied by a hundred. Such mountains! Such coloring! Leaving Mastilejo, one ascends by easy stages to the ridge behind the town from which is obtained an incomparable view of the entire Bobadilla Valley. It was here that, in 1476, the Moors—

Mrs. R.: The Moorish relics in Granada—

Mr. B.: The Moorish relics in Granada are like something you buy from Sears Roebuck compared to the remains in Tuna. You saw Tuna, of course?

Mrs. R.: Well, no (*lying her head off*), we were going there, but Harry thought that it would just be repeating what—

Mr. B.: The biggest mistake of your life, Mrs. Reetaly, the biggest mistake of your life! Unless you have seen Tuna, you haven't seen Spain.

Mrs. R.: But Carcassonne—

Mr. B.: Ah, Carcassonne! Now you're talking! Did you ever see anything to beat that old diamond mill in the *Vielle Ville*? Would they let you go through it when you were there?

Mrs. R.: Why, I don't think that we saw any old diamond mill. We saw an old—

Mr. B.: I know what you're going to say! You saw the old wheat sifter. Isn't that fascinating? Did you talk with the old courier there?

Mrs. R.: Why, I don't remember—

Mr. B.: And the hole in the wall where Louis the Neurotic escaped from the Saracens?

Mrs. R.: Yes, wasn't that—? (*Very weak.*)

Mr. B.: And the stream where they found the sword and buckler of the Man with the Iron Abdomen?

Mrs. R. (*Edging away*): Yes, indeed.

Mr. B.: And old Vastelles? You visited Vastelles, surely? . . . Mrs. Reetaly, come back here, please! I just love talking over these dear places with someone who has just been there. . . . May I call on you some day soon and we'll just have a feast of reminiscence? . . . Thank you. How about tomorrow?

And from that day to this, I am never bothered by Mrs. Reetaly's European trip, and you needn't be, either, if you will only study the above plan carefully.

The other method is based on just the opposite theory—that of no offense, or defense, at all. It is known as "dumb submission," and should be tried only by very phlegmatic people who can deaden their sensibilities so that they don't even hear the first ten minutes of the traveler's harangue. The idea is to let them proceed at will for a time and then give unmistakable evidence of not having heard a word they have said. Let us say that Mr. Thwomly has accosted me on the train.

MR. T.: It certainly seems funny to be riding in trains like this again. We have been all summer in France, you know, and those French trains are all divided up into compartments. You get into a compartment—*compartimon,* they call them—and there you are with three or five other people, all cooped up together. On the way from Paris to Marseilles we had a funny experience. I was sitting next to a Frenchman who was getting off at Lyons—Lyons is about half way between Paris and Marseilles—and he was dozing when we got in. So I—

MR. B.: Did you get to France at all when you were away?

MR. T.: This was in *France* that I'm telling you about. On the way from Paris to Marseilles. We got into a railway carriage—

MR. B.: The railway carriages there aren't like ours here, are they? I've seen pictures of them, and they seem to be more like compartments of some sort.

MR. T. *(a little discouraged)*: That was a French railway carriage I was just describing to you. I sat next to a man—

MR. B.: A Frenchman?

MR. T.: Sure, a Frenchman. That's the *point.*

MR. B.: Oh, I see.

MR. T.: Well, the Frenchman was asleep, and when we got in I stumbled over his feet. So he woke up and said something in French, which I couldn't understand, and I excused myself in English, which *he* couldn't understand, but I saw by his ticket that he was going only as far as Lyons—

MR. B.: You were across the border into France, then?

MR. T. *(giving the whole thing up as a bad job)*: And what did *you* do this summer?

Whichever way you pick to defend yourself against the assaults of people who want to tell you about Europe, don't forget that it was I who told you how. I'm going to Europe myself next year, and if you try to pull either of these systems on *me* when I get back, I will recognize them at once, and it will just go all the harder with you. But, of course, *I* will have something to tell that will be worth hearing.

More Songs for Meller

AS SENORITA RAQUEL MELLER sings entirely in Spanish, it is again explained, the management prints little synopses of the songs on the program, telling what each is all about and why she is behaving the way she is. They make delightful reading during those periods when Señorita Meller is changing mantillas, and, in case she should run out of songs before she runs out of mantillas, we offer a few new synopses for her repertoire.

(1) ¿ Voy Bien?
(AM I GOING IN THE RIGHT DIRECTION)

When the acorns begin dropping in Spain there is an old legend that for every acorn which drops there is a baby born in Valencia. This is so silly that no one pays any attention to it now, not even the gamekeeper's daughter, who would pay attention to anything. She goes from house to house, ringing doorbells and then running away. She hopes that some day she will ring the right doorbell and will trip and fall, so that Prince Charming will catch her. So far, no one has even come to the door. Poor Pepita! if that is her name.

(2) Camisetas de Flanela
(FLANNEL VESTS)

Princess Rosamonda goes nightly to the Puerta del Sol to see if the early morning edition of the papers is out yet. If it isn't she hangs around humming to herself. If it is, she hangs around humming just the same. One night she encounters a young matador who is returning from dancing school. The finches are singing and there is Love in the air. Princess Rosamonda ends up in the Police Station.

(3) La Guia
(the time-table)

It is the day of the bull fight in Madrid. Everyone is cockeyed. The bull has slipped out by the back entrance to the arena and has gone home, disgusted. Nobody notices that the bull has gone except Nina, a peasant girl who has come to town that day to sell her father. She looks with horror at the place in the Royal Box where the bull ought to be sitting, and sees there instead her algebra teacher, whom she had told that she was staying at home on account of a sick headache. You can imagine her feelings!

(4) No Puedo Comer Eso
(i can not eat that!)

A merry song of the Alhambra—of the Alhambra in the moon-light—of a girl who danced over the wall and sprained her ankle. Lititia is the ward of grouchy old Pampino, President of the First National Banco. She has never been allowed further away than the edge of the piazza because she teases people so. Her lover has come to see her and finds that she is fast asleep. He considers that for once he has the breaks, and tiptoes away without waking her up. Along about eleven o'clock she awakes, and is sore as all get-out.

(5) La Lavandera
(the laundryman)

A coquette, pretending to be very angry, bites off the hand of her lover up to the wrist. Ah, naughty Cirinda! Such antics! However does she think she can do her lessons if she gives up all her time to love-making? But Cirinda does not care. Heedless, heedless Cirinda!

(6) Abra Vd. Esa Ventana
(open that window)

The lament of a mother whose oldest son is too young to vote. She walks the streets singing "My son can not vote! My son is not old enough!" There seems to be nothing that can be done about it.

Compiling an American Tragedy

SUGGESTIONS AS TO HOW THEODORE DREISER MIGHT WRITE
HIS NEXT HUMAN DOCUMENT AND SAVE FIVE YEARS' WORK

CHAPTER I

UP EAST DIVISION STREET, on a hot day in late July, walked
two men, one five feet four, the other, the taller of the two, five
feet six, the first being two inches shorter than his more elongated
companion, and consequently giving the appearance to passers-by
on East Division Street, or, whenever the two reached a cross street,
to the passers-by on the cross street, of being at least a good two
inches shorter than the taller of the little group.

Walking up East Division Street they came, in two or three
minutes, to Division Street proper, which runs at right angles and
a little to the left of East Division Street, but not so much to the left
as Marcellus Street, or Ransome Street, for that matter. As the two
continued strolling, in that fashion in which two men of their respective heights are likely to stroll, they came in succession to—

(NOTE TO PRINTER: *Attached find copy of Thurston's Street Guide.
Print names of every street listed therein, beginning with East Division and up to, and including, Dawson.*)

CHAPTER II

That these two men, presented in the last chapter, would eventually stop walking up Division Street and enter a house of some
sort or description, might well be anticipated by the reader, and,
in fact, such was the case.

It was, indeed, the house of the shorter of the two, of the one
whom we have seen in the last chapter to have been five feet four, if,

111

indeed, he was. It was a typical dwelling, or home, of a man of the middle class in a medium-sized city such as the one in which these men found themselves living.

(NOTE TO PRINTER: *Attached find insurance inventory of household effects and architect's specifications. Reproduce in toto.*)

CHAPTER III

Reaching the living room described above, Tom Rettle, for such was the name of the shorter of the two—the one to whom the house, or home, or dwelling, belonged—was greeted by his wife, Anna, a buxom woman of perhaps thirty-four or thirty-five, certainly not *more* than thirty-five, if one were to judge by her fresh, wholesome color and the sparkle of her brownish-gray eyes, or even by her well-rounded form, her—

(*Print attached passport description of Anna Rettle.*)

"Well, hello, Anna," said Tom, pleasantly, for Tom Rettle was, as a matter of fact, a very pleasant man unless he were angered, and his blue eyes smiled in a highly agreeable manner.

"Well, hello, Tom," replied Anna, for it was indeed Anna who spoke, in a soft, well-modulated voice, too, giving the impression of being an extremely agreeable sort of a woman.

"Anna, I want you to meet a very good friend of mine, Arthur Berolston, a very good friend of mine," said Tom, politely, looking, at the same time, at both Anna and Berolston.

"I'm very happy to meet Mr. Berolston," added Anna, genially, although one could see that in her heart she wished that Tom would bring a little different type of friend home, a thing she had often spoken to him about when they were alone, as they often were.

"Dat's very good of yer ter say, Missus Rettle," replied Berolston, in modern slang, which made him sound even more uncouth than he looked, which was uncouth enough. "For de love o' Mike!"

At this indication of a rough bringing-up on the part of her husband's acquaintance, Anna Rettle winced slightly but showed no other sign of her emotions. Tom was such a kind-hearted fellow! So good! So kind-hearted! Tom was.

"What is there for supper tonight, Anna?" asked Tom, when the wincing had died down. "You know how well I like cole slaw, and have always liked it."

"I certainly do know your fondness for cole slaw, Tom," replied his wife, but with a note of regret in her voice, for she was thinking that she had no cole slaw for supper on the particular night of which we are speaking. "But you will remember that we had cole slaw last night with the cold tongue, and night before last with the baked beans and—"

(*Run attached "Fifteen Midsummer Menus for Cole Slaw Lovers."*)

CHAPTER IV

Prepared as Tom was not to have cole slaw for supper, he could not hide his disappointment. Anna had been a good wife to him.

But somehow tonight, when he had brought Arthur Berolston home to supper, his disappointment was particularly keen, for he and Arthur had been discussing cole slaw all the way up East Division Street, across Division Street and through to the southwest corner of Dawson and Margate, where Tom lived, and each had said how much he liked it.

Should he strike Anna for failing him at this juncture? He, Tom Rettle, strike his wife, Anna Rettle? And, even if he should decide to strike her, *where* should he direct the blow? Tom's mind was confused with all these questions.

(*Reprint the above paragraph twenty-five times.*)

CHAPTERS V-LXXXII INCLUSIVE

TO PRINTER: *With the above copy you will find a briefcase containing newspaper clippings giving the complete testimony of Anna Rettle, Thomas Rettle and Arthur Berolston in the case of "ANNA RETTLE VS. THOMAS RETTLE," tried in the Criminal Court of Testiman County, September 2-28, 1925. There is also a transcript of the testimony of three neighbors of the Rettles' (Herman Nordquist, Ethel Nordquist and Junior Nordquist), and of Officer Louis M. Hertzog of the Fifth Precinct. Reprint all these and, at the bottom of the last page, put "THE END."*

Inter-office Memo

IT WILL always be a mystery to me why I was asked "into conference" in the first place. I am more the artistic type, and am seldom consulted on the more practical aspects of life. I have given up wearing soft collars and can smoke a cigar, if it is a fairly short one, but I don't seem able to give off any impression of business stability. I am just one of the world's beautiful dreamers.

So when McNulty called me up and asked me if I could come over to his office for a conference with somebody named Crofish or Cronish of Detroit, I was thrown into a fever of excitement. At last I was going to sit in on a big business conference! I think there was some idea that I, as a hay-fever sufferer, might have a suggestion or two on handkerchiefs that might be valuable. For the conference was on the marketing of a steel handkerchief which the Detroit people were about to put out.

So all in a flutter I rushed over to McNulty's office, determined to take mental notes on the way in which real business men disposed of real business in the hope that one day I might extricate myself from the morass of inefficiency in which I was living and perhaps amount to something in the business world. At least, I would have caught a glimpse of how things ought to be done.

Mr. Crofish or Cronish (whose name later turned out to be Crolish) was already there, with his briefcase open in front of him and a lot of papers piled up on the desk. He and McNulty were both so bustly and efficient-looking that it hardly seemed worth while for me to sit down. This conference couldn't last more than a minute and a half!

"Sorry to bother you, Bob, old man," said McNulty, briskly, "but we thought that you might be able to help us out a little in this scheme for getting the Beau Brummel Steel Handkerchief before

114

the public . . . Sit down won't you? . . . Perhaps Mr. Crolish can state his problem better than I can, and then we will get your angle on it."

Mr. Crolish looked at his papers and cleared his throat. "Well, here is the situation we are faced with," he began.

"Just a minute, Mr. Crolish," interrupted McNulty, "I think it might be well, before you begin, to find out from Reemis just what magazines we are going to use, so that Mr. Benchley will have a little better idea of what type of copy we shall need." And he turned to the telephone. "Get me Mr. Reemis, will you please, Miss Fane?"

Mr. Reemis's line seemed to be busy, so McNulty propped the receiver up against his ear and reached in the drawer for some cigars, while waiting.

"Another couple of days like this and spring will be here," he announced tentatively.

"That's right," said Mr. Crolish, which didn't leave much for me to say unless I wanted to fight the statement.

Mr. Reemis was very busy, so McNulty, still holding the receiver, tried something else to pass the time.

"Mrs. McNulty and I saw one of the worst shows I've ever seen last night. *Rolling Raisins*. Did you ever see it?"

I said that I hadn't and Mr. Crolish said that he hadn't but that he had heard about it.

"No wonder people don't go to the theatre more," said McNulty, "when they put . . . oh, hello! . . . Reemis? . . . say, could you step into my office for just a minute, please?"

While we were waiting for Mr. Reemis, McNulty explained the plot of *Rolling Raisins*. And, as Mr. Reemis was evidently coming into the office by a route which led him down into the street and up the back stairway, Mr. Crolish told the plot of a show which had opened in Detroit last week. I had just started in on the plot of a show we had once put on in college when Mr. Reemis appeared.

"This is Mr. Benchley, Mr. Reemis . . . I guess you know Mr. Crolish. . . . What we wanted to find out was just what magazines we are going to use in this Beau Brummel campaign."

"Well, there have been some changes made since we went over

it with you, Mr. McNulty," said Mr. Reemis. "I'm not quite sure of the list as it stands. I'll shoot back to my desk and get it."

So Mr. Reemis shot back, and Mr. Crolish walked over to the window.

"They certainly are tearing up this old town, aren't they?" he asked. "Every time I come here there is a new building up somewhere. I suppose they'll be tearing down the Woolworth Building next."

"I understand they've started already," said McNulty, "but they don't quite know where to begin."

This was a pretty fair line and it got all the laugh that it deserved. The thing was beginning to take on the air of one of those easygoing off-hours which we impractical artists indulge in when we are supposed to be working. It was interrupted by Mr. Reemis shooting back with the list.

"Here we are," he said, brightly. "Now, as I understand it, this is a strictly class appeal we are trying to make and we don't want to bother with the old-fashioned handkerchief users; so we thought that—"

Here the door opened and one of the partners came in.

"Sorry to butt in, Harry," he said, "but have you seen this statement of the Mackbolter people in the *Times?*"

"I just glanced at it," said McNulty, ". . . you know Mr. Benchley, Mr. Wamser? . . . I guess you know Crolish."

Mr. Wamser and I shook hands.

"Are you any relation to the Benchley who used to live in Worcester?" he asked.

I admitted that I had relatives in Worcester.

"I'll never forget the night I spent in Worcester once," he said, seating himself on the edge of McNulty's desk. "We were motoring to Boston and a thunderstorm came up; so we put in at Worcester—what's the name of that hotel?"

"The Bancroft?" I suggested.

"I don't think it was the Bancroft," he said. "What are some of the others? I'll know the name if I hear it."

Two young men bearing a layout came in

I said that so far as I knew there weren't any others since the old Bay State House had been torn down.

"Well, maybe it was the Bancroft."

Mr. Crolish suggested that it might have been the Worthy.

"The Worthy is in Springfield," said McNulty.

At this point two young gentlemen bearing a layout came in.

"Sorry to interrupt," said one of them, "but do you want the package played up in this Meer-o page or just show the girl playing tennis?"

The two young gentlemen were introduced and turned out to be Mr. Rollik and Mr. MacNordfy.

"Hoagman is handling that more than I am," said Mr. Wamser. And going to the telephone he asked to have Mr. Hoagman step into Mr. McNulty's office for a minute. While waiting for Mr. Hoagman, Mr. Rollik asked the gathering (which was, by now, assuming the proportions of a stag smoker) if they had seen what Will Rogers had in the paper that morning.

"I can always get a laugh out of that guy Rogers," said Mr. Crolish.

"What I like about him is that he gets a lot of common sense into his gags. They *mean* something." It was Mr. MacNordfy who thought this.

"Abe Martin is the one I like," said McNulty. Mr. Wamser was of the opinion that no one had ever been able to touch Mr. Dooley. To prove his point he quoted a fairish bit of one of Mr. Dooley's dissertations in very bad Irish dialect. Mr. Hoagman, having entered during the recitation, waived the formality of introductions and began:

"If you like Irish jokes, I heard one yesterday that I thought was pretty clever. I may be wrong."

He was wrong, and so got down to business. "What was it you wanted to see me about?" he asked, as soon as he had stopped laughing.

"The boys here want to know whether the Meer-o people want the package played up in this layout or to subordinate it to the girl playing tennis?"

I made unnoticed for the elevator

"Oh, you've got to play the package up," said Mr. Hoagman, thereby making the first business decision of the morning. This gave him such a feeling of duty-done that he evidently decided to knock off work for the rest of the morning and devote his time to story-telling.

The room was so full by this time that I had completely lost sight of Mr. Crolish, who was, at best, a small man and was in his original seat on the other side of the room, still sitting in front of his open briefcase. Mr. McNulty was talking on the telephone again and seemed good for fifteen minutes of it. The rest of the staff were milling about, offering each other cigarettes, telling anecdotes and in general carrying on the nation's business.

I looked at my watch and found that I was already late for a lunch date; so picking up my hat, I elbowed my way quietly out of the room unnoticed and made the elevator.

Later in the week I heard that McNulty had told someone that I was a nice guy but that there was no sense in trying to do business with me. I guess I shall always be just a dreamer.

Fascinating Crimes

THE STRANGE CASE OF THE VERMONT JUDICIARY

RESIDENTS of Water Street, Bellows Falls (Vt.), are not naturally sound sleepers, owing to the proximity of the Bellows Falls Light and Power Co. and its attendant thumpings, but fifteen years before the erection of the light-and-power plant there was nothing to disturb the slumbers of Water Streetites, with the possible exception of the bestial activities of Roscoe Erkle. For it was Mr. Erkle's whim to creep up upon people as they slept and, leaping on their chests, to cram poisoned biscuits into their mouths until they died, either from the poison or from choking on the crumbs.

A tolerant citizenry stood this as long as it could decently be expected to, and then had Roscoe Erkle arrested. It is not this phase of his career in which we are interested, however, so much as the remarkable series of events which followed.

His trial began at St. Albans, Franklin County, on Wednesday morning, May 7, 1881. Defending Erkle was an attorney appointed by the Court, Enos J. Wheefer. Mr. Wheefer, being deaf, had not heard the name of his client or he would never have taken the case. He thought for several days that he was defending Roscoe Conkling, and had drawn up his case with Conkling in mind.

Atty. Herbert J. McNell represented the State and, as it later turned out, a tragic fate gave the case into the hands of Judge Alonso Presty for hearing.

Judge Presty was one of the leaders of the Vermont bar at the time and a man of impeccable habits. It was recalled after his untimely death that he had been something of a rounder in his day, having been a leader in barn-dancing circles while in law school,

121

but since donning the sock and buskin his conduct had been propriety itself. Which make the events that we are about to relate all the more puzzling.

On the opening day of the trial, Atty. McNell was submitting as evidence passages from the prisoner's diary which indicated that the murders were not only premeditated but a source of considerable delight to Mr. Erkle. It might perhaps be interesting to give a sample page from the diary:

"*Oct.* 7—Cool and fair. Sharp tinge of Fall in the air. New shipment of arsenic arrived from W. Spent all day powdering biscuits and then toasting them. Look good enough to eat.

"*Oct.* 8—Raw, with N. E. wind. Betsy came in for a minute and we did anagrams. (EDITOR's NOTE: *Betsy was Erkle's cow.*)

"*Oct.* 9—Still raw. Cleaned up Water Street on the left-hand side, with the exception of old Wassner who just wouldn't open his mouth. Home and read till after midnight. That man Carlyle certainly had the dope on the French Revolution, all right, all right."

As Atty. McNell read these excerpts from the diary in a droning voice, the breath of Vermont May-time wafted in at the open windows of the courtroom. Now and then a bee hummed in and out, as if to say, "Buz-z-z-z-z-z-z!" Judge Presty sat high above the throng, head resting on his hand, to all intents and purposes asleep.

Suddenly the attorney for the defendant arose and said, "I protest, Your Honor. I cannot hear what my learned colleague is saying, but I don't like his expression!"

There was silence while all eyes turned on the Judge. But the Judge did not move. Thinking that he had fallen asleep, as was his custom during the May term, the attorneys went on. It was not until he had gradually slipped forward into the glass of water which stood before him on his desk that it was discovered that he was dead!

The trial was immediately halted and an investigation begun. Nothing could be discovered about the Judge's person which would give a clue to his mysterious lapse except a tiny red spot just behind his right ear. This, however, was laid to indigestion and the Judge was buried.

Another trial was called for October 10, again in St. Albans. This time Judge Walter M. Bondy was presiding, and the same two attorneys opposed each other. Roscoe Erkle had, during the summer, raised a red beard and looked charming.

On the second day of the trial, while Atty. McNell was reading the prisoner's diary, Judge Bondy passed away quietly at his bench, with the same little red spot behind his right ear that had characterized the cadaver of his predecessor. The trial was again halted, and a new one set for the following May.

By this time, the matter had become one for serious concern. Erkle was questioned, but his only reply was: "Let them mind their own business, then." He had now begun to put pomade on his beard and had it parted in the middle, and, as a result, had married one of the richest spinsters in that section of Vermont.

We need not go into the repetitious account of the succeeding trials. Suffice it to say that the following May Judge Rapf died at his post, the following October Judge Orsenigal, the May following that a Judge O'Heel, who had been imported from New Hampshire without being told the history of the case, and the succeeding solstices saw the mysterious deaths of Judges Wheefer (the counsel for the defense in the first trial, who had, in the meantime, been appointed Judge because of his deafness), Rossberg, Whelan, Rock, and Brady. And, in each case, the little telltale mark behind the ear.

The State then decided to rest its case and declare it *nol-prossed*. Judges were not so plentiful in Vermont that they could afford to go on at this rate. Erkle was released on his own recognizance, took up the study of law, and is, at latest accounts, a well-to-do patent attorney in Oldham. Every May and every October he reports at St. Albans to see if they want to try him again, but the Court laughingly postpones the case until the next term, holding its hand over its right ear the while.

Back to the Game

THIS is about the time of year (it would be a good joke on me if this chapter were held over until Spring) when the old boys begin thinking of going back to college to the Big Game. All during the year they have never given a thought to whether they were alumni of Yale or the New York Pharmaceutical College, but as soon as the sporting pages begin telling about O'Brienstein of Harvard and what a wonderful back he is, all Harvard men with cigar ashes on their waistcoats suddenly remember that they went to Harvard and send in their applications for the Yale Game. There is nothing like a college education to broaden a man.

Going back to the old college town is something of an ordeal, in case you want to know. You think it's going to be all right and you have a little dream-picture of how glad the boys will be to see you. "Weekins, 1914," you will say, and there will be a big demonstration, with fireworks and retchings. The word will go round that Weekins, 1914, is back and professors in everything but Greek will say to their classes, "Dismissed for the day, gentlemen. Weekins, 1914, is back!" And a happy crowd of boys will rush pell-mell out of the recitation hall and down to the Inn to take the horses from your carriage (or put horses into it) and drag you all around the Campus. (My using the word "Campus" is just a concession to the rabble. Where I come from "Campus" is a place where stage-collegians in skull-caps romp around and sing "When Love Is Young in Springtime" in four-part harmony. The reservation in question is known as "the Yard," and I will thank you to call it that in future.)

Anyone who has ever gone back to the old college town after, let us say, ten years, will realize that this country is going to the dogs, especially as regards its youth in the colleges. You get your tickets

*A couple of young men come in and, seeing you, go
right out again*

for the Big Game and you spend a lot of money on railroad fare.
(That's all right; you have made a lot of money since getting out.
You can afford it.) When you get to the old railroad station you
can at least expect that Eddie, the hack driver, will remember you.
Eddie, however, is now pretty fat and has five men working for him.
You can't even get one of his cabs, much less a nod out of him.
O. K. Eddie! The hell with you!

You go to the fraternity house (another concession on my part
to my Middle West readers) and announce yourself as "Weekins,
1914." (My class was 1912, as a matter of fact. I am giving myself a
slight break and trying to be mysterious about this whole thing.)
A lone junior who is hanging around in the front room says, "How
do you do? Come on in," and excuses himself immediately. The
old place looks about the same, except that an odd-looking banner

on the wall says "1930," there being no such year. A couple of young men come in and, seeing you, go right out again. Welcome back to the old House, Weekins!

A steward of some sort enters the room and arranges the magazines on the table.

"Rather quiet for the day of the Big Game," you say to him. "Where is everybody?"

This frightens him and he says, "Thank you, sir!" and also disappears.

Well, after all, you *do* have a certain claim on this place. You helped raise the money for the mission furniture and somewhere up on the wall is a stein with your name on it. There is no reason why you should feel like an intruder. This gives you courage to meet the three young men who enter with books under their arms and pass right by into the hall.

"My name is Weekins, 1914," you say. "Where is everybody?"

"Classes are just over," one of them explains. "Make yourself at home. My name is Hammerbiddle, 1931."

Somehow the mention of such a year as "1931" enrages you. 1931 what? Electrons? But the three young men have gone down the hall, so you will never know.

A familiar face! In between the bead portières comes a man, bald and fat, yet with something about him that strikes an old G chord.

"Billigs!" you cry.

"Stanpfer is the name," he says. "Think of seeing you here!"

You try to make believe that you knew that it was Stanpfer all the time and were just saying Billigs to be funny.

"It must be fifteen years," you say.

"Well, not quite," says Stanpfer, "I saw you two years ago in New York."

"Oh, yes, I know, *that!*" (Where the hell did you see him two years ago? The man is crazy.) "But I mean it must be fifteen years since we were here together."

"Fourteen," he corrects.

"I guess you're right. Fourteen. Well, how the hell are you?"

"Great! How are you?"

"Great! How are you?"

"Great! Couldn't be better. Everything going all right?"

"Great! All right with you?"

"Great! All right with you?"

"You bet."

"That's fine! Kind of quiet around here."

"That's right! Not much like the old days."

"That's right."

"Yes, sir! That's right!"

Perhaps it would be better if the 1931 boys came back. At least, you wouldn't have to recall old days with them. You could start at scratch. Here comes somebody! Somebody older than you, if such a thing is possible.

"Hello," he says, and falls on his face against the edge of the table, cutting his forehead rather badly.

"Up you get!" you say, suiting the action to the word.

"A very nasty turn there," he says, crossly. "They should have that banked."

"That's right," you agree. You remember him as a senior who was particularly snooty to you when you were a sophomore.

"My name is Feemer, 1911," he says, dabbing his forehead with his handkerchief.

"Weekins, 1914," you say.

"Stanpfer, 1914," says Billigs.

"I remember you," says Feemer. "You were an awful pratt."

You give a short laugh.

Feemer begins to sing loudly and hits his head again against the table, this time on purpose. Several of the undergraduates enter and look disapprovingly at all three of you.

By this time Feemer, through constant hitting of his head and lurching about, is slightly ill. The general impression is that you and Stanpfer (or Billigs) are drunk too. These old grads!

The undergraduates (of whom there are now eight or ten) move unpleasantly about the room, rearranging furniture that Feemer has upset and showing in every way at their disposal that they wish you had never come.

"What time is the game?" you ask. You know very well what time the game is.

Nobody answers.

"How are the chances?" Just why you should be making *all* the advances you don't know. After all, you are fourteen years out and these boys could almost be your sons.

"I want everybody here to come to Chicago with me after the game," says Feemer, tying his tie. "I live in Chicago and I want everybody here to come to Chicago with me after the game. I live in Chicago and I want everybody here to come to Chicago with me after the game."

Having made this blanket invitation, Feemer goes to sleep standing up.

The undergraduate disapproval is manifest and includes you and Billigs (or Stanpfer) to such an extent that you might better be at the bottom of the lake.

"How are the chances?" you ask again. "Is Derkwillig going to play?"

"Derkwillig has left college," says one of the undergraduates, scornfully. "He hasn't played since the Penn State game."

"Too bad," you say. "He was good, wasn't he?"

"Not so good."

"I'm sorry. I thought he was, from what I read in the papers."

"The papers are crazy," says a very young man, and immediately leaves the room.

There is a long silence, during which Feemer comes to and looks anxiously into each face as if trying to get his bearings, which is exactly what he is trying to do.

"We might as well clear the room out," says one of the undergraduates. "The girls will be coming pretty soon and we don't want to have it looking messy."

Evidently "looking messy" means the presence of you, Feemer and Stanpfer. This is plain to be seen. So you and Stanpfer each take

There is no sign of recognition on either side

an arm of Feemer and leave the house. Just as you are going down the steps (a process which includes lurching with Feemer from side to side) you meet Dr. Raddiwell and his wife. There is no sign of recognition on either side.

There is a train leaving town at 1:55. You get it and read about the game in the evening papers.

The Typical New Yorker

ONE of the most persistent convictions reported by foreign commentators on the United States (a group which evidently embraces all unoccupied literates of England and the more meditative sections of the Continent) is that the real America is represented by the Middle West. Aside from the not entirely adventitious question of who is to decide just what "the real America" is, there arises a fascinating speculation for breeders and students of climatic influence as to why a man living in Muncie, Indiana, should partake of a more essential integrity in being what he is than a man living in New York City. Why is the Middle Westerner the real American, and the New Yorker the product of some complicated inbreeding which renders him a sport (in the biological sense) and a man without a country?

Of course, at the bottom of it all is the generally accepted theory (not limited by any means to visiting scribes but a well-founded article in our national credo) that there is something about the Great Open Spaces which makes for inherent honesty and general nobility of character. Hence the firmly rooted superstition that a boy who has been raised on a farm is somehow finer and more genuine than a boy who has been raised in the city.

I remember once a mother whose three children were being brought up in the country (and very disagreeable and dishonest children they were, too) saying, with infinite pity of the children of a city acquaintance, "Just think, those kiddies have probably never seen a cow!" Just what sanctity or earnest of nobility was supposed to attach itself to the presence of a cow in a child's life

I never could figure out, but there was an answer which might have been made that her own kiddies had never seen the Woolworth Building or the East River bridges at night. Among the major inquiries that will one day have to be made is one into the foundation for this belief that intimacy with cows, horses, and hens or the contemplation, day in and day out, of great stretches of crops exerts a purifying influence on the souls of those lucky enough to be subjected to it. Perhaps when the answer is found, it may help solve another of the pressing social problems of the day—that of Rural Delinquency.

However, so ingrained is this faith in the efficacy of livestock and open spaces in the elevation of the race, that even to question it is to place oneself under suspicion of being a character who will bear watching by the authorities. So it will be perhaps just as well to pass quickly on to the second, and more specific, reason for our guest writers' impression that the Middle West is America and that New York is just New York.

In most cases this is easily explained by following the New York itinerary of the guest writer (and the word "guest" is used advisedly —it has been estimated that the total personal expenditures of visiting authors during their stay in America, if pooled, might possibly buy one American author one breakfast at the Savoy in London). The New York about which they write is the New York they have seen or have been told about by their hosts, and for even the most conscientious among them, this cannot constitute more than a quarter of even the Borough of Manhattan.

Ford Madox Ford has even been so explicit as to call his recent book *New York Is Not America*, and yet he admits in the course of his argument that, for him, "New York is intimately and solely the few miles . . . along Fifth Avenue and Broadway from the Battery." And, at that, Mr. Ford knows his New York much better than most foreigners who prescribe for it. The customary laboratory and field work entered into by New York diagnosticians from abroad consists of a luncheon at the Coffee House Club, visits to several of the more accessible night clubs, a peep into Greenwich Village, and a series of dinners more or less under the auspices of Otto H. Kahn. If they are really in earnest, they may be taken up into Harlem and shown the negro exhibit, or over to Long Island City and shown how Sunshine Biscuits are made. They ask questions of their dinner partners, and those answers which they cannot use in a "vignette" of New York they embody in a searching and comprehensive analysis of the American Woman. This is generally considered ample investigation on which to base a broad survey entitled *The Meaning of New York*, or, as Mr. Ford has put it, *New York Is Not America*.

For most visitors to Manhattan, both foreign and domestic, New York is the Shrine of the Good Time. This is only natural, for outsiders come to New York for the sole purpose of having a good time, and it is for their New York hosts to provide it. The visiting Englishman, or the visiting Californian, is convinced that New York City is made up of millions of gay pixies, flitting about constantly in a sophisticated manner in search of a new thrill. "I don't see how you stand it," they often say to the native New Yorker who has been sitting up past his bedtime for a week in an attempt to tire his guest out. "It's all right for a week or so, but give me the little old home town when it comes to *living*." And, under his breath, the New Yorker endorses the transfer and wonders himself how he stands it.

The New York pixie element is seen by visitors because the visitors go where the pixie element is to be found, having become, for the nonce, pixies themselves. If they happen to be authors in search of copy, they perhaps go slumming to those places where they have heard the Other Half lives. They don't want to be narrow about the thing. There are the East Side pushcarts, which they must see and write a chapter about under the title of "The Melting Pot." Greenwich Village they have heard about, but that only fortifies their main thesis that New York is a gay, irresponsible nest of hedonists. Wall Street comes next, with its turmoil and tall buildings—rush-rush-rush-money-money-money! These ingredients, together with material gathered at the Coffee House Club and private dinners, and perhaps a short summary of the gang situation, all go into a word picture called "New York," and the author sails for home, giving out an interview at the pier in which he says that the city is pleasure-mad and its women are cold and beautiful.

Typical of the method by which the actualities of New York are taken by writers and translated into material for the New York of their dreams is the fantasy indulged in by Mr. Ford (in common, it must be admitted, with most of our domestic writers) of attributing the lights in the buildings along lower Manhattan to some province of fairyland.

"By day the soaring cliffs," writes Mr. Ford, "that rise joyously over behind the Battery are symbols not merely of hope but of attainment; after dark, and more particularly in the dusk, they are sheer fairyland. There is something particularly romantic in a Germanic sort of way about mountains illuminated from within . . . the million-wise illumination of New York is a lighter, gayer affair . . . the mind on seeing it connotes not subterranean picks and sweat but lighter more tenuous occupations—the pursuits of delicate, wayward beings."

Our visitors are confronted with so much gaiety in New York, especially where the lights are brightest, that they fall into the literary error of ascribing any metropolitan utilization of voltage to the pursuit of pleasure. And it *is* difficult to look at the lighted windows at the end of the island and not idealize them into some sort of manifestation of joy and exuberance. But if the writers who thrill so at the sight and translate it into terms of New York's light-heartedness could, by some sardonic and unkind force, be projected along any one of those million beams of fairy light, they would find that it came directly from an office peopled by tired Middle Westerners, New Englanders, and Southerners, each watching the clock as lighting-up time comes, not to start out on a round of merrymaking but to embark on a long subway ride uptown. And this ride will take them on past the haunts that the visitors and their hosts know, past the clubs and theatres and squash courts, to an enormous city above One Hundred and Twenty-fifth Street, where life is, with the exception of a certain congestion in living quarters, exactly the same as life in Muncie, Indiana, or Quincy, Illinois. For the inhabitants of this city have come direct from Muncie and Quincy and have never become assimilated into the New York of the commentators. It is not even picturesque, as the East Side is picturesque. It is a melting pot where the ingredients refuse to melt. The people are just as much New Yorkers as those in the Forties, and they outnumber the "typical" New Yorkers to so great an extent that an intramural battle between the two elements could not possibly last for more than twenty minutes, even if the pixies had machine guns.

I am not speaking of Harlem or the Bronx, where the standard of living is radically different from that of the much-advertised denizens of pleasure. Up in the Heights and beyond, as well as in the side streets farther down town, there are hundreds of thousands of men and women who go to bed at ten o'clock for the same reason that residents of Dodge City, Kansas, go to bed at ten o'clock—because they can't think of anything else to do, and because they have to be up at seven. There are streets north of Central Park through which a cooler breeze blows in summer than many a Mid-Western hamlet can boast, where life is quiet and its pace even. These streets are peopled by the very types who are supposed to make the Middle West the "real America," as alien to the New York of the magazine articles as their kinsfolk back home. They are in New York for many reasons, chiefly to make more money or because the head office in South Bend sent them there, and many of them wish that they had never come. But there they are, just as much New Yorkers as the patrons of Webster Hall or the Embassy Club, and a great deal more numerous.

I am not creating a New York out of my imagination as do those writers who find a filmy fairyland in the New York Edison Company's service along Pine and Nassau Streets. I have lived in New York's Middle West. During my early days as a metropolitan rounder (fresh from Massachusetts) I was under the wing of a kindly family from Canton, Ohio, who lived in Washington Heights, and it was a great comfort to me in my nostalgia to feel that here, in this neighborhood, I was, to all intents and purposes, among home folk. My first dissipation in New York was a church supper, so identical with the church suppers I had known in New England that it was impossible to imagine that farther down on this same island was the gay Gomorrah I had heard and been warned so much about. The people at this bacchanalia of chicken salad and escalloped oysters matched to a man the people I had eaten chicken salad and escalloped oysters with in my home town. There was the same aroma of coffee and hot rolls as one entered the vestry, and the same satyristic little boys were chasing the same coy little girls around the Sunday School room with as much vigor and obnoxiousness as if they had all been raised on a farm. Practically all of those present were small-town people, with small-town outlooks, and I venture to say that not one of them would have been recognized by a specialist in New Yorkese as a New Yorker. And yet there they were, they and their kind, a million strong.

Life in the New York Middle West goes along in its middle-class way with a dull rhythm which is in no way different from its model in Ohio or Michigan. Its pleasures are simple and inexpensive— movies, stock-company productions, church suppers, Masonic dances, and Sunday automobile riding in the country. When the day's work is done (and, as I understand it, even the real Americans in the Middle West have to attend to some sort of office work during the day aside from contemplating Nature in its more magnificent aspects) the same odor of cooking pervades the front halls, the same evening paper is read around the sitting-room table, the same problem of the evening's entertainment arises, ending in a general dozing in arm chairs and early retiring. Of sophistication there is none, of restlessness there is none (unless it be a restlessness to get back to Kansas or Massachusetts some day), and of the carefree fountain-fay that is the New Yorker of the correspondents you could go from one block to another all night long and not find a trace. There are simply dull, solid, one-hundred-percent Americans, who have never been in a night club in their lives and have no desire to be in one, whose bridge game has barely progressed from the bid-whist stage, and whose evening clothes are still in the trunk in the cellar and couldn't be worn anyway.

Whatever mysterious qualities the Middle Westerner has which fit him for the rôle of "real American," his brother in New York possesses to an equal degree, although with perhaps not quite so much volubility. Just what the real America is supposed to be is a bit hard to define, for each commentator has a different idea. But almost all agree that the America of the Middle West is made up of bustling Babbitts, children of energy, forward-looking perhaps in politics but incurably chauvinistic and provincial in their world outlook. All of which might be a word picture of the rank and file of New York's great Region of Respectability.

For, when the final house-to-house analysis is made of New York, the Typical New Yorker will emerge as quite a disappointing and colorless figure. In a rather wavering and indefinite career in that city I have lived and worked in many sections. While trying to "find myself" (a search which I ultimately gave up) I have had jobs in Wall Street, the negro district of Harlem, the Tenderloin, and Park Row. At night I have gone home to Washington Heights, an East Side Settlement House, Greenwich Village, the roaring Forties, and Chelsea. About the only districts in which I have not, at one time or another, stayed are the wharf districts along the North and East Rivers, and certain sections of the Bronx and San Juan Hill. And, after fifteen years of this sort of thing, I still look a second time at the sight of a man in evening dress, waving toy balloons in a night club, and think: "Perhaps now I am seeing the New York life I have heard so much about." I still look a second time at a gunman, although I have given several their start in life in my boys' club days. And, although my present work—and play—takes me almost nightly into the slightly lopsided maelstrom of the pixie activities in the theatres and night clubs, I can never bring myself to feel that this can be the gay, lighthearted New York Life that produces the Typical New Yorker. It is all so Middle Western and tentative.

The New Yorker at whom one does not look a second time, because there are so many of him and, furthermore, because he would not justify a second look, is a composite of the small-town qualities of every State in the Union. He wears his soft felt hat in winter and his straw hat in summer and, when his day's work is done, reads the same things in the New York *Evening Sun* or *World* that he read in his home-town evening paper before he came to New York: the domestic news on the front page (nothing with a foreign dateline) and the sporting news. He has a vague feeling that he is not *au courant* with the world's events and thoughts, and so subscribes to *The Literary Digest* or *Time*—which his wife reads. He votes for Hoover because Smith is a Catholic, or for Smith because Hoover is an Anglophile, and feels much less strongly about the issue of Prohibition than the zealots on either side think. If anything touches his business interests, however, he is roused into action and becomes a Moving Force. He has two children and wants them to have a good education. He is one-hundred-percent American, one-hundred-percent business and one-hundred-percent dull. And much as he dislikes New York, he would live in no other place.

On a scale such as statisticians draw showing the comparative sizes of the standing armies of Europe, this man would tower over the small figures of the night-club rounder, the sophisticated *literatus*, the wage slave of the East Side, and the other popular conceptions of the New Yorker as the S. S. *Majestic* standing on end towers above a soldier in a Swiss uniform. He cannot be called a "typical New Yorker" because there is no such thing, but, if the man seen in the Middle West by the visiting writers is a "typical American," then this man is one too. Furthermore, he is the product of no one section of the country but of all sections.

All of which would seem to give New York a right to claim that within its boundaries alone can be found the real, composite America. But New York does not apparently care enough to make such a claim, which lack of civic pride and booster-spirit is perhaps the most un-American thing about New York.

Carnival Week in Sunny Las Los

YOU have all doubtless wanted to know, at one time or another, a few of the quaint customs which residents of the continent of Europe seem to feel called upon to perpetuate from one century to another. You may know about a few of them already, such as child-bearing (which has been taken up on this continent to such an alarming extent) and others of the more common variety of folk mannerisms, but I am very proud and happy to be able to tell you today of some of the less generally known customs of the inhabitants of that medieval Spanish province Las Los (or Los Las, as it was formerly called, either way meaning "The The" *pl.*) where I have had the extremely bad fortune to be spending the summer.

Las Los, nestling, as it does, in the intercostal nooks of the Pyrenees, makes up into one of the nicest little plague-spots on the continent of Europe. Europe has often claimed that Las Los was *not* a part of it, and in 1356 Spain began a long and costly war with France, the loser to take Los Las and two outfielders. France won and Spain built an extension onto the Pyrenees in which to hide Los Las. They succeeded in hiding it from view, but there was one thing about Los Las that they forgot; so you always know that it is there.

It was in this little out-of-the-way corner of the world, then, that I set up my easel and began painting my fingers and wrists. I soon made friends with the natives (all of whom were named Pedro) and it was not long before they were bringing me their best Sunday knives and sticking them in my back for me to try and tell which was which. And such laughter would go up when I guessed the wrong one! All Latins, after all, are just children at heart.

But I am not here to tell you of the many merry days I myself spent in Las Los, but of some of the native customs which I was privileged to see, and, once in a while, take part in. They rather resent an outsider taking part in most of them, however, for there is an old saying in Las Los that "when an outsider takes part, rain will surely dart" (meaning "dart" from the clouds, you see) and above all things rain is abhorred in that section of the country, as rain has a tendency to cleanse whatever it touches, and, as another old proverb has it, "clean things, dead things"—which isn't exactly accurate, but appeals to these simple, childish people, to whom cleanliness is next to a broken hip.

First of all, then, let us tiptoe up on the natives of Las Los during their carnival time. The carnival week comes during the last week in July, just when it is hottest. This makes it really ideal for the Los Lasians, for extreme heat, added to everything else, renders their charming little town practically unbearable. This week was chosen many hundreds of years ago and is supposed to mark the anniversary of the marriage of old Don Pedro's daughter to a thunderbolt, a union which was so unsatisfactory to the young lady that she left her husband in two days and married a boy named Carlos, who sold tortillas. This so enraged the thunderbolt that he swore never to come to Los Las again, and, from that day to this (so the saying goes, I know not whether it be true or not) that region has never had any locusts. (This would almost make it seem that the repulsed bridgegroom had been a locust, but the natives, on being questioned, explained that the *patois* for "thunderbolt" [*enjuejoz*] is very much like the *patois* for "locust" [*enjuejoz*] and that the thunder god, in giving his order for the future of Los Las, put the accent on the wrong syllable and cut them off from locusts instead of thunderstorms.) This may, or may not, be the truth, but, as I said to the old man who told me, "Who the hell cares?" The first day of the Carnival of the Absence of Locusts (just why they should be so cocky about having no locusts is not clear. Locusts would be a godsend compared to some the things they *have* got) is spent in bed, storing up strength for the festival. On this day all the shops, except those selling wine, are closed. This means that a little shop down by the

"For the love of God, shut up that incessant banging!"

river which sells sieves is closed. People lie in bed and send out to the wine shops for the native drink, which is known as *wheero*. All that is necessary to do with this drink is to place it in an open saucer on the window sill and inhale deeply from across the room. In about eight seconds the top of the inhaler's head rises slowly and in a dignified manner until it reaches the ceiling where it floats, bumping gently up and down. The teeth then drop out and arrange themselves on the floor to spell "Portage High School, 1930," the eyes roll upward and backward, and a strange odor of burning rubber fills the room. This is followed by an unaccountable feeling of intense lassitude.

Thus we may expect nothing from the natives for the first two days of the carnival, for the second day is spent in looking for bits of head and teeth, and in general moaning. (A sorry carnival, you will say—and *I* will say, too.) But later on, things will brighten up.

On the third day the inhabitants emerge, walking very carefully in order not to jar off their ears, and get into a lot of decorated ox carts. They are not very crazy about getting into these ox carts, but it is more or less expected of them at carnival time. Pictures are taken of them riding about and are sent to the London illustrated papers, and if they were to pass up one year without riding in decorated ox carts, it wouldn't seem like carnival week to the readers of the London illustrated papers. You can hardly blame a man with a *wheero* hangover, however, for not wanting to bump around over cobblestones in an old two-wheeled cart, even if it has got paper flowers strong all over it. One of the saddest sights in the world is to see a native, all dressed up in red and yellow, with a garland of orange roses around his neck, jolting and jouncing along over hard stone bumps with a girl on his knee, and trying to simulate that famous Spanish smile and gay abandon, all the time feeling that one more bump and away goes that meal he ate several days ago, along with his legs and arms and portions of his lower jaw. No wonder Spaniards look worried.

However, there is a great deal of shouting and cawing among those who can open their mouths, and occasionally someone hits a tambourine. This is usually frowned upon by the person standing next to the tambourine-hitter and a remark, in Spanish, is made which could roughly be translated as "For the love of God, shut up that incessant banging!"

The carnival, which is known as *Romeria*, is supposed to be a festival of the picnic type combined with a religious pilgrimage to some sort of shrine. This shrine, however, is never reached, as along about noon of the third day some desperate guy, with a hangover no longer to be borne, evolves a cure on the "hair of the dog that bit you" theory, and the *wheero* is brought out again. The village watering trough is filled with it and a sort of native dance is held around the trough, everyone inhaling deeply. Those who are still unable to inhale are carried to the edge of the trough and a little *wheero* is rubbed on their upper lips, just under the nose. Then it is "good-night all, and a merry, merry trip to Blanket Bay," for the festive villagers, and the carnival is shot to hell. A week later business is quietly resumed.

On the fifth day of the carnival there is supposed to be a bull chase through the streets. The principle of the thing is that a bull is let loose and everyone chases it, or vice versa. As, however, there was nobody fit to chase a butterfly, much less a bull, on the fifth day of this carnival, I had to take care of the bull myself. The two of us sat all alone in the public square among the cadavers drinking a sort of lemon squash together.

"A dash of *wheero*?" I asked the bull.

Well, you should have heard him laugh! After that, I got up on his back and rode all around the town, visiting the points of interest and climbing several of the better-looking mountains. Pretty soon we were in Turkey, where we saw many interesting sights and then, swinging around through the Balkans, I got back just in time for me to scramble into bed. I must have hit my head on the footboard while pulling up the sheet, for the next morning (or whenever it was) when I awoke, I had quite a bad headache. Thank heaven I knew enough to lay off that *wheero*, however. I'm no fool.

Another Uncle Edith Christmas Story

UNCLE EDITH said, "I think it is about time that I told you a good old-fashioned Christmas story about the raging sea."

"Aw, nuts!" said little Philip.

"As you will," said Uncle Edith, "but I shall tell it just the same. I am not to be intimidated by a three-year-old child. Where was I?"

"You were over backwards, with your feet in the air, if I know anything about you," said Marian, who had golden hair and wore it in an unbecoming orange ribbon.

"I guess that you probably are right," said Uncle Edith, "although who am I to say? Anyway, I *do* know that we sailed from Nahant on the fourteenth March."

"What are you—French?" asked little Philip. "The fourteenth March."

"The fourteenth *of* March, then," said Uncle Edith, "and if you don't shut up I will keep right on with the story. You can't intimidate me."

"Done and done," said little Philip, who bled quite a lot from a wound in his head inflicted a few seconds before by Uncle Edith.

"We set sail from Nahant on the fourteenth *of* March (nya-a-a-a-a) on the good ship *Patience W. Littbaum,* with a cargo of old thread and bound for Algeciras."

"End of story!" announced Marian in a throaty baritone.

"It is *not* the end of the story, and I will sue anyone who says that it is," petulated Uncle Edith. "You will know well enough when I come to the end of the story, because I shall fall over on my face. Now be quiet or Uncle Edith will give you a great big abrasion on the forehead."

"I can hardly wait," said little Philip, or whichever the hell one of those children it was. I can't keep them all straight, they are all so much alike.

"Aboard," continued Uncle Edith, "aboard were myself, as skipper—"

"Skippered herring," (*a whisper*).

"—Lars Jannssenn, first mate; Max Schnirr, second mate; Enoch Olds, third base; and a crew of seven whose names you wouldn't recognize. However, there we were.

"The first seven hundred and nine days were uneventful. The sailmaker (a man by the name of Sailmaker, oddly enough) made eleven sails, but, as we had no more ships to put them on, and as our sails were O.K., we had to throw them overboard. This made the men discontented, and there were rumors of mutiny. I sent a reporter up to see the men, however, and the rumors were unconfirmed; so I killed the story. NO MUTINY was the head I put on it in the ship's paper that night, and everybody was satisfied."

"You great big wonderful animal," said Marian, running her tiny hand through Uncle Edith's hair.

"It was nothing," said Uncle Edith, and everybody agreed that it certainly was.

"However," continued the old salt pork, "everyone on board felt that something was wrong. We were at that time at Lat. seventy-eight, Long. seventy-eight, which cancelled each other, making us right back where we started from—"

"Don't tell me that we are back at Nahant again," said little Philip, throwing up.

Max Schnirr, second mate

"Not exactly Nahant," said Uncle Edith, "but within hailing distance of a Nahanted ship."

"You just used Nahant in the first place so that you could pull that gag," said Primrose, who, up to this time, had taken no part in the conversation, not having been born.

"So help me God," said Uncle Edith, "it came to me like *that!*" And he snapped a finger, breaking it. "The ha'nted ship lay just off our starboard bow, and seemed to be manned by mosquitoes. As we drew alongside, however, we found that there was not a soul on board. Not a soul on board."

"That is the second time you have said that," said little whatever-his-name-is—Philip.

Uncle Edith made no reply other than to throw nasty little Philip into irons.

" 'Prepare to board!' was the order given. And everybody, ignoring the chance for a pun, prepared to board the derelict. In a few seconds we were swarming over the side of the empty ship and searching every nook and cranny of her. The search, however, was fruitless. The ship's log was found in the wheelhouse, but, as the last entry read, 'Fair and warm. Billy said he didn't love me as much as he does Anna' we discarded that as evidence. In the galley we found a fried egg, done on only one side, and an old bo'sun who was

no good to anybody. Other than these two things, the mystery was complete."

"Not that I give a damn," said Marian, "but what was the explanation to this almost complete mystery?"

"If you will shut your trap," said Uncle Edith, "I will tell you. As I may not have told you, the mystery ship was full of sleeping Hessian troops, such as were used against the colonists in the Revolutionary War. They were very gay in their red coats and powdered wigs, and, had they been awake, might have offered some solution of the problem which now presented itself to us.

" 'What shall I do, cap'n?' asked Lars Jannssenn, who had been promoted to purser.

" 'What would you *like* to do, Lars?' I asked him.

" 'Me, I would like to have three wishes,' was the typically Scandinavian reply. (Lars had belonged to the Scandi-navy before he joined up with us.)

" 'They are yours,' I said, more on the spur of the moment than anything else. 'You take your three wishes and put them in your hat and pull it down over your ears. Anybody else?'

"Suddenly there was a scream from below decks. I have heard screams in my day, but never anything like this one. It was dark by

now, and there were a lot of couples necking in the lifeboats. But this scream was different. It was like nothing human. It came from the bowels of the ship, and you know that's bad.

" 'All hands below!' I cried, and just as everybody was rushing down the hatchways there came a great explosion, seemingly from the jib.

" 'All hands to the jib!' I cried in my excitement.

" 'What is all this—a game?' asked the crew, as one man.

" 'I am captain here,' I said, boxing the compass roundly, 'and what I say goes! In the future please try to remember that fact.'

"Well, this sort of thing went on for hours. Up and down the ship we went, throwing overboard Hessians in our rush, until finally the cook came to me and said, 'Cap'n, I frankly am sick of this. Are there, or are there not, any reasons why we should be behaving like a pack of schoolboys?"

"This was a poser. I called the crew together and we decided to go back to the *Patience W. Littbaum*. But, on looking over the side, we found a very suspicious circumstance. *The Patience W. Littbaum was gone!*"

"I don't believe it!" said little Philip, from the brig.

Uncle Edith turned sharply. "I thought you were in irons," he said.

"You think a lot," replied little Philip, and the entire casino burst into a gale of laughter, although it was a pretty lousy comeback, even for a three-year-old.

"Very well, then," said Uncle Edith. "I am sorry if you feel that way. For I was just going to end the story by saying that we sailed the mystery ship back to Nahant."

"And where does Christmas come in?" piped up Marian, who hadn't heard a word of Uncle Edith's story.

"Who the hell said anything about Christmas?" asked Uncle Edith in a rage.

And who the hell did?

If These Old Walls Could Talk!

IN PASSING by the old Waldorf the other day (or, to be exact, just as they were beginning to tear it down) I realized, with a slight catch in my throat, that some of the dullest hours of my life had been spent within its crumbling walls and, as I stopped to look for the last time at its historic front, I would have murmured *"Eheu fugaces!"* if I had been sure whether the "g" is pronounced hard or soft.

The Grand Ballroom of the Waldorf! What a flood of tiresome memories come tumbling to mind at the thought of that long speakers' table and the deadly hooey that had been delivered across its parapet! For six solid months, as a reporter for the daily press, I was forced nightly to attend banquets there, writhing with my colleagues at the little table down at the left; sleeping sometimes with my little head pillowed in my arms, sometimes supported by a numbing elbow, but always restless and uneasy and deriving none of that refreshing repair which sleep is supposed to bring. For always in my ear there was the steady, rhythmic drone of the speakers saying, "I do not want to take up more of your time, but there *is* one more point which I would like to make, and that is this—"

If only those old walls could talk, how boring they would be! No walls can take the beating that those walls took, decade after decade, without absorbing some of the deadly words and ponderous phrases with which the air was saturated and giving off something of the ennui which settled like a pall over that room at nine-thirty every night for years. Probably no walls of their age would have as little that was worthwhile to repeat.

Come, let us all turn into pumpkins and roll upstairs again into that old ballroom and see what ghosts are there! All right, then, let's not!

But if we *were* to visit the place again some night at midnight, just before the wreckers let the last of the royal boxes crash to the place where the floor used to be, I am sure that we would see a sight which would repay us for our trouble—and a hell of a lot of trouble it would be, too, climbing up stairs which aren't there any more.

For there, at the end of the long room, in the eerie half-light, we would see the speakers' table, with its mounds of carnations and plates of melting ice cream studded with cigar ends, and rising above it, behind badly bent shirt fronts, would be the row of guests, each running over in his mind the torture he is about to inflict on his audience and each making believe listen to the one who happens to have the floor at the time.

And who is that youth, sitting over at the table in the corner, along with other youths of the same ilk and informal dress, drawing little pictures on his menu and now and again muttering under his breath, "Ah, nuts!"? It is the ghost of the Boy I Used to Be, the boy whose fresh young soul was seared and calloused with a premature cynicism, whose eyes were even then narrowing with bitter distrust of mankind, because night after night he was forced to listen to the great minds of the nation giving expression to palpable bologna just in order that his section of the metropolitan press might go roaring to print with all the horrid details for the next morning's breakfast tables. (As a matter of fact, out of perhaps two hundred banquets covered, my paper used not more than three stories of mine and only a couple of sticks of those.)

And what are these ghost words which come floating out from nowhere, rustling through the empty shell of the great room? Listen carefully and you will hear them.

". . . and, just so long as this great nation, supreme in its devotion to the ideals of that Liberty established by our fathers . . . with annual imports for the year 1915 running into tens of millions of dollars . . . founded on the principle, based on the idea, conceived in the theory that no organization, no institution, no body of men can ... now, gentlemen, I feel in a way like that Irishman in being here with you tonight, because ... over against this is, as I see it, America's debt to France, a debt which can never ... this does not include that work done by outside organizations which have handled the thing very ably in their own way ... leaving six billions of dollars which this country ... get hung, nigger, get hung ... I have only a few more minutes at my disposal, your chairman having warned me before I began that ... the Class of 1918 has already raised more than its quota and I am sure that each and every one of you here tonight ... and I want to tell you tonight of a case which Dr. Gilley brought to my attention ... it has been said that the teacher of Martin Luther always stood before his pupils ... a little boy in the back of the room raised his hand ... into sixteen millions of dollars annually ... just as surely as if he had died in the trenches ... glowing with American ideals, fortified with new concepts of character, trained as children never have been trained in all the long history of the Near East ... making a total of three hundreds of millions of dollars ... I thank you."

And, as we listen to these words, echoes of a few of the hundreds of thousands of speeches which have reverberated through the old Waldorf ballroom, let us tip-toe quietly away, as so many auditors have done in the past, and, getting our hat and coat from the ghost of a check-room boy, leave the scene to those memories which have made it. But, as we go, perhaps it will be possible for us to give the last remaining wall a push so that it will fall in the direction of the speakers' table.

Happy Childhood Tales

WE HAVE had so many stories lately dealing with the sordid facts of life, about kitchen sinks and lynchings and young girls thrown out into the streets by mean old farmers who live in horsehair trunks, to say nothing of incidental subjects, such as gin and cold oatmeal and unfortunate people who have only one glove apiece, that a reaction is taking place in the mind of the reading public and a demand is going up for some of the fanciful happy tales of our youth.

"Enough of these stories of crime and unhappiness!" the people are crying. "Tell us again some of the ancient myths of an older day, the gay little legends on which we were brought up before the world grew grim and sordid."

And so, my little readers, I am going to try to recall to you some of the charming fairy tales, or, at any rate, to make up some like them, and I hope that after this little trip back into the Never-Never Land of our youth, those little cheeks of yours will be blooming again and that you will shut your traps. For, after all, there must be *some* good in the world, else why were erasers put on the ends of lead pencils?

Endremia and Liason

(*From the Greek Mythology*)

Endremia was the daughter of Polygaminous, the God of Ensilage, and Reba, the Goddess of Licorice. She was the child of a most unhappy union, it later turned out, for when she was a tiny child her father struck her mother with an anvil and turned himself into a lily pad to avoid the vengeance of Jove. But Jove was too sly for Polygaminous and struck him with a bolt of lightning the size of the Merchants Bank Building, which threw him completely off his

152

balance so that he toppled over into a chasm and was dashed to death.

In the meantime, Little Endremia found herself alone in the world with nobody but Endrocine, the Goddess of Lettuce, and her son Bilax, the God of Gum Arabic, to look after her. But, as Polygaminous (her father; have you forgotten so soon, you dope?) had turned Endremia into a mushroom before he turned himself into a lily pad, neither of her guardians knew who she was, so their protection did her no good.

But Jove had not so soon forgotten the daughter of his favorite (Reba), and appeared to her one night in the shape of a mushroom gatherer. He asked her how she would like to get off that tree (she was one of those mushrooms that grow on trees) and get into his basket. Endremia, not knowing that it was Jove who was asking her, said not much. Whereupon Jove unloosed his mighty wrath and struck down the whole tree with a bolt of lightning which he had brought with him in case Endremia wouldn't listen to reason.

This is why it is never safe to eat the mushrooms which grow on trees, or to refuse to get into Jove's basket.

MILGRIG AND THE TREE WILFS
(Something like Hans Christian Andersen)

Once upon a time there was a little girl named Milgrig, believe it or not. She lived in the middle of a deep dark forest with her three ugly sisters and their husbands, who were charcoal burners. Every night the three ugly sisters used to take little Milgrig and pull out a strand of her golden hair, so that by the time she was thirteen years old she looked something awful. And after the three sisters had pulled out her hair, their three husbands (I forgot to tell you that the three husbands were even uglier than the three sisters and much nastier) would stick pins into little Milgrig until she looked like a war map.

One night, when little Milgrig was so full of pins that she couldn't see straight, a fairy prince came riding up to the door of the charcoal burners' hut and asked if he had lost his way.

"How should I know?" replied the oldest sister, who was uglier than all the rest. "What was your way?"

"My way was to the king's castle," replied the prince, "and I must get there before midnight, for my father is torturing my mother with red-hot irons."

"Your father sounds like a good egg," replied the oldest husband, who was uglier than all the rest. "We must ask him down some night."

The prince, however, did not think that this was very funny and asked if little Milgrig might not be allowed to show him the way to the castle.

The ugly husbands and sisters, thinking that Milgrig would not know the way and would get the prince lost in the forest, agreed heartily to this suggestion, and the pins were pulled out of Milgrig to make it possible for her to walk.

"Good luck and a happy landing!" they all called out after the two young people as they set forth on their perilous journey.

But the prince was no fool, and knew his way through the forest as well as you or I do (better, I'll wager), and he took little Milgrig to the palace just as fast as his palfrey would carry him.

She wasn't particularly crazy about going, but a prince is a prince, and she knew enough to keep her mouth shut.

When they reached the palace and the prince found that his father had already killed his mother, he turned to little Milgrig and said:

"Now you are queen."

At this, little Milgrig was very pleased and immediately dispatched messengers to the charcoal burners' hut, where her three ugly sisters and three still uglier brothers-in-law were burned alive in a slow fire. Little Milgrig and the prince, happy in this termination to their little affair, lived happily ever after.

And so now, my readers, you must toddle off to bed, for we have had an evening with the happy, happy story-tellers of an earlier day and have had a vacation, for one night at least, from the drab, unpleasant sordidness of present-day writing.

The Sunday Menace

I AM not a gloomy man by nature, nor am I easily depressed. I always say that, no matter how much it looks as if the sun were never going to stop shining and no matter how long the birds carry on their seemingly incessant chatter, there is always a good sleet storm just around the corner and a sniffly head cold in store for those who will only look for it. You can't keep Old Stepmother Nature down for long.

But I frankly see no way out of the problem of Sunday afternoon. For centuries Sunday afternoon has been Old Nell's Curse among the days of the week. Sunday morning may be cheery enough, with its extra cup of coffee and litter of Sunday newspapers, but there is always hanging over it the ominous threat of 3 P.M., when the sun gets around to the back windows and Life stops dead in its tracks. No matter where you are—in China, on the high seas, or in a bird's nest—about three o'clock in the afternoon a pall descends over all the world and people everywhere start trying to think of something to do. You might as well try to think of something to do in the death house at Sing Sing, however, because, even if you do it, where does it get you? It is still Sunday afternoon.

The Blue Jeebs begin to drift in along about dessert at Sunday dinner. The last three or four spoonfuls of ice cream somehow lose their flavor and you begin crumbling up your cake instead of eating it. By the time you have finished coffee there is a definite premonition that before long, maybe in forty or fifty minutes, you will be told some bad news, probably involving the death of several favorite people, maybe even yourself. This feeling gives way to one of resignation. What is there to live for, anyway? At this point, your dessert begins to disagree with you.

155

On leaving the dining room and wandering aimlessly into the living room (living room indeed; there will be precious little living done in that room this afternoon), every one begins to yawn. The drifts of Sunday papers on the floor which looked so cozy before dinner now are just depressing reminders of the transitory nature of human life. Uncle Ben makes for the sofa and promptly drops off into an unattractive doze. The children start quarreling among themselves and finally involve the grownups in what threatens to be a rather nasty brawl.

"Why don't you go out and play?" someone asks.

"Play what?" is their retort, and a good one, too.

This brings up the whole question of what to do and there is a half-hearted attempt at thinking on the part of the more vivacious members of the party. Somebody goes to the window and looks out. He goes back to his chair, and somebody else wanders over to another window and looks out there, pressing the nose against the pane and breathing absent-mindedly against the glass. This has practically no effect on the situation.

In an attempt to start conversation, a garrulous one says, "Heigh-ho!" This falls flat, and there is a long silence while you look through the pile of newspapers to see if you missed anything in the morning's perusal. You even read the ship news and the book advertisements.

"This life of Susan B. Anthony looks as if it might be a pretty good book," you say.

"What makes you think so?" queries Ed crossly. Ed came out to dinner because he was alone in town, and now wishes he hadn't. He is already thinking up an excuse to get an early train back.

There being no good reason why you think that the life of Susan B. Anthony might be interesting, you say nothing. You didn't really think that it might be interesting, anyway.

A walk is suggested, resulting in groans from the rest of the group. The idea of bridge arouses only two out of the necessary four to anything resembling enthusiasm. The time for the arrival of Bad News is rapidly approaching and by now it is pretty fairly certain to involve death. The sun strikes in through the window and you notice that the green chair needs reupholstering. The rug doesn't look any too good, either. What's the use, though? There would be no sense in getting a lot of new furniture when every one is going to be dead before long, anyway.

It is a funny thing about the quality of the sunshine on a Sunday afternoon. On other days it is just sunshine and quite cheery in its middle-class way. But on Sunday afternoon it takes on a penetrating harshness which does nothing but show up the furniture. It doesn't make any difference where you are. You may be hanging around the Busy Bee lunch in Hong Kong or polishing brass on a yacht in the North Sea; you may be out tramping across the estate of one of the vice-presidents of a big trust company or teaching Indians to read in Arizona. The Sunday afternoon sunlight makes you dissatisfied with everything it hits. It has got to be stopped.

When the automobile came in it looked as if the Sunday afternoon problem was solved. You could climb in at the back door of the old steamer and puff out into the country, where at least you couldn't hear people playing "Narcissus" on the piano several houses away. (People several houses away are always playing "Narcissus" on the piano on Sunday afternoons. If there is one sound that is typical of Sunday afternoon, it is that of a piano being played several houses away.) It is true, of course, that even out in the country, miles away from everything, you could always tell that it was Sunday afternoon by the strange behavior of the birds, but you could at least pick out an open field and turn somersaults (first taking the small change out of your pockets), or you could run head-on into a large oak, causing insensibility. At least, you could in the early days of automobiling.

But, as soon as everybody got automobiles, the first thing they did naturally was to try to run away from Sunday afternoon, with the result that every country road within a hundred miles of any city has now taken the place of the old-time county fair, without the pleasure of the cattle and the jam exhibits. Today the only difference between Sunday afternoon in the city and Sunday afternoon in the country is that, in the country, you don't know the people who are on your lap.

Aside from the unpleasantness of being crowded in with a lot of

I really have no remedy for Sunday afternoons

strangers on a country road and not knowing what to talk about during the long hours while the automobiles are waiting to move ahead, there is the actual danger of an epidemic. Supposing some one took a child out riding in the country on Sunday and while they were jammed in line with hundreds of thousands of other pleasure riders the child came down with tonsilitis. There she would be, a carrier of disease, in contact with at least two-thirds of the population, giving off germs right and left and perhaps starting an epidemic which would sweep the country before the crowds could get back to their homes and gargle. Subways and crowded tenements have long been recognized as breeding grounds for afflictions of the nose and throat. Are country roads on Sunday afternoons to be left entirely without official regulation?

I really have no remedy for Sunday afternoon, at least none that I have any confidence in. The only one that might work would be to set fire to the house along about 1:30 P.M. If the fire were nursed along, it would cause sufficient excitement to make you forget what day it was, at least until it was time to turn on the lights for the evening. Or you might go down into the cellar right after dinner and take the furnace apart, promising yourself to have it put together again by supper time. Here, at least, the sunlight couldn't get at you. Or you could rent a diver's suit and go to the nearest body of water and spend the afternoon tottering about under the surface, picking sea anemone and old bits of wreckage.

The method which I myself have tried with considerable success and little expense, however, is to buy a small quantity of veronal at the nearest druggist's, put it slyly in my coffee on Saturday night, and then bundle off to bed. When you wake up on Monday morning you may not feel crisp, but Sunday will be over.

And that, I take it, is what we are after.

Can We Believe Our Eyes?

IT IS pretty generally agreed by now that Seeing is not Believing. Along with those exploded saws (watch out for exploding saws!) that Old Friends Are Best and the Longest Way Round is the Shortest Way Home (I could kill the guy who made that one up —it cost me eight dollars and a half in taxi fare once), the old dictum about seeing and believing has been shown to be just another flash in the pan.

In fact, according to scientists, if your eyes tell you that a thing is so, it is a very good reason for believing the opposite.

This will eventually make for a lot of trouble in the world.

However, all you have to do is to read the Sunday papers to see what little monkeys your eyes really are. Even the advertisements are getting into the game of confusing us with pictures showing large arrows and small arrows with captions like "Which is the larger of these two arrows?" Of course, it is perfectly obvious which is the larger, but when you come to measure them you find that, through some trickery, they are both the same size.

I will put up with just so much of this sort of thing, and then I will stop measuring. This unreliability on the part of visual images is only one part of Nature's way of making saps out of us, her children.

You may see two girls at a party, or two wire-haired fox terriers in a dog-shop window, and you say, pointing deliberately to one, "The one on the right is the one for me. I can tell just by looking that this is what I have been searching for all my life." If you want to know what this leads to all you have to do is read the divorce notices or the list of wire-haired fox terriers for sale "cheap."

For example, take Figure 1 of the accompanying illustrations. Which of these acorns would you say was the taller? (One is a hydrant, but you are not supposed to know that.) You would naturally say that the acorn on the left was at least twice as tall as the one on the right. Taller and handsomer.

Well, you would be right. But, when you see two objects like these in an eye test, you *think*: "There is a trick here! I am supposed to say that the one on the left is taller, so it can't be. I will say the one on the right, much against my better judgment." And so you lose five dollars.

FIG. 1

This is only one of the fascinating things that you can do with your eyes. Another is to wink one of them very slowly at a young lady sitting at the next table in a restaurant, and, the first thing you know, the other eye will be all blue and bulging and *very* sore, owing to her escort having shown you that optical illusion isn't everything. (See Figure 2.)

In Figure 3 we have another common form of self-deception. If you will take these concentric circles and rotate them slowly in front of your eyes, you will soon be dizzy enough to be quite ill. (In order to rotate the circles it will be necessary for you to buy another copy of this book and cut out the diagram with a pair of scissors. If you try rotating the whole book, you will find, not only that you will get tired quickly, but that you will be unable to read the type matter. And as in the type matter are contained the directions for *stopping* the rotary movement, you may go on twirling the paper for hours without knowing what to do next.) But after you have rotated the concentric circles for some time, you will find yourself believing that the thing is *actually turning itself!* After a while you will think that you are on a bicycle and will start working your feet on the pedals. If you keep the thing up much longer, you will faint.

Thus we see that our eyes play their pranks—as well as our other senses—and that the best thing to do with them is to keep them shut entirely.

FIG. 2

There is a well-known case of optical illusion recorded in the files of the British War Office at the Old Vic. It seems that during the Crimean War a detachment of British troops was isolated in a lonely village in a clump of trees. (The natives were tree dwellers, silly as it may seem.)

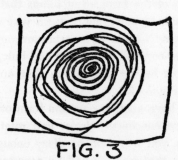

FIG. 3

They had nothing to do but drink a sort of mixture of heartsease (absinthe) and wormwood (absinthe) which the local doctor put up for people who had rather be dead.

Thus the days wore on.

One night when three subalterns were sitting around a fire and sipping at this strange mixture (no longer strange to them, however; more like a mother), one, a sergeant (British spelling), Villiers, turned to his companions and said,

"Don't look now, boys, but there go the Devonshire Reds, all but O'Day."

(The Devonshire Reds was a regiment that was stationed in Ottawa at the time, and O'Day was the only man in the regiment whom Villiers knew.)

"I rather doubt if the Devonshire Reds are over here in the Crimea right at this minute," said Athoy, one of the three, "but I see what you mean. It is a body of moving figures going quickly, in a swaying motion, from left to right, but it is my guess that they are penguins.

"See! See! There is a penguin now—leading the band!"

The third member of the party, a Leftenant Merley, who had said nothing up until this time, still said nothing. It was later discovered that his mouth had, in some unaccountable way, sunk into his cartridge belt, making it impossible for him to talk. Furthermore, he didn't care.

But the two who had seen the passing regiment (of either Devonshire Reds or penguins) argued far into the night over the phantom marchers, and finally decided that they had been really nothing but a crowd of rather ungainly sheep, walking on their hind legs.

In the morning, however, it was found that, as far as the sentries knew, *nobody had passed through the camp at all!*

This, one of the most famous examples of optical illusion, is only one item in the testimony to back up the contention that we cannot believe our eyes. And if we cannot believe our eyes, what *can* we believe?

The whole thing becomes frightening once you start to think of it. So don't think of it.

The King's English:
Not Murder but Suicide

BEING by nature and carefully acquired tastes something of an Anglophile, the following rather bitter outburst is going to hurt me more than it hurts England. In fact when, in the old days before I began filling out, I was occasionally told by strangers that I looked as if I might be English, I very often did nothing to correct the impression and even went so far as to throw in a word like "shedule" or "*cement*" deliberately to strengthen it. England has no better friend in the world than I am, even though I sometimes appear out of patience. That is because I am tired.

But, royalist though I am at heart, I find myself taking the old musket down from the wall and priming it for a determined stand against the redcoats who continue to assail our right to pronounce words as they are spelled. For years we colonists have submitted meekly to the charge that we speak the English language badly. We know that it is true in a way, that our voices are harsh and loud, that some of us roll our "r's" while others say "boid" and "erl," and we also know that, in the matter of vocabulary we are mere children lisping "cat," "doggie" and "O.K." exclusively. And the knowledge of these shortcomings, together with the venomous scorn with which our English friends point them out, has bred an inferiority in us which is nothing short of craven. We never think of turning on our tormentors and saying, "You're not so hot yourselves!"

British nausea at American pronunciation reached an almost active stage after the invasion of England by Hollywood-made talking-pictures. London editorial writers took the matter into their own hands and urged an embargo on American films on the charge of corrupting their youth. They saw the complete degradation of the English language in fifty years if little English children were allowed to listen at their movies to the horrid sound of Americans talking.

There was some idea of limiting the sale of tickets to those of his Majesty's subjects who were safely established in the traditional English habits of speech, barring at the door all those in the formative stage. Others would have had the pictorial parts of the films made in Hollywood (since England seemed to be having a little trouble in making any that would sell) but the sound-tracts made in Elstree by strictly British voices, the two being synchronized to produce a picture which might be listened to by English tots without fear of contamination. The whole island was evidently on the verge of a panic such as might arise at the approach of a fleet of cholera-ridden ships up the Thames.

No one in America will deny that many of the beautiful young gentlemen and ladies of Hollywood should never have been called upon to talk. Neither will anyone deny that a large number of American actresses and actors who go to London in the spoken drama might well offend the sensitive British ear. They have offended even the cauliflower ear of New York.

But is England entirely without sin in the matter of language distortion? Might New York never justifiably be distressed by the sounds made by the countless English casts which came over here to earn twice what they could earn at home? Is the frequent confusion in the minds of American audiences as to just what the English actors are saying on the stage due to the fact that our auditory faculties are not attuned to pure English or to the fact that the English actors are not pronouncing the words properly as they are spelled? If spelling means anything at all in the pronunciation of a word, then the English are at fault. If it doesn't, then they are at fault anyway.

Of course, there can be no argument (and let us have this understood at the start, please) over the comparative mellifluousness of English and American speech. Even the most incompetent English actor, coming on the stage briefly to announce the presence below of Lord and Lady Ditherege, gives forth a sound so soft and dulcet as almost to be a bar of music. But sometimes that is all there is. The words are lost in the graceful sweep of the notes. I have heard entire scenes played by English actors (especially juveniles) in which absolutely nothing was distinguishable except a series of musical notes ranging in cadenzas from B to G sharp and back to B again. It is all very pretty, but is it the English language?

This slurring of words into a refined cadence until they cease to be words at all is due partly to the Englishman's disinclination to move his lips. Evidently the lips and teeth are held stationary for the most part, open just wide enough to let in air for breathing (many Englishmen must breathe through their mouths, otherwise they would not breathe at all) with an occasional sharp pursing of the lips on a syllable which does *not* call for pursing the lips. This lethargic attitude toward articulation makes more or less of a fool out of a word which is dependent on pronunciation for its success. It makes a rather agreeable sound of it, but practically eliminates it as an agent for expressing thought.

I am not dealing now with cockney or other perversions of the British manner of speaking, although Englishmen are not so fair as to remember that much of the speech which they call "American" on the stage and in pictures is deliberately vulgarized and harshened by the American actors themselves to imitate gangsters, newspaper reporters, and others of the non-classical group. I am speaking of the more "refayned" type of English actor, and even of the ordinary well-educated Englishman. They distort good old Anglo-Saxon words into mere blobs of sound, eliminating letters and syllables at will. And what they do to *French* words must not be mentioned here because that is not strictly within the range of this thesis. Neither is it important.

But it is safe to predict that a comparative tabulation of words in common use in England and America, analyzed phonetically as pronounced in each country, would give America a startling lead over the mother country in accuracy. Saying them through the nose, as many Americans do, may not be so pleasant as saying them through the large palate, as many Englishmen do, but the words themselves get a better break and, at least, the integrity of the sentence is preserved.

The time is about ripe for someone to write a skit for an American revue, lasting perhaps three minutes, in which are reproduced the sounds made by a group of English juveniles such as came over here every year in plays of post-war younger-generationism, bounding on and off the stage carrying tennis racquets and giving off exuberance to the point of combustion. If I were writing such a sketch I would open the scene with two or three young gentlemen and ladies lying about on window-seats and porch chairs in careless fashion, with the conversation running something like this:

At this point Reggie would come bursting into the room, with his shirt open at the neck, fresh from badminton and would call, swinging his body lithely from the hips:

Things would go on like this for a minute or two with absolutely no word being spoken, just a series of British sounds with a great deal of bounding about and quick, darting movements of the heads and arms. The young men would stand with feet wide apart and hands jammed down into the side pockets of their coats, while the young ladies would stand with their feet not quite so far apart and their hands jammed down into the pockets of their sweaters. It would all have to be played very fast and loosely and might end with their all putting their heads together and doing the thing in harmony, still with no words. Or a canary, which had been hanging in a cage throughout the act, might join in with them until it fell dead from exhaustion. Or almost anything might happen, provided no sense was given to the lines.

Some time ago I heard *Major Barbara* done by an English company. The young man who played Cusins was a particularly vicious example of the songster-actor so prevalent on the English stage. Although I took no notes and am not very good at carrying a tune, I should say that one of his speeches ran something like this: (The key was C sharp and the range was from B to G sharp in an almost continuous cadenza):

"Eetsnottth'sao ehvmeh seuhl thett trehbles meh; Eh hev seuhld et teuh efften teh care abeht thett. Eh hev seuhld et fereh preuhfes-sorshep. Eh hev seuhld et tescep beinempressoned feh refusin t'peh texes fer hengmen's reuhps end ehnjust wehrs end things thet ehabheuh. Wot es ehl humen cehnduct beht th'daioy end heuhrly sao of ehur seuhls f'trehfles? Wot ehem neuh seoinet feh is neither meneh ehr pesition nehr kemfet, bet freelity and fpeuher."

Is that any kind of English for our children to hear? Are we to sit by and let minors absorb this sort of distortion of our mother tongue and perhaps grow up to speak it themselves? We pay good money to have them taught to say "don't" and "donkey." Are they to be led by outlanders into saying "dehn't" and "dehnkey"? We have been brought up to believe that dropping the final "g" is the mark of a vulgarian. Are our children to hear "nice people" from England saying "runnin'" and "singin'"? No, a theuhsend tehms Neuh!

The fact is that neither Americans nor English have anything to boast of in the matter of pronunciations of their common tongue. There are a few people in each country who have got the hang of it, but for the most part a pretty bad job has been made of the whole thing. Probably the best English is spoken by foreigners who have taken the pains to learn it correctly.

"One Minute Please!"

I AM known as a bad business man from one end of the country to just a little beyond the same end. Practically every one in my class in kindergarten went into business after graduation, and when I say business I mean business. Whenever I see them now they are always dressed up in stiff shirts and are making marks on the backs of envelopes. Get me a hundred of my old schoolmates together and let them talk from 9 A.M. until almost dinner time and I won't understand a word they are saying. It is only around dinner time that I begin to catch a glimmer of sense and then they have to come right out and say "Martini" or "Green turtle soup." At this point I join the party.

But not until I have had it said to me eight or a dozen times that I ought to be more businesslike. "Good old Bob," they say (those of them who remember that my name is "Bob"), "you are just a sucker to be so impractical. Why don't you let us take some of your money and triple it for you?"

Leaving aside the question "What money?" I am frankly at a loss for something to say. Here I am, just a dreamer, and there they are, captains of industry, or, at any rate, second lieutenants. They have the advantage of me.

Of course, if I wanted to, I might point out that out of a possible $5000 which I have made since I left school I have had $3000 worth of good food (all of which has gone into making bone and muscle and some nice fat), $1500 worth of theatre tickets, and $500 worth of candy; whereas many of my business friends have simply had $5000 worth of whatever that stock was which got so yellow along about last November.

169

I was sympathetic with all the boys at that time and even advanced a little cash in a sparing manner, but I couldn't help remembering the days during the summer when I had to sit and listen to them say, "Well, I made $650,000 over the week-end. What will you have, Bob, old man?" And all the time I was, in my old impractical way, sinking my money into silk neckties (which I still have) and throwing it away on life-giving beefsteaks.

I do not intend to dwell on this phase of life's whirligig, however. Who can tell, perhaps some day even we spendthrifts may find ourselves short of cash. In the meantime, those of us who have nothing but fripperies to show for our money have had a good laugh. At least we've got the fripperies.

What I do want to dwell on is the point that there are still a great many practices which are considered businesslike and efficient and which any one of us old dreamers could improve upon and speed up. Now you sit still and read this. I have sat still and listened to you long enough.

First, there is the question of business telephoning. During the last five or six years there has spread throughout the business world a method of telephoning which, so far as I am concerned, bids fair to destroy all channels of business communication. If it keeps up, I, for one, will go back to the old Indian runner and carrier pigeon methods. I won't stand for this another day. In fact, I stopped standing for it a year ago.

I refer to the delayed-pass play, so popular among busy executives. In this play your busy executive, when he wants to get me on the telephone (why he should want to get me on the telephone is a mystery), says to his secretary, "Get me Mr. Benchley on the wire, Miss Whatney." You see, he hasn't got the time to get me himself, what with all those stocks he has to tend to; so he has Miss Whatney do it for him. So far, pretty good. Miss Whatney looks up my number in the book and gives it to the operator at the switchboard, thereby releasing the busy executive for other duties, such as biting off the end of a cigar or drawing circles on his scratch pad.

The scene now changes and we see me, the impractical dreamer, sitting at an old typewriter with nothing to do but finish an article which was due the day before. My telephone rings and I, in my slipshod, impractical way, answer it. And what do I get for my pains?

"Is this Vanderbilt 0647? Is Mr. Benchley there? Just a minute, please!"

Having nothing to do but wool-gather, I wait. In about two minutes I hear another female voice saying, "Is this Mr. Benchley? Just a minute, please, Mr. Kleek wants to speak to you."

Remember, it is Mr. Kleek who is calling *me* up. I don't want to speak to Mr. Kleek. I wouldn't care if I never spoke to him. In fact, I am not sure that I know who Mr. Kleek is.

"Just a minute, please," comes the voice again. "Mr. Kleek is talking on another wire."

Now, fascinating as this information is, it really wasn't worth getting up out of my chair for. Mr. Kleek could be busy on eight other wires and my life would go on just about the same. Am I to be called away from my work to be told that a Mr. Kleek is talking on another wire? I think this out as I stand there waiting.

Finally, after several minutes, I hear a man's voice.

"Hello," it says gruffly, "who is this?" I am not only to be told to wait until Mr. Kleek is ready to speak to me, but I am to be treated by Mr. Kleek as if I had infringed on his time. At this point I frankly flare up.

"Who is this yourself?" I snarl. "This was your idea, not mine!"

Then evidently Miss Whatney tells Mr. Kleek that she has got Mr. Benchley on the wire, and he is somewhat mollified. But I want to tell you, Mr. Kleek, that by that time I am not on the wire any longer and you can stick that telephone ear-piece into the side of your head. Furthermore, from now on, the minute I am called to the telephone and told to wait a minute, that Mr. Anybody wants to speak to me, I hang up so quickly that the hook drops off. If Mr. Kleek or any other busy executive wants to speak to me he can be there within four seconds after I answer or he can put in the call again. I may be just an old wool-gatherer, but I want to gather my wool somewhere else than at a telephone receiver.

It is possible that the telephone has been responsible for more

business inefficiency than any other agency except laudanum. It
has such an air of pseudo-efficiency about it that people feel efficient
the minute they take the receiver off the hook. A business man could
be talking with Ajax, the mechanical chess player, on the other
end of the wire and still feel he was getting somewhere, simply
because to anyone passing the door he looks as if he were very
busy. There is something about saying "O.K." and hanging up the
receiver with a bang that kids a man into feeling that he has just
pulled off a big deal, even if he has only called up Central to find out
the correct time. For this reason business men use the telephone
exclusively when almost any other form of communication would be
quicker.

In the old days when you wanted to get in touch with a man you
wrote a note, sprinkled it with sand, and gave it to a man on horseback. It probably was delivered within half an hour, depending on
how big a lunch the horse had had. But in these busy days of rush-
rush-rush, it sometimes is a week before you can catch your man
on the telephone. The call is put in, but he is out. You tell your
secretary to keep calling, but, if the man takes any kind of care of
himself at all, he is out most all day in the fresh air. So day after day
the secretary keeps calling and, in this way, autumn turns into
winter and winter to spring. Perhaps you never get him.

A busy executive said to me the other day in an exasperated tone,
"Aren't you ever in? I have been trying to get you on the telephone
for five days. What do you do with your time, cut lawns?" You see,
I am the one who was in the wrong. I was the impractical one.

I might have told him about that new invention called the "typewriter," whereby, if you can't get a man on the telephone, you can
drop him a note which will reach him the next morning. Or I also
might have told him that I was in my office all the time, but was so
busy working that I had left word with the telephone operator not
to bother me with time-wasting calls from business men. In either
case, dropping me a note would have saved him four days of
telephoning. But apparently note-dropping is considered a relic of
Civil War days and is not to be considered in the bustle of modern

business. You must use the telephone, even if it doesn't get you anywhere.

The telephone is the particular pet of the go-getter who won't take no for an answer. He has a passion for long-distance calls. Let us say that his organization is getting up a dinner in Chicago and wants to get an after-dinner speaker from New York. The go-getter is, of course, chairman of the dinner committee because he gets things done. He guarantees to get the New York speaker. "Leave it to me," he says, knowingly. And, even as he says it, he is putting in a long-distance call for New York. Bingo—like that! The New York man answers and gets the following:

"This is Ferley of the Autumn Coat and Suit speaking! We're holding a dinner here on February 10th, and you're coming out to speak for us!—O, yes, you are! I won't take no for an answer. . . . O, yes, you can—I'll call those people up and tell them you're coming to us. . . . Now, not another word!—See you on the 10th!"

With this he hangs up and reports to the committee that he has the speaker sewed up. The fact that the New York man can't go to Chicago on the 10th and has no intention of going doesn't enter into the calculations at all. No one is supposed to be able to resist the man with the telephone personality. He sweeps everything before him.

The only drawback is that, two days before the dinner, when it is found out that the New York speaker meant what he said and really isn't coming, the go-getter has to go-get somebody through a local agency to do card tricks for the diners. "That's the trouble with dealing with these literary guys," he thunders. "You can't count on them!" And he puts in another long-distance call just to quiet his nerves.

And so it goes through life. There are the doers and the dreamers, the men who make every second count and the men who waste their time with nothing to show for it. The first are the business men of the country, the others are the impractical fellows who write and draw pictures. Or perhaps it is just the other way 'round. I always get these things mixed.

Looking Shakespeare Over

AT THE end of the current theatrical season, the trustees of the Shakespeare estate will probably get together at the Stratford House and get pie-eyed. It has been a banner year for "the Immortal Bard," as his wife used to call him. Whatever the royalties are that revert to the estate, there will be enough to buy a couple of rounds anyway, and maybe enough left over to hire an entertainer.

There was a time during the winter in New York when you couldn't walk a block without stepping on some actor or actress playing Shakespeare. They didn't all make money, but it got the author's name into the papers, and publicity never hurt anyone, let alone a writer who has been dead three hundred years and whose stuff isn't adaptable for the movies.

The only trouble with acting Shakespeare is the actors. It brings out the worst that is in them. A desire to read aloud the soliloquy (you know the one I mean) is one of the first symptoms a man has that he is going to be an actor. If ever I catch any of my little boys going out behind the barn to recite this speech, I will take them right away to a throat specialist and have their palates removed. One failure is enough in a family.

And then, too, the stuff that Will wrote, while all right to sit at home and read, does *not* lend itself to really snappy entertainment on the modern stage. It takes just about the best actor in the world to make it sound like anything more than a declamation by the young lady representing the Blue and the Gray on Memorial Day. I know that I run counter to many cultured minds in this matter, but I think that, if the truth were known, there are a whole lot more of us who twitch through two-thirds of a Shakespearean performance than the last census would lead one to believe. With a company con-

sisting of one or two stars and the rest hams (which is a good liberal
estimate) what can you expect? Even Shakespeare himself couldn't
sit through it without reading the ads on the program a little.

But you can't blame the actor entirely. According to present
standards of what constitutes dramatic action, most of Will's
little dramas have about as much punch as a reading of a treasurer's
report. To be expected to thrill over the dramatic situations incident
to a large lady's dressing up as a boy and fooling her own husband,
or to follow breathlessly a succession of scenes strung together like
magic-lantern slides and each ending with a perfectly corking
rhymed couplet, is more than ought to be asked of anyone who has,
in the same season, seen *Loyalties* or any one of the real plays
now running on Broadway.

It is hard to ask an actor to make an exit on a line like:

> "I am glad on't: I desire no more delight
> Than to be under sail and gone tonight"

without sounding like one of the characters in Palmer Cox's Brownies
saying:

> "And thus it was the Brownie Band,
> Came tumbling into Slumberland."

That is why they always have to exit laughingly in a Shakespearean production. The author has provided them with such
rotten exits. If they don't do something—laugh, cry, turn a hand-
spring, or something—they are left flat in the middle of the stage
with nothing to do but say, "Well, I must be going." In *The
Merchant of Venice*, the characters are forced to keep up a running fire of false-sounding laughter to cover up the artificial nature
of what they have just said:

> "At the park gate, and therefore haste away
> For we must measure twenty miles today.
> A-ha-ha-ha-ha-ha!" (*Off l. c.*)

To hear Lorenzo and Gratiano walking off together you would
have thought that Lorenzo had the finest line of funny stories in
all Venice, so loud and constantly did they laugh, whereas, if the

truth were known, it was simply done to save their own and Shakespeare's face. Now my contention is that any author who can't get his stuff over on the stage without making the actors do contortions, is not so good a playwright technically as Eugene Walters is. And now for the matter of comedy.

An actor, in order to get Shakespeare's comedy across, has got to roll his eyes, rub his stomach, kick his father in the seat, make his voice crack, and place his finger against the side of his nose. There is a great deal of talk about the vulgarity and slapstick humor of the movies. If the movies ever tried to put anything over as horsy and crass as the scene in which young Gobbo kids his blind father, or Falstaff hides in the laundry hamper, there would be sermons preached on it in pulpits all over the country. It is impossible for a good actor, as we know good actors today, to handle a Shakespearean low comedy part, for it demands mugging and tricks which no good actor would permit himself to do. If Shakespeare were alive today and writing comedy for the movies, he would be the headliner in the Mack Sennett studios. What he couldn't do with a cross-eyed man!

Another thing that has made the enjoyment of Shakespeare on the stage a precarious venture for this section of the theatre-going public at least, is the thoroughness with which the schools have desiccated his works. In *The Merchant of Venice*, for example, there was hardly a line spoken which had not been so diagnosed by English teachers from the third grade up that it had lost every vestige of freshness and grace which it may once have had. Every time I changed schools, I ran into a class which was just taking up *The Merchant of Venice*. Consequently, I learned to hate every word of the play. When Bassanio said:

> "Which makes her seat of Belmon Colchis' strand,
> And many Jasons come in quest of her"

in my mind there followed a chorus of memories of questions asked by Miss Mergatroid, Miss O'Shea, Miss Twitchell, Mr. Henby, and Professor Greenally, such as: "Now what did Shakespeare mean by 'Colchis strand'?" "Can anyone in the room tell me why Portia's lovers were referred to as 'Jasons'? Robert Benchley, I wonder if you can leave off whispering to Harold Bemis long enough to tell me what other Portia in history is mentioned in this passage?"

Perhaps that is the whole trouble with Shakespeare anyway. Too many people have taken him up. If they would let you alone, to read snatches from his plays now and then when you wanted to, and *stop* reading when you wanted to, it might not be so bad. But no! They must ask you what he meant by this, and where the inflection should come on that, and they must stand up in front of scenery and let a lot of hams declaim at you while you are supposed to murmur "Gorgeous!" and "How well he knew human nature!" as if you couldn't go to Bartlett's *Quotations* and get the meat of it in half the time. I wouldn't be surprised, if things keep on as they are, if Shakespeare began to lose his hold on people. I give him ten centuries more at the outside.

How I Create

IN AN article on How Authors Create, in which the writing methods of various masters of English prose like Conrad, Shaw, and Barrie are explained (with photographs of them in knickerbockers plaguing dogs and pushing against sun-dials), I discover that I have been doing the whole thing wrong all these years. The interviewer in this case hasn't got around to asking me yet—doubtless because I have been up in my room with the door shut and not answering the bell—but I am going to take a chance, anyway, and tell him how I do my creative work and just how much comes from inspiration and how much from hashish and other perfumes. I may even loosen up and tell him what my favorite hotweather dishes are.

When I am writing a novel I must actually live the lives of my characters. If, for instance, my hero is a gambler on the French Riviera, I make myself pack up and go to Cannes or Nice, willy-nilly, and there throw myself into the gay life of the gambling set until I really feel that I *am* Paul De Lacroix, Ed Whelan, or whatever my hero's name is. Of course this runs into money, and I am quite likely to have to change my ideas about my hero entirely and make him a bum on a tramp steamer working his way back to America, or a young college boy out of funds who lives by his wits until his friends at home send him a hundred and ten dollars.

One of my heroes (Dick Markwell in *Love's How-do-you-do*), after starting out as a man about town in New York who "never showed his liquor" and was "an apparently indestructible machine devoted to pleasure," had to be changed into a patient in the Trembly Ward of a local institution, whose old friends didn't recognize him and furthermore didn't want to.

But, as you doubtless remember, it was a corking yarn.

This actually living the lives of my characters takes up quite a lot of time and makes it a little difficult to write anything. It was not until I decided to tell stories about old men who just sit in their rooms and shell walnuts that I ever got around to doing any work. It doesn't make for very interesting novels, but at any rate the wordage is there and there is something to show the publishers for their advance royalties. (Publishers are crotchety that way.

They want copy, copy, copy all the time, just because they happen to have advanced a measly three hundred dollars a couple of years before. You would think that printing words on paper was their business.)

And now you ask me how I do my work, how my inspiration comes? I will tell you, Little Father. Draw up your chair and let me put my feet on it. Ah, that's better! Now you may go out and play.

Very often I must wait weeks and weeks for what you call "inspiration." In the meantime I must sit with my quill pen poised in air over a sheet of foolscap, in case the divine spark should come like a lightning bolt and knock me off my chair onto my head.

*Very often I must wait weeks and weeks for
what you call "inspiration"*

(This has happened more than once.) While I am waiting I mull
over in my mind what I am going to do with my characters.

Shall I have Mildred marry Lester, or shall Lester marry Evelyn?
("Who is Evelyn?" I often say to myself, never having heard of her
before.) Should the French proletariat win the Revolution, or
should Louis XVI come back suddenly and establish a Coalition
Cabinet? Can I afford to let Etta clean up those dishes in the
sink and get them biscuits baked, or would it be better to keep
her there for another year, standing first on one foot and then on
the other?

You have no idea how many problems an author has to face
during those feverish days when he is building a novel, and you
have no idea how he solves them. Neither has he.

Sometimes, while in the throes of creative work, I get out of
bed in the morning, look at my writing desk piled high with old
bills, odd gloves, and empty ginger-ale bottles, and go right back

to bed again. The next thing I know it is night once more, and time for the Sand Man to come around. (We have a Sand Man who comes twice a day, which makes it very convenient. We give him five dollars at Christmas.)

Even if I do get up and put on a part of my clothes—I do all my work in a Hawaiian straw skirt and a bow tie of some neutral shade—I often can think of nothing to do but pile the books which are on one end of my desk very neatly on the other end and then kick them one by one off on to the floor with my free foot.

But all the while my brain is work, work, working, and my plot is taking shape. Sometimes it is the shape of a honeydew melon and sometimes a shape which I have never been quite able to figure out. It is a sort of amorphous thing with two heads but no face. When this shape presents itself, I get right back in bed again. I'm no fool.

I find that, while working, a pipe is a great source of inspiration. A pipe can be placed diagonally across the keys of a typewriter so that they will not function, or it can be made to give out such a cloud of smoke that I cannot see the paper. Then, there is the process of lighting it. I can make lighting a pipe a ritual which has not been equaled for elaborateness since the five-day festival to the God of the Harvest. (See my book on Rituals: the Man.)

In the first place, owing to twenty-six years of constant smoking without once calling in a plumber, the space left for tobacco in the bowl of my pipe is now the size of a medium body-pore. Once the match has been applied to the tobacco therein, the smoke is over. This necessitates refilling, relighting, and reknocking. The knocking out of a pipe can be made almost as important as the smoking of it, especially if there are nervous people in the room. A good, smart knock of a pipe against a tin wastebasket and you will have a neurasthenic out of his chair and into the window sash in no time.

The matches, too, have their place in the construction of modern literature. With a pipe like mine, the supply of burnt matches in one day could be floated down the St. Lawrence River with two men jumping them.

When the novel is finished, it is shipped to the Cutting and Binding Room, where native girls roll it into large sheets and stamp on it with their bare feet. This accounts for the funny look of some of my novels. It is then taken back to the Drying Room, where it is rewritten by a boy whom I engage for the purpose, and sent to the publishers. It is then sent back to me.

And so you see now how we creative artists work. It really isn't like any other kind of work, for it must come from a great emotional upheaval in the soul of the writer himself; and if that emotional upheaval is not present, it must come from the work of any other writers which happen to be handy and easily imitated.

First—Catch Your Criminal

WITH the increase in crime during the past decade has come a corresponding increase in crime prevention. Or perhaps it is vice versa. At any rate, we are awfully busy down at our laboratory trying to find out who is a criminal and who isn't. (You can imagine the surprise of the head of our Research Department the other day when he reacted to one of his own tests, thereby proving himself to be a "lingoidphrensic" type, or man-eating shark. He immediately resigned his portfolio and gave himself up to the authorities; but as he is seventy-one years old, they didn't want him.)

Our theory of crime prevention has a strictly psychological basis but we will listen to anything. It is our idea to take the criminal *before* he becomes a criminal and to chivvy him about the laboratory until he is too tired and disgusted to commit the crime. A great many times we have converted potential criminals into hermits and deep-sea divers by making them want to get away from it all and just be alone. The man who runs the lighthouse at Salt Mackerel Rock, Maine, is one of our graduates. He won't even let people bring him newspapers.

This man is a rather interesting case of a reformed "rhombusmanic," or "inverted nailbiter" type; that is, instead of wanting to bite his own nails he wanted to bite other people's. Perhaps I should say that his *tendencies* were in that direction, for we caught him before he had really started on anything that could be called a career in that field. Following was our course of experimentation: Mr. X, as we will call him (although his real name is Mr. Y), was a patient in the Nursing Home on City Island, having been brought there suffering from a three days' beard. He had been shaved, and was lying in his cot rubbing his chin with the tips of his fingers, when discovered by our Dr. Altschu, who was browsing about among the charity patients looking for types. Dr. Altschu immediately detected in Mr. X the indications of a rhombusmanic (low frontal elevation, pendent ear lobes, and absence of pupils in the eyes) and effected a transfer of the patient from the Nursing Home to the Crime Prevention laboratory. We gave a third baseman in exchange.

Once in the laboratory, Mr. X was put into a hot bath with a rubber walrus and told to get himself nice and clean. He was then dressed in a suit of blue denim and taken into the Chart Room, where he was seated in an easy chair (or what he thought was an easy chair) and told to watch the words that were thrown on the screen in front of him.

As a matter of fact, the chair was a special invention of Dr. Altschu's, with a delicate registering device concealed in the arms and an invisible wire stretching across the patient's neck, so that each fluctuation in his breathing and each quickening of his pulse was registered. Also the wire across his neck gradually choked him until he jumped up yelling, "Let's get the hell out of here!" At this point another registering device, which had in some unaccountable way become attached to his ankles to indicate ankle fluctuation, became suddenly rigid and threw him to the ground, where his weight and preference in flowers were taken simultaneously.

The room was then darkened and a series of jokes were flashed on the screen. It was the patient's reactions to these jokes, as indicated on a dial in the Control Room, which determined just which type of rhombusmanic he belonged to. (There are three types of rhombusmanic—the A type, or introvert; the B type, or extravert; and the D type, or Old Man River. There used to be a C type, or Life on the Oregon Trail; but we had to drop it, as it began to edge over into the lower thermo-depressive type, which gets us into Juggling and Sleight-of-Hand.)

There was considerable confusion in the case of X, however, as he would not laugh at *any* of the jokes which were flashed on the screen. He just sat and asked when the newsreel came on. We couldn't get him to react in the slightest degree, and the man in the Control Room kept popping his head out and saying, "O. K.; Start 'er up!" But X wouldn't start.

We tried the one about the man who had three daughters that he wanted to get married, the one about the Scotchman, the Irishman, and the Jew, and the one ending: "Lie down; do you want to make a fool out of the doctor?" But all that X would do was to keep asking about the newsreel and saying, "I like Mickey Mouse." This in itself was significant, but we couldn't decide of what.

So we took Mr. X out of the Joke-Registration Room and put him in the Blank-Filling-Out Clinic. We set great store by our blanks, or questionnaires, especially the pink ones. If we can get a patient to fill out one of our pink questionnaires, answering every question without once dashing it to the floor and screaming, "Of all the damned nonsense!" we feel that we have done a lot toward the preservation of Society. So far we haven't been able to find one patient who could keep his temper long enough to answer every question on the sheet. This makes it difficult to keep our records straight.

Mr. X was no exception to the rule, even though we began him on the blue questionnaire. His aversion to the questions, however, took the form of frivolity and sneering, which is even harder to cope with than rage. For example, the first question on the blue form was: "You are (*a*) Mohammed, (*b*) Disraeli, (*c*) Mussolini, (*d*) yourself. Cross out the wrong ones." On this the only name that X would cross out was Mussolini's, because he said that Mussolini was the only one who was wrong. To all the other questions he answered simply "Yes" or else drew a thumb-nail sketch of a sailboat and labeled it "My vacation sport."

It was obvious that X was no ordinary rhombusmanic, but it was equally obvious that he ought not to be allowed at large with as many questionnaires as are being put out today. Here was a man who was evidently in a way to become either a menace to

Society or else darned good company. We couldn't decide which, so we subjected him to further tests. By this time we had him in the Shipping Room.

Here he had little electric bulbs flashed before his eyes and was told to say the first word which popped into his mind at each flash. All he would say was "Ooops!" every time. He was told to shut his eyes and twirl around on his heel three times and then walk straight ahead and place his finger on the center of a wall chart. He shut his eyes as we told him, but kept on twirling round and round without stopping, maintaining that he liked it. When he was finally persuaded to stop, he walked forward and stuck his finger in Dr. Altschu's mouth, keeping on until Dr. Altschu gagged.

He was shown cards of different colors and asked to explain what they reminded him of, but on the first card (which was green) he launched forth into such a long reminiscence that we finally had to stop him and hide the rest of the cards.

By this time the patient was beginning to get restless, and we of the examining staff were frankly upset. So we came right out and asked him if he didn't think that he might possibly be a criminal in the making, and he said that he was sure of it. In fact, he said it was only a question of minutes before he killed us all.

It was then that he asked us if we thought that we could get him a job as a lighthouse keeper where he wouldn't have to see anyone ever again, and the position at Salt Mackerel Rock was found for him.

It is along these lines that we are trying to build our system of crime prevention, on the theory that, if we can catch the criminal before he commits the crime, there would be no crime. What we need right now, however, are more experimental chairs and lots more colored bulbs.

The Noon Telephone Operator

AT THE sound of the noon whistle, the pixies come down and take charge of most of the telephone switchboards in our apartment houses and offices. One pixie is assigned to each switchboard, and, from the sounds which come up over the extension when one tries to telephone between the hours of twelve and one, they are very old pixies who never were much good at steering a thistledown or ravishing a honeysuckle. In their youth they must have been pixies with low thyroid, whose teachers didn't understand them. Today they constitute the less efficient group of the elfin tribe and are therefore put on telephone switchboards while the regular operator is out at lunch.

I feel that they are pixies because they sound like nothing particularly human and bear no vocal resemblance to the elevator boy or superintendent who would naturally be supposed to take the board in an emergency. And furthermore, if you rush down to the ground floor to catch them at their work, either for the purpose of slitting their throats or merely seeing who it is that has so little feeling for the art of telephone operating, you will find that there is *no one at all* there. This points to something impish, you must admit.

Let us say that at about twelve forty-five you want to put in a call. You lift the receiver and, instead of the prompt "Number, please" of your regular operator (especially before Christmas), there is a dead, almost unpleasant, silence. Continued wiggling of the hook results in nothing until, all of a sudden, there is a crashing which sounds as if a heavy body had lurched into a pile of tin pie-plates. This is followed by the noise of heavy breathing and a scratching sound as of a heavily mustached lip colliding with the mouthpiece downstairs. Sometimes there is even a bump of front teeth, indicating that the pixie's balance is none too good.

Then, in a conversational, almost controversial tone: "Hello!"

Unless you are careful you will reply, "Hello, yourself," but, if you have your wits about you, you will give your number: "Wickersham 1259, please."

"Murray Hill 12593?" This is in the form of a query.

"No, no! Wickersham 1259."

There is more crashing among the pie-plates and then, suddenly, a dead silence, indicating that the machinery has completely ceased to function. You are right back where you started from.

More jiggling of the hook brings down more horrendous crashings and heavy breathing.

"Did you get your number?"

"I'm sorry. No," you say. "I wanted Wickersham 1259."

At this point, the entire switchboard below seems to burst into flames, necessitating the calling out of the militia and dozens of men with fire buckets. The excitement over, there is a slight passage of words between the mysterious operator below and the operator belonging to the telephone company. This dialogue is complicated by the fact that the operator below has a strong Scandinavian accent, although every employee of the house that you have ever talked to is either colored or Irish.

"I wan' Veeker sam wan——"

"Number, please," asks Central very nicely.

This discourages the pixie and he gives the whole thing up in dismay. A crash into the pots and pans indicates that he has perhaps fainted at his post. To make the thing simpler, the line goes dead.

Now, if it is not particularly important that you get your number until after the regular operator comes back on duty, you will do well to give up too. If it is a matter of life and death, you must keep at it. But, in this event, you must wait for quite a while, until the emergency operator has recovered from his swoon and put in the number again.

This time you will hear strange mutterings on his part. He is frankly baffled. Operating a telephone switchboard is not in his line and he never agreed to do it when he took the job (whatever his job is). He hates this hour from twelve to one and looks forward to it with dread all day. Without the horror of this task hanging over him, he would be a comparatively happy pixie all the day long. With it, he is a nervous wreck. This you can feel as you hear him muttering and wheezing below. It seems to him as if the regular operator never *would* come back. She must be having a seven-course lunch. It also seems that way to you.

If, by any chance, you *do* get your number, you can almost hear the sigh of relief that goes up from the little man downstairs. If, as is more likely, you do not get it, you know that he has assigned the whole horrid affair to the limbo of those things "which can't be helped," and, if you are wise, you will do the same.

And the mysterious part of it is that, as you go out to lunch yourself, there is nobody at the switchboard. He is either hiding under the desk, or the banshees have been at work. If it is the banshees, it is high time that there was an official investigation. This sort of thing can't go on in a city of the size of New York in the Twentieth Century.

Fall In!

IT MAY be because I do not run as fast, or as often, as I used to, but I seem to be way behind on my parades. It must be almost a year since I saw one, and then I was in it myself. I don't mean that I started out marching in it, but I got caught up in it and became confused and had to march several blocks before I could get out. It was horrible.

But in spite of the fact that I haven't been out watching them go by, I know that there have been parades, because I have heard the bands. Nothing makes a man feel older than to hear a band coming up the street and not to have the impulse to rush downstairs and out on to the sidewalk. I guess that this symptom of senility comes on after about twenty-five years of rushing downstairs and out on to the sidewalk only to find that it is the Reuben Lodge of the local Order of Reindeer marching by in brown sack suits and derby hats. After a while, this sort of disappointment makes a cynic of a person.

I think that not only was the last parade I ran after made up of men in brown sack suits and derby hats, but the *band* had on brown sack suits and derby hats as well! That definitely crushed me, and now I wouldn't even take my head out of my hand (where it is most of the time) to look out the window at the finest band music that could pass my house ... Well, I might just *look*.

The American people, however, are still pretty unswerving in their allegiance to any organization which feels like walking up and down the street to music. And as for the police and city officials, they will go out of their way to help make it a gala occasion.

Our municipalities spend thousands of dollars and tear out great

190

handfuls of hair trying to figure out some way of relieving traffic congestion. They arrest pedestrians who don't hold out their hands when making a left turn, and chase automobilists who go straight ahead when they should go around in a circle. They arrange red lights and green lights and orange-by-southeast and blue-by-southwest lights, with systems of bells which only a Swiss bell-ringer can understand, and all in an attempt to straighten out the tangle in our streets which modern automotive civilization has brought down upon us.

And yet, let the National Association of Cyclone Underwriters petition for a permit to march up the main street of the city and throw traffic into a five-hour chaos, and not only do they get their permit but the police get out their riot machine guns and help them to spread confusion. There is a flaw somewhere.

In the old days parading was more simple. If the morning paper announced that the circus or the local cavalry troop was to start their parade at the Fair Grounds at 10 A.M., the entire route, all the way along Main Street, through Elm, up Center and down Walnut, would be cleared by 9:45, and the sidewalks lined with expectant throngs hours before the marshals had arrived at the starting point.

"It said in the paper that they would pass by the City Hall about ten-twenty," was the whisper which ran along the curbing. "That would bring them along here about ten twenty-five." The smaller children would start crying shortly after ten-five, and the older ones would begin darting out into the street and tripping over their balloons by ten-fifteen. One would hardly have believed it possible for children to get so smeared with molasses and popcorn in fifteen minutes. In fact, one would hardly have believed it possible for there to have been so many children, and so unattractive.

"Listen, Norman, mamma'll take you right home this minute if you don't stand up here on the sidewalk. Come *here!*" But Norman, knowing that Mamma wouldn't give up her place on the curbing for anything short of a cash bonus, was never impressed. And neither was Evelyn, Harold, Stanley, or Ralph, Junior. They knew that until that parade had gone by Mamma was as good as planted right there, no matter what they did. So they did it.

Then, as the minutes dragged by and no parade appeared, the parents would join their children in little abortive excursions out into the middle of the street to look in the direction of the Fair Grounds. By this time all traffic had entirely disappeared from Main Street, which meant that Dakin's Fish Market was making its deliveries over another route and that it would be noon before McCann & Stodder got their groceries around.

Every now and again some of the older boys would yell, "Here they come!"—at which children would be yanked in from the gutters and hats would topple off as their owners tried to crane their necks to see. But these false alarms soon ceased to have their effect, especially as someone who lived across the street from the Fair Grounds telephoned down that the parade hadn't even started yet, owing to one of the horses refusing to get up or the man who carried the front end of the drum being unable to get up. When this word had been passed around, everyone sat down on the curbing and waited, the comical ones pretending to go to sleep, the more serious-minded ones finishing what they had brought along to eat.

But no one went home. And no traffic passed through the restricted area. It was probably eleven or eleven-thirty before the band was finally heard in the distance and the excitement, for the eighth consecutive time, reached a fever heat. But it made no difference to anyone how long they waited. In those days, *nothing* made any difference to anyone. And civilization is supposed to progress!

Today a parade is no joke. Next to a big fire, there is probably nothing worse than a parade for jamming things up. There are still a lot of people who will wait on a curbing for hours to see one, but there are also a lot of people who *can't* wait on a curbing for hours. Today there are trains to be caught and dates to be kept, and a man who has to catch a train or keep a date never seems to enter into the parade spirit—not when he is held by the necktie and prevented from crossing the street by a large cop while phalanx after phalanx of strangers wearing red sashes and carrying bamboo canes shuffle past. To have one section of a city's populace lining the streets cheering and another section held in check by the police, fuming, is a state of affairs which tends to civic unrest.

Then there is the question of saluting the colors. In the old days, two flags were enough for one parade, and it was a pleasure, not unaccompanied by a thrill, to doff the hat. But today, when every chapter of an organization representing every state in the Union carries the national banner, the thing loses a little of its impressiveness. It is better just to keep your hat in your hand and perhaps genuflect a little at each passing flag.

Of course, if you are in an office and have work to do, there is an almost irresistible urge to rush to the window and hang out whenever a band is heard. I used to do that myself until I got an office over a radio store. For the first two months, every time I heard the martial strains of *Under the Double Eagle* coming from the street below, I would drop everything and tear to the window. It took me two months to discover that the band music came from the loudspeaker projecting from the store below.

It is too bad that the parade as an institution has lost its glamour. If I were police commissioner I would issue parade permits only to those organizations which wore brilliant red coats or could promise to ride camels. Then they would be worth watching. If they could be induced both to wear red coats and ride camels, I might be induced to march with them.

For, in spite of my aversion to parades in general, I have always had a sneaking feeling that I could cut rather a dashing figure in one myself.

"Could You Tell Me...?"

I HAVE often wondered what makes young men, with their whole lives before them, go to work in a tourist bureau. Not that the work isn't clean, and possibly well-paid, and run at gentlemanly hours. But the people, the customers! I'll bet, if the truth were known, a great many of the unsolved murder mysteries could be traced to tourist-agency clerks who have followed tourists outside and killed them.

It probably isn't so bad in the offices in the United States, although I am ready to believe that it is bad enough. But those unfortunate young men who have to cope with customers who have already been traveling in Europe for a month or two and who are cross and tired and sooty, these are the young men who must have murder constantly in their hearts. And who could blame them?

There is probably no more unlovely sight in the world than an Anglo-Saxon family (a phrase slyly contrived to include the English as well as American) which has been on the go long enough to be tired of the whole thing and to want to go home. There is a father and mother (or, if the father has had any sense, just a mother), two daughters and one son. They all hate each other, especially the young son. They have been to England, if they are Americans, and have seen the Tower, and Shakespeare's birthplace, and the lions in Trafalgar Square. Then they have gone to Paris or Berlin. Here they discover that part of their little group wants to go on somewhere else and part wants to stay right where they are. Or maybe two-thirds of them want to go home. And they go around to the office of the tourist company.

Here you will find them, lined up against the counter, all trying to talk at once, except the young son who is sulking and won't talk at all.

"We want to know," begins the mother, not quite sure whether or not the clerk speaks English, "if we can get a good train from here to Interlaken—"

"Not Interlaken, Mother!" says one of the daughters, in evident disgust at her mother's gaucherie, "*Lauter*brunnen."

"Your uncle said 'Interlaken'," insists the mother. "Didn't he, Miriam?"

Miriam is also disgusted with her mother. " 'Lauterbrunnen,' he said, Mother."

The mother gets out a letter from Uncle Harcourt and reads it while the clerk waits.

"My daughter just graduated in June from Miss Teasdale's school," explains the mother to the clerk. "We thought it would be very nice for them to see as much of Europe as they can while they are young. Their Uncle Harcourt, who wrote this letter, is in the London branch of the U. S. Steel and Wire Co. their father's brother—"

"Very nice, I'm sure, Madame," responds the clerk politely. At this point he is accosted by another, and larger lady, who has pushed her way up from the left.

"I want you to tell me," she begins, "how long it will take me—"

"I'm sorry, Madame, but I am busy right now."

"We're using him," says Mother, with considerable hauteur, in the same breath with that of the young man. Then she adds, "The nerve of some people."

It looks for a minute as if Mother and the large lady are in for a short, sharp round of fisticuffs but the two daughters close in around Mother and the large lady is lost from view.

"Mother, don't you think it would be better to wait until we see whether Harry is coming to Paris this week or not—"

"Now, Ethel, we had that all out at the hotel. If you want to wait here until Harry comes, (*to the clerk*) Harry is her cousin— you may do so. But it will spoil the summer for Miriam and me—"

"My summer is spoiled already," says Miriam. "Look in your letter, Mother, and see what Uncle said."

It is then discovered that the letter is lost. The clerk looks through the sheets and timetables on the counter, and it is only after a thorough search that Mother realizes that she has put it back in her bag in the excitement.

"Oh, *Mother!*" says Miriam, accusingly. If she was disgusted with her parent before, she is practically weeping with chagrin now.

"Where was it you wanted to go from wherever you wanted to go first," suggests the young man.

"That was what we wanted you to tell us," says Mother. "Now here it is—(*reading aloud from letter*) 'if you and the girls want a good quiet time to sandwich in between your stay in Paris and your trip home—and if I know anything about the girls they will need a little rest—'"

"Mother, *don't* read all that! *Here!* Let *me* see the letter!"

A bit of a struggle results in Mother's keeping the letter, but before she can find the part where Uncle Harcourt makes his important revelation, three young ladies have barged their way up to the counter and accosted the clerk in no uncertain tones.

"Can we get any passage back to America on the *Nausea* which sails tomorrow?" one of them asks.

"I'm sorry, Madame," says the clerk, "but. . . ."

His excuses are not heard, however, for the three young ladies suddenly discover that they know the two young lady daughters and there is a chorus of screaming which makes any conversation impossible for a period of five minutes.

"Miriam *Goodney!* What are *you* doing here?"

"*Alice!* Mother, here's Alice!"

"Ethel, my *dear!* This *couldn't* be more divine!"

"Helen Wasservogle! Don't *tell* me you've been here all the time! Where are you staying?"

The clerk, by this time, has given up and is making little marks with his pencil on a timetable. The young son has left in a pet.

And right here is where the killing should take place, if it ever is going to be done. To let the victims live until they have gone through the whole thing over again, is only cruelty to the clerk. To kill them will save a great deal of future trouble for other clerks and for the young ladies' fathers. But, so far as statistics show, no travel-bureau clerk has ever reached under the counter and pulled out a blackjack and with four quick whacks in succession cleaned the thing right up then and there. And it would be so easy to do.

Things like this cannot go on, year in and year out, without bringing on another war. All the conferences in the world, and all the sunken battleships, will not protect the nations of the earth from an armageddon so long as families of one nation are allowed to visit tourist offices of other nations and behave as they do now.

I would do something more definite about the matter than simply writing a protest, but I have to go down to the steamship office right now and engage passage for my own family. And the young man behind the counter had better be pretty civil or I shall report him to the manager.

The Wreck of the Sunday Paper

WHAT is to be done with people who can't read a Sunday paper without messing it all up? I just throw this out as one of the problems with which we are faced if we are to keep our civilization from complete collapse.

There is a certain type of citizen (a great many times, I am sorry to have to say, one of the "fair" sex) whose lack of civic pride shows itself in divers forms, but it is in the devastation of a Sunday newspaper that it reaches its full bloom. Show me a Sunday paper which has been left in a condition fit only for kite flying, and I will show you an antisocial and dangerous character who has left it that way.

Such a person may not mean deliberately to do the things to a newspaper that he or (pardon my pointing) *she* does. They really couldn't achieve such colossal disarrangement by any planning or scheming. It has to come from some cataclysmic stroke of a giant force, probably beyond their control. Let them but touch a nice, neat Sunday edition as it lies folded so flat and cold on the doorstep, and immediately the rotogravure section becomes entwined with the sporting section and the editorial page leaps out and joins with the shipping news to form a tent under which a pretty good-sized child could crawl. The society page bundles itself up into a ball in the center of which, by some strange convulsion, the real-estate news conceals itself in a smaller and more compact ball. It is the Touch of Cain that these people have, and perhaps we should not blame them for it.

But they needn't *leave* this mound of rumpled newsprint this way. They could recognize their failing and at least try to correct its ravages before handing the paper on to someone else.

198

I once knew a man whose wife was a newspaper builder. She built things out of newspapers when she read them. There wasn't much to show for it when she had finished in the way of definite objects; that is, you couldn't quite make out just what she had thought she was building. But there had very evidently been some very clear idea of making each section of the newspaper into an object of some sort—anything so long as it made the newspaper absolutely unsuited for reading purposes.

Now the man usually tried to get down on Sunday morning ahead of his wife so that he could have first crack at the paper before the Great Disintegration set in. But, owing to a habit he had formed in his youth of staying out late on Saturday nights, he found it difficult to beat her to it. By the time he got downstairs the room looked like a militia encampment.

"What do you do with a newspaper?" he once asked her, as quietly as he could. "Try to dress yourself in it? You'll never get anywhere without buttons, you know."

But she didn't seem to mind his taunts, and, in fact, more or less put him on the defensive by calling him "an old maid"; so he decided that the time had come for action. He ordered *two* editions of each Sunday paper, one for his wife to mux about with and one for himself.

It was then that he discovered that his helpmeet's rolling herself up in the paper was not just an unconscious weakness on her part but a vicious perversion from which she got a fiendish pleasure. She would sneak upstairs and get his personal edition before he was awake and give it the works, pretending that she couldn't find her own.

She was simply doing it to be mean, that was all. Often her own copy would be untouched and he would find it on Monday morning hidden away behind the sofa in its pristine smoothness.

I suppose, in a way, that the inability to read a newspaper which someone else has wrapped around himself or which is in any way disarranged is a sign of abnormality in itself and that we sensitive ones are in the wrong. All right, then—*I'm* the one to blame. *I'm* the enemy to society and the one to be locked up. But the fact remains that I am going to stand just so much more of this thing and then away *some*body goes to the police station.

What—No Budapest?

A FEW weeks ago, in this space, I wrote a little treatise on "Movie
Boners," in which I tried to follow the popular custom of picking
technical flaws in motion pictures, detecting, for example, that
when a character enters a room he has on a bow tie and when
he leaves it is a four-in-hand.

In the course of this fascinating article I wrote: "In the picture
called *Dr. Tanner Can't Eat* there is a scene laid in Budapest.
There is no such place as Budapest."

In answer to this I have received the following communication
from M. Schwartzer, of New York City:

"Ask for your money back from your geography teacher. There
is such a place as Budapest, and it is not a small village, either.
Budapest is the capital of Hungary. In case you never heard of

Hungary, it is in Europe. Do you know where Europe is? Respectfully yours," etc.

I am standing by my guns, Mr. Schwartzer. There is no such place as Budapest. Perhaps you are thinking of Bucharest, and there is no such place as Bucharest, either.

I gather that *your* geography teacher didn't tell you about the Treaty of Ulm in 1802, in which Budapest was eliminated. By the terms of this treaty (I quote from memory):

"Be it hereby enacted that there shall be no more Budapest. This city has been getting altogether too large lately, and the coffee hasn't been any too good, either. So, no more Budapest is the decree of this conference, and if the residents don't like it they can move to some other place."

This treaty was made at the close of the war of 1805, which was unique in that it began in 1805 and ended in 1802, thereby confusing the contestants so that both sides gave in at once. Budapest was the focal point of the war, as the Slovenes were trying to get rid of it to the Bulgks, and the Bulgks were trying to make the Slovenes keep it. This will explain, Mr. Schwartzer, why there is no such place as Budapest.

If any word other than mine were needed to convince you that you have made a rather ludicrous mistake in this matter, I will quote from a noted authority on non-existent cities, Dr. Almer Doctor, Pinsk Professor of Obduracy in the university of that name. In his *Vanished Cities of Central Europe* he writes:

"Since 1802 there has been no such place as Budapest. It is too bad, but let's face it!"

Or, again, from *Nerdlinger's Atlas* (revised for the Carnation Show in London in 1921):

"A great many uninformed people look in their atlases for the city of Budapest and complain to us when they cannot find it. Let us take this opportunity to make it clear that there is no such place as Budapest and has not been since 1802. The spot which was once known as Budapest is now known as the Danube River, by Strauss."

I would not rebuke you so publicly, Mr. Schwartzer, had it not been for that crack of yours about my geography teacher. My geography teacher was a very fine woman and later became the mother of four bouncing boys, two of whom are still bouncing. She knew about what happened to Budapest, and she made no bones about it.

In future communications with me I will thank you to keep her name out of this brawl.

Mind's Eye Trouble

AMONG other personal shortcomings (a list of which will be furnished on application to any one of my host of friends) I seem to have been endowed at birth by a Bad, Bad Fairy with a paucity of visual imagination which amounts practically to a squint. The delicate surface of my mind's eye, so well compared to the film of a camera in the vivid phraseology of our school-teachers, must have stopped recording images when I was fifteen years old, for I have about eight exposures with which to work in conjuring up scenes in my mind for the stories I read. I seem to be quite unable to evolve any new pictures for myself.

To those who go about picturing new scenes in their imagination for every novel they read, this may sound a little incredible. I do not expect to gain any admirers through such a confession of weakness. I want only to give some idea of the handicap I have had to fight in my plucky struggle to acquaint myself with the best in the world's literature, and perhaps explain why I have more or less given the whole thing up and devoted myself to the reading of gentlemen's essays and the daily newspapers.

This limitation of mine might not be so cramping in its effect if the few visual images which I have were not confined almost exclusively to street scenes in Worcester, Massachusetts, the fortunate city which gave me birth and fostered me until I was seventeen. Now Worcester, Massachusetts, is a splendid city, with an excellent school system and a wide range of manufacturing interests, but it is not the ideal locale for the *Chanson de Roland* or the adventures of Ivanhoe. It does not have quite the bucolic atmosphere essential to a complete feeling for the Wessex of Hardy, and, elm-shaded and pleasant though many of its streets are, it is not likely that Hugo had any such place in mind when he wrote *Les Misér-ables*. However, regardless of what Hugo had in mind, *I* have Front Street, Worcester, in mind when I read it.

Probably the most perverted of my imaginary localities is the one in which I have, for all time, placed the rise and fall of the Roman Empire. During that period of my youth when I was first writing tiny English words over the lines of Latin in a small volume called *Gates to Caesar*, and was looking up the Furniss notes in the back of Shakespeare's historical drama of a somewhat similar name, I was spending my romping hours with a noisy group of young people who gathered in the driveway and under the *porte-cochère* of a white house at the corner of May and Woodland Streets. (I might add that the little lady who lived in the white house later grew so accustomed to having me around that she finally married me, which may account for my preoccupation with this particular *mise en scène*.)

It is here, in the middle of this driveway, that I pictured every scene of Roman life, even to the feasts of Lucullus, which, so far as I know, were really held indoors. Caesar was murdered under the *porte-cochère* and Antony made his speech standing on the fence post at the end of the driveway, with the mob of Romans tossing high their sweaty caps in air in such numbers that they extended way over across the street to the front lawn of the Congregational Church parsonage. And, in spite of my reason telling me that the subsequent military action must surely have taken place some distance from the Forum, I am unable to whip my imagination into anything less parochial than to picture Brutus's tent as being pitched on the other corner of the parsonage lawn, easily visible to those wives and sweethearts who stayed at home in the shade of Romulus and Remus by the *porte-cochère*. Even the phrase "Caesar's wife," which one hears so much nowadays (usually in a misquotation) brings to my mind the corner of May and Woodland Streets in Worcester, and whenever I hear it I wonder what ever became of Dr. Scott, the Congregational parson.

Once in a while I do shift the Roman scene to the map of Italy as it used to be in the Rand, McNally textbook which was furnished free by the lavish School Board. I am willing to concede that the invading hordes of Goths and Visigoths could not have come very impressively over the back fence at No. 30 May Street; so, by a terrific wrench of the imagination, I lift myself bodily into the air above the old map of the Italian Boot as I remember it (which is probably not accurately) and look down on them charging out from the cockroach chain of Alps in a sort of impersonal array of pinheads. This far I will go in admitting that Rome was not located at the corner of May and Woodland Streets, but it is only in the emergency of extensive military operations involving the Alps. When I return to Maurice Baring's *Diminutive Dramas* and the dinner parties of Calpurnia and Lucullus, I am back again under the *porte-cochère*, for there, and there alone, lies the grandeur that was Rome.

For my Dickens settings I am transported on the one lame wing of my imagination perhaps two blocks from Rome, to the foot of Shepard Street hill. Here it was that I myself lived at such times as I was not hanging around the white house at the corner of May and Woodland. Practically every tale out of Dickens takes place, in my mind's eye, on the second floor of this house, although it in no possible way resembles even a tyro's idea of London in the thirties and forties. Our "sitting-room" could not, by the stretch of any imagination except mine, be associated with Scrooge's office, nor could the bay window ever have served as deskroom for Bob Cratchit. But so long as I hear *A Christmas Carol* read aloud (which looks as if it might go on now for some years), it is in these unbelievable surroundings that I am forced to place my friends.

The fact that I have seen London offices which would be better, and London dwellings which would be more appropriate, as settings for my Dickens, cannot alter the imperishable conviction in the camera obscura of my mind that Bob Cratchit and Barnaby Rudge and David Copperfield all made their exits and their entrances by the door at the left of the stairway and delivered all their speeches in front of the fireplace in the "sitting-room" of this house at No. 3 Shepard Street, Worcester, Massachusetts.

For some reason, probably because *A Tale of Two Cities* is not real Dickens, I have yielded enough to place the execution of Sydney Carton on the Worcester Common, directly back of the City Hall. I can account for this vagary only by recalling a bronze plate in this vicinity which announces that, on this spot, on such and such a date (*you* know) the Declaration of Independence was read to the assembled citizens of Worcester. I must have somehow confused the War of the American Revolution with the French Revolution (a quite natural mistake in a mind so informally thrown together as mine) and taken it for granted that the guillotine stood on the site now occupied by the equestrian statue of General Devens.

You must not think, however, that the neighborhood of No. 3 Shepard Street is limited to Dickens' lore. Between Nos. 3 and 5 there was what is known as a "side yard." It was perhaps as big as a small miniature golf course, but it served as a screaming and chasing ground for such children as were not at the moment screaming and chasing up in the May Street driveway. This territory represents, to my mind, the Solid South. In it are included acres and acres of cotton fields and miles and miles of levees. On the tar walk which led to the clothes reel in the back yard, Simon Legree whipped Uncle Tom into admitting that, belong his body to whom it might, his soul belonged to God. Eliza, in her heroic flight, had only to run from the clothes reel to the extension of the tar walk which led to the cellar bulkhead, and she was safe in Canada. And even Stonewall Jackson, pausing in his march from Frederick (or was it *to* Frederick?) to make his gallant gesture in the direction of the Old Gray Head, found himself and his troops directly under the bay window from which Bob Cratchit, had he cared to look on a cool September morn, could have witnessed the whole inspiring incident and might even have given Barbara Frietchie an encouraging pat on the back and said, "'Atta girl!"

I can offer no possible explanation of why, within exactly these same precincts, Werther wrestled with his sorrows. Perhaps no explanation is needed.

Side yards seem to figure prominently in this stunted imagination

of mine. My aunt, having come into closer contact with the manufacturing interests of Worcester than my mother, had a larger side
yard on her Woodland Street property. It was so large that it had no
fence around it, although a horse named (for a reason which I have
never before thought to question) Drex was often turned out to
graze in it. Drex must have been a particularly trustworthy horse,
for Woodland Street was far from being a rural thoroughfare, and
escape would have been but a matter of a fairly quick bound for
him. However that may be, this side yard of my aunt's became,
almost before I was able to read, the scene of every story connected
with the West (or Australia). Beginning quite logically with *Black
Beauty*, I placed—and still place—every scene of round-ups,
Indian massacres, Santa Fe trailing and even Yukon exploration,
right in this side yard of my Aunt Mary Elizabeth's. I do not even
remember what her house was like (except that in her kitchen I
was taught how to tell time by the consecutive positions taken up
by the hands of the clock), for she moved from there before I was
six years old. But her side yard is still with me and will be so long
as I read tales of the Wild West and of Man's struggle to tame the
elements. The fact that, directly across from it, was one of those
white houses with a porch and small tower (in which the sewing-
room was located) so popular in New England in the nineties, does
not seem to cramp my vision in its stubborn attempt to make the
vicinity into a replica of the Great Open Spaces. To me it is the
West, and the West had better accommodate itself to my whim.

No amount of travelling or sightseeing can shift me from this
visionary inertia. I have been in Venice, but the Venice of bookland
is to me simply King Street flooded with water. Byron lived in his
elaborate and complicated sin in a house at the corner of King and
Shepard Streets, with gondolas plying their creaking way directly
up King Street hill in defiance of all man-made laws of gravity.
Clarissa Harlowe carried on her incessant correspondence sitting
in a room overlooking the playground of the Woodland Street
School, a playground which was also the scene of Tom Sawyer's
evasions of Aunt Polly, Katherine Mansfield's garden, Swinnerton's

Nocturne and Walpole's *Fortitude.* I might say, in weak extenuation of this unaccountable hodge-podge, that the playground did have a high board fence which separated it from the fairly impressive grounds of an estate belonging to the man who owned the first automobile ever seen in Worcester (a little thing of his own invention). I don't know just what this explains, but somehow it all seems very logical to me.

The question now arises, in those circles in which any interest at all is evinced, what am I to do about all this? What is the sense in going on reading if everything is to take place in the South End of Worcester, Massachusetts? I have tried travel and I have tried osteopathy. I have deliberately said to myself, when I find that I am sending Proust walking up and down Woodland Street with Albertine, "Come, come, man! This is not Normandy!" But always I go back in my mind's eye to a district as parochial as Yorkville or Chelsea, from which there is no escape.

My solution at one time was to stick to the daily papers. I caught myself, however, placing Moscow on the Common back of the Worcester City Hall and locating Galveston as a black spot on a red state on a Rand, McNally map. Perhaps I had just better give up reading entirely. But then what else is there to do?

How to Understand Music

WITH people having the Very Best Music interpreted for them every Sunday afternoon over the radio by the Very Best Experts, it will soon be so that we can't hear *Turkey in the Straw* without reading a meaning into it. With so much attention being paid to *leitmotifs* and the inner significance of what the bassoons are saying, it would not be surprising if, after a while, we forgot to beat time. And if you don't beat time, where is your music?

I would like to take up this afternoon an analysis of Bach's (*Carry Me Back to Old Virginny*) symphonic tschaikovski in C minor, one of the loveliest, and, at the same time, one of the most difficult exercises for three-and-a-half fingers ever written. I may have to stop and lie down every few minutes during my interpretation, it is so exciting. You may do as you like while I am lying down.

In the first place, I must tell you that the modern works of Schönberg, although considerably incomprehensible to the normal ear (that is, an ear which adheres rather closely to the head and *looks* like an ear) are, in reality, quite significant to those who are on the inside. This includes Schönberg himself, his father, and a young man in whom he confides while dazed. What you think are random noises made by the musicians falling over forward on their instruments, are, when you understand them, really steps in a great, moving story—the Story of the Traveling Salesman who came to the Farmhouse. If you have heard it, try to stop me.

We first have the introduction by the wood-winds, in which you will detect the approach of summer, the bassoons indicating the bursting buds (summer and spring came together this year, almost before we were aware of it) and the brasses carrying the idea of winter disappearing, defeated and ashamed, around the corner. Summer approaches (in those sections where you hear the "tum-tiddy-ump-ump-tum-tiddy-ump-ump." Remember?) and then, taking one look around, decides that the whole thing is hardly worth while, and goes back into its hole—a new and not entirely satisfactory union of the groundhog tradition with that of the equinox. This, however, ends the first movement, much to the relief of everyone.

You will have noticed that during this depicting of the solstice, the wind section has been forming dark colors right and left, all typical of Tschaikovski in his more wood-wind moods. These dark colors, such as purple, green, and sometime W and Y, are very lovely once they are recognized. The difficulty comes in recognizing them, especially with beards on. The call of the clarinet, occurring at intervals during this first movement, is clearly the voice of summer, saying, "Co-boss! Co-boss! Co-boss!" to which the tympani reply, "Rumble-rumble-rumble!" And a very good reply it is, too.

The second movement begins with Strephon (the eternal shepherd, and something of a bore) dancing up to the hut in which Phyllis is weaving honey, and, by means of a series of descending six-four chords (as in Debussy's *Reflets dans l'eau* which, you will remember, also makes no sense), indicating that he is ready for a romp. Here we hear the dripping coolness of the mountain stream and the jump-jump-jump of the mountain goat, neither of which figures in the story. He is very eager (tar-ra-ty-tar-ra-ty-tar-ra-ty) and says that there is no sense in her being difficult about the thing, for he has everything arranged. At this the oboes go crazy.

I like to think that the two most obvious modulations, the dominant and the subdominant respectively, convey the idea that, whatever it is that Strephon is saying to Phyllis, nobody cares. This would make the whole thing much clearer. The transition from the dominant to the subdominant (or, if you prefer, you may stop over at Chicago for a day and see the bullfights) gives a feeling of adventure, a sort of Old Man River note, which, to me, is most exciting. But then, I am easily excited.

We now come to the third movement, if there is anybody left in the hall. The third movement is the most difficult to understand, as it involves a complete reversal of musical form in which the wood-winds play the brasses, the brasses play the tympani, and the tympani play "drop-the-handkerchief." This makes for confusion, as you may very well guess. But, as confusion is the idea, the composer is sitting pretty and the orchestra has had its exercise. The chief difficulty in this movement lies in keeping the A strings so tuned that they sound like B-flat strings. To this end, small boys are employed to keep turning the pegs down and the room is kept as damp as possible.

It is here that Arthur, a character who has, up until now, taken no part in the composition, appears and, just as at the rise of the sixth in Chopin's *Nocturne in E Flat* one feels a certain elation, tells Strephon that he has already made plans for Phyllis for that evening and will he please get the hell out of here. We feel, in the descent of the fourth, that Strephon is saying "So what?" Any movement in which occurs a rise to the major third suggests conflict (that is, a rise from the key-note to the major third. Get me right on that, please) and a similar rise to the minor third, or, if you happen to own a bit of U. S. Steel, a rise to 56, suggests a possibility of future comfort. All this, however, is beside the point. (Dorothy Angus, of 1455 Granger Drive, Salt Lake City, has just telephoned in to ask "what point?" Any point, Dorothy, any point. When you are older you will understand.)

This brings us to the fourth movement, which we will omit, owing to one of the oboes having clamped his teeth down so hard on his mouthpiece as to make further playing a mockery. I am very sorry about this, as the fourth movement has in it one of my favorite passages—that where Strephon unbuttons his coat.

From now on it is anybody's game. The A minor prelude, with its persistent chromatic descent, conflicts with the *andante sostenuto*, where the strings take the melody in bars 7 and 8, and the undeniably witty theme is carried on to its logical conclusion in bars 28 and 30, where the pay-off comes when the man tells his wife that he was in the pantry all the time. I nearly die at this every time that I hear it. Unfortunately, I don't hear it often enough, or long enough at a time.

This, in a way, brings to a close our little analysis of whatever it was we were analyzing. If I have made music a little more difficult for you to like, if I have brought confusion into your ear and complication into your taste, I shall be happy in the thought. The next time you hear a symphony, I trust that you will stop all this silly sitting back and taking it for what it is worth to your ear-drums to your emotions, and will put on your thinking caps and try to figure out just what the composer meant when he wrote it. Then perhaps you will write and tell the composer.

The King and the Old Man

BEING A WHIMSICAL LEGEND, WRITTEN WITHOUT
APOLOGIES TO THE LONDON CHRISTMAS WEEKLIES

FOR you must know that in those days there was a King ruling in the land who was very great, so great even that he was called "Pepin Glabamus," or "Pepin Flatfoot," and there were in his kingdom anywhere from twenty-and-four to twenty-and-eight maidens who were in sore distress and concerning whom no one, not even the youth of the university, had any interest whatsoever. Now the King grieved greatly at this, and so great was his grief that he became known far and wide as "Pepin Glubabo" or "Pepin Red-Eye." He was also known as "That Old Buzzard."

Now there came to the castle one night an Old Man, who begged admittance on the grounds that he represented the Fuller Brush Company and would like to show the King a thing or two about brushing. But the King, who was still in high dudgeon (the low dudgeons being full of paynims and poor white trash left over from the Fifth, or Crucial, Crusade), sent out word that he had already been brushed and to get the hell out from under that portcullis. But the Old Man paid no heed to the King's command, but instead sent back word that he had some very nice mead which was guaranteed to make the drinker's ears fly out and snap back, all to the count of "one-two-one-two." So the King, it being Christmas Eve and being sorely troubled in spirit, sent down word, "Oh, well." And so the Old Man came up.

And so the Old Man came up. (A very medieval and mystic effect is gained by repeating the same sentence twice, as you will find out by reading farther in this tale, you sucker.) And when he had reached the King's chamber, he encountered the Chamberlain who, lest the Queen should take to prowling of a night, was always stationed by the door in possession of a loud gong and a basket of red fire. And, at the sound of the gong and the sight of the red fire over the transom, the King was accustomed to open a secret passageway like a flash, and into this secret passageway could dart any business friends who might be sharing a friendly nightcap with His Majesty. Only one night, being sore confused and in something of a daze, the King himself had darted into the secret passageway, leaving the business friend behind on top of the silken canopy, very uncomfortable from the pointed spearheads which held the canopy in place. It was from this unhappy incident, or so said the jester and court winchell, that the Royal Museum acquired its rare collection of golden tresses and slightly damaged neck ornaments, listed in the catalogue under the head of "Or Else."

At last the Old Man came into the presence of the King and, what with opening his sack of mead and testing it himself (the King being no fool), and what with giving of it to the King for him to taste, and what with trying it first with juice of half a lemon and then with effervescent waters to see which way it went best, it was no time at all before both the King and the Old Man were going through the King's supply of neckties to see which ones they should send to the Pope for Christmas.

"Here is one that I have worn only once," said the King.

"How did you ever happen to do that?" asked the Old Man, looking at its tapestry design and screaming with laughter.

And the King screamed, too, not once but eleven times—and the evening was on. The evening was on, and the night was on, and the morning, up until ten-thirty, was on, and, by that time, the Queen was on and had packed up and gone to her mother's.

And so it happened that late on Christmas Day the King rolled over and, finding his head where it had bounced under the bed, replaced it on one shoulder and rubbed his eyes, which he found in the pocket of his waistcoat, and then said:

"Old Man, who *are* you?"

But the Old Man had gone on, rather, it looked to the King as if he had gone, but he was all the time in the open bureau drawer with the neckties.

And so, to this day, no one ever found out who the Old Man really was, but there are those who say that he was the West Wind, and there are those who say that he was the Down from a Thistle, but there are older and wiser ones who say that he was just a naughty Old Man.

The Real Public Enemies

I HAVE now reached an age when I feel that I am pretty well able to take care of myself against animate enemies. By "animate enemies" I mean living people, like burglars, drunks, or police—people who set out with a definite idea in their minds of getting me. Mind you, I don't mean that I can lick these people in a hand-to-hand encounter, but I do know, in a general way, what to do when they attack me, even if it is only to run.

It is the inanimate enemies who have me baffled. The hundred and one little bits of wood and metal that go to make up the impedimenta of our daily life—the shoes and pins, the picture books and door keys, the bits of fluff and sheets of newspaper—each and every one with just as much vicious ill-will toward me personally as the meanest footpad who roams the streets, each and every one bent on my humiliation and working together, as on one great team, to bedevil and confuse me and to get me into a neurasthenics' home before I am sixty. I can't fight these boys. They've got me licked.

When I was very young and first realized the conspiracy against me on the part of these inanimate things, I had a boyish idea that force was the thing to use. When a shoestring had clearly shown that it was definitely *not* going to be put through the eyelet, I would give it a yank that broke it in two, and feel that the bother of getting a new lace was not too much to pay for the physical pain which the old lace must have suffered. In fact, as I put in the new one I had an idea that it was pretty well frightened at the example of its predecessor and would jolly well behave itself or suffer the same fate.

But after years of getting out new laces and buying new fountain pens (my method, when a pen refused to work, was to press down on it so hard that the points spread open like a fork and then to rip the paper in a frenzied imitation of writing), I gradually realized that I was being the sucker in the battle and that the use of force didn't pay in the long run.

I then started trying subtlety. If there is one field in fighting in which a human ought to be able to win out over a piece of wood, it is in tricky maneuvering. Take, for example, when you are trying to read a newspaper on top of a bus. We will start with the premise

that the newspaper knows what you are trying to do and has already made up its mind that you are not going to do it. Very well, Mr. Newspaper, we'll see! (Later on you don't call it "Mr. Newspaper." You call it "you —— ——!" But that is after you know it better.)

Suppose you want to open it to page four. The thing to do is not to hold it up and try to turn it as you would an ordinary newspaper. If you do, it will turn into a full-rigged brigantine, each sheet forming a sail, and will crash head-on into your face, blinding you and sometimes carrying you right off the bus.

The best way is to say, as if talking to yourself, "Well, I guess I'll turn to page seven." Or better yet, let the paper overhear you say, "Oh, well, I guess I won't read any more," and make a move as if to put it away in your pocket. Then, quick as a wink, give it a quick turn inside out before it realizes what is happening.

It won't take it long to catch on, but, thinking that you want to turn to page seven, as you said, it will quite possibly open to page four, which was the one you wanted.

But even this system of *sotto voce* talking and deceit does not always work. In the first place, you have to have a pretty young newspaper, who hasn't had much experience, for all the older ones will be on to your game and will play it back at you for all it is worth.

The only way to be safe about the thing is to take it all very calmly and try to do your best with deliberate fierceness, folding each page over under your feet very slowly until you come to the right one. But by that time you have got the paper in such a condition that it cannot be read—so you lose anyway.

Of course, after years of antagonizing members of the inanimate underworld, you are going to get an active conspiracy against you, with physical violence on *their* part as its aim. It then becomes, not an aggressive campaign on your part, but one of defense to save yourself from being attacked.

For example, I have a pair of military brushes which have definitely signed up to put me on the spot and will, I am afraid, ultimately kill me. I have taken those brushes from the bureau and held them in a position to brush my hair, without an unkind thought in my mind, and have had them actually fly out of my hands, execute a pretty take-off of perhaps a foot and a half, and then crash into my forehead with as deft a "one-two" as any heavy-weight ever pulled on a groggy opponent.

I have placed slippers very carefully under my bed, only to have them crawl out during the night to a position where I will step into them the wrong way round when leaping out of bed to answer the telephone.

These things don't just happen, you know. They are proofs of a very clear conspiracy to hurt me physically which exists among household objects, and against which I have no defense. All that I

can do is to walk about all day crouched over with one elbow raised to ward off the heavier attacks which are being aimed at me. This gives a man a cringing look which so becomes a personal characteristic.

It is this element of physical danger which has entered my struggle with these things which has got me worried. I will match myself in an unequal fight to open a can of sardines or a bottle of water, if the issue is to be merely whether I get it open or not. But I can't face the inevitable gashing and bleeding which always follow my failure. I will tackle the closing of a trunk or suitcase, but I am already licked by the knowledge that, no matter how the fight turns out, the metal snaps are going to reach out and nip my fingers.

The only thing that I can do, as old age and experience bear down on me, is to sit with my hands in my pockets and try nothing.

I have said that, in my youth, I gave up the use of force when little things thwarted me. I *should* have given it up, but there is one enemy which I still lash out at in futile bludgeonings. It is the typewriter on which I am writing this article. In putting on a ribbon

I lose myself entirely, and invariably end up completely festooned like Laocoön, ripping and tearing madly with ink-stained fingers at a ribbon which long before I had rendered useless. I am also thrown into raging fits of physical violence when, owing to some technical fault which I do not understand, the letters begin getting dimmer and dimmer, finally becoming just shells of their natural selves. On such occasions I start very quietly hitting the keys harder and harder, muttering, "Oh, you won't, won't you?" until I am crashing down with both fists on the keyboard and screaming, "Take that—and *that!*"

In fact, as I write this, I detect a weakening in the pigment of the ribbon, and, as I strike each key, less and less seems to be happening. I will try to be calm.

I must try to remember that it does no good to inflict pain on inanimate things and that the best that I can do is break the typewriter . . . But really . . . after all . . . you xxxxx you xxxxxxxxxxxx take that xxxxxxxxxxxx and *that* xxxxxxxxxxxx.

Matinees—
Wednesdays and Saturdays

TO THE Inveterate First-nighter (of which there are perhaps four, aside from the critics who don't count because they don't dress) a play is either good or bad. As he walks out of the theatre, dropping his muffler behind him on the way up the aisle, he nods his head either from side to side or up and down, meaning "It won't do!" or "It's in!" All of which goes to show just how much the Inveterate First-nighter (this time *including* the critics) knows about it.

For behind him, through the succeeding weeks, comes a line of strange people whom he has never seen at first-nights, most of them ladies with boxes of candy clutched under their arms, who can take his pontifical judgment and attach a neat tail to it, giving it exactly the appearance of a monkey. That little line of diamond type in the theatrical advertisements which reads, "Matinees Wednesdays and Saturdays," and all that it implies, is what the first-nighter does not take into consideration when he hands down his judgment. In fact, there is something slightly revolting to a first-nighter about the idea of a matinee, especially a Wednesday one. He would prefer not to think about it, to pretend that such things do not exist. But they do exist, and the wise producer takes them seriously into consideration.

Not that matinees alone can make a play a success by any means, and not that a success can make matinees go. Some of the best shows in town have what is known as "weak matinees." But the elements which make the ladies like a play in the afternoon, if present in a play to sufficient extent, can transform what looks like a Sock and Buskin Club production on the opening night into a good, solid, rent-paying proposition before the season is over.

And these elements of matinee success, if you ladies don't mind my saying so, are the tutti-frutti ice cream of the theatre, the simple pleasures of childhood, the most elementary form of entertainment. By that I mean good old-fashioned slap-stick, slap-stick comedy, slap-stick tragedy and slap-stick sex. Here we do not find the male character, with a delicate regard for the subtler points of romantic psychology, saying to the female as he looks out over the Bay of Naples, "What are we going to do about this, you and I?" For the ladies of the matinee he can go right up and grab her and say, "I love you, you great big, marvelous thing!" and never once be accused of being obvious. They eat it up. And, when the moment for comedy comes, he need not look at the back of his hand and say cryptically, "Life to me seems a little like something which life is not at all like." All that he has to do is to exit and reappear shortly in a white nightshirt and the house crashes about his ears in a storm of delight.

One of the most clarifying experiences that a wise first-nighter can have is to pocket his pride and go back to see the second or third matinee of a play which he has condemned to oblivion in his own judgment. He will first be surprised, and a little shocked, to see so many people waiting in the lobby. (The first fifteen minutes of a matinee are always consumed by ladies waiting in the lobby for each other. Why they don't go to luncheon together and come to the theatre at the same time is one of the mysteries of matinee-going. One always seems to be waiting for the other—and in not very good humor either.) Why, asks the first-nighter in disgust, should there be so many people wasting their money at a play which must, by now, be known far and wide as bad? This is like an honest, God-fearing man asking why so many women waste their time on a man who is known far and wide as being a charlatan. He shouldn't ask himself. He should ask the women.

Inside the theatre he will always find that the curtain has not yet gone up. No matter how late you arrive at a matinee, the curtain has never gone up. Just as an incidental point of advice in theatrical matters, I would say that one may go to any matinee as late as two fifty-five and still have time to join the bedlam of conversation, unlimber the chocolate caramels (pronounced "car-mels" at matinees) and read the "Who's Who" in the program before the lights are finally lowered and the exhausted orchestra stops its fifth consecutive rendering (verse and two choruses) of *Zwei Herzen*.

Even when the lights are down, it is several minutes before the crinkling of bonbon coverings and the buzz of feminine checkings-up can be quelled. Next to an old-fashioned church social, or possibly a monster bridge party, there is no buzz that can equal the sibilant buzz of a matinee. Ladies *en masse* always seem to be conversing exclusively in words beginning and ending with the letter "s." Even after the curtain has gone up, there are several little groups scattered over the house who doggedly stick it out and take part themselves in the first few minutes of the act, sometimes, if the cast is an English one, more distinctly than the actors themselves. The buzzing is resumed at various points during the performance whenever it is necessary for one to tell her neighbor what she has suddenly divined as the next step in the plot. Sometimes, at a tense moment, one can hear, almost in unison, the house whisper "He's going to shoot her!" or "She's just outside the door!" This helps keep the actors themselves in touch with the play.

It is an axiom among people of the theatre that lines which fall flat at the evening show may go big at a matinee, and *vice versa*. It is also true that whole sections of a play are received in entirely different spirit at night and in the afternoon. *The Animal Kingdom*, which dealt with refined infidelity, with the husband's ex-mistress finally winning out, was resented by the married ladies of a matinee. Not that the play itself was resented, for it held too many passages of genteel sex not to appeal to a lady-audience. But Miss Frances Fuller, who played the role of the mistress, was conscious of an antagonism from out front which was quite lacking in the evening, an antagonism which the author really designed for the wife and which arose from that instinct, usually attributed to the male, of sticking together.

Of course, there is nothing like a house full of women for a good salacious play like *The Command to Love* or *Experience Unnecessary*. One of the most embarrassing experiences that a man can have is to find himself alone at a matinee where Sex is rampant on the stage in either double, or simple *entendre*. Scenes of seduction, like those in *Fata Morgana* for example, which in the evening are taken with at least a modicum of the seriousness intended by the author, become, at matinees, occasions for giggling and obscene hilarity, making the lone male feel that perhaps, in spite of its traditional temporary advantages, the whole institution of Sex has been a mistake. Woman, however lovely she may be in stooping to folly in individual cases, is never so unlovely as when giggling at it in a group over boxes of chocolates. Of course, some of this gaiety at salacity and seduction may be due to a hysterical and nervous embarrassment on the part of the ladies themselves, for they are also given to laughing at tense moments in melodramas and even tragedies (I once heard a woman laugh at that most tragic moment in all drama, the off-stage shot in *The Wild Duck*, and I afterward had her killed, so there will be no more of that out of *her*). But, on the whole, the laughter at dirty comedies and serious sex plays, seems to spring from something less charming than hysteria, and we must regretfully conclude that, as a sex, the ladies cannot be trusted with anything more intimate in the theatre than a minuet.

This is, of course, not to say that the men do not laugh at dirty jokes in revues and burlesque shows for the evidence is there to refute any such wild statement. But these jokes were meant to be laughed at, and there is no possible suspicion of deviousness about them. The actual business of seduction is too serious to the male to be treated lightly. He has a tough enough time as it is.

This may explain why the scattered male members of a matinee audience wince at the ladies' levity in the face of the Facts of Life, but the main thing to be explained about men at matinees is how they happen to be there at all. Who are they? Never by any chance is there a familiar face among them. They sit, usually in solitary unimpressiveness, on the side aisles, looking very uncomfortable and out of place, and never, by any chance, seem to be enjoying the show. Are they out-of-town salesmen whiling away two hours until their prospects get back from lunch? Or husbands left, as children used to be left in the Eden Musee, while the womenfolk do some shopping? Whatever they are, they might much better be out in the fresh air getting some exercise, or even in a good speakeasy building up a bun. Matinees should be left to the ladies, to giggle and cry and buzz to their hearts' content. And then, when the last fur-piece has been turned in at the box-office and the last caramel covering has been swept up from the floor, the sophisticates and grown-ups can come in for the evening entertainment and the show can go on as intended.

The Chinese Situation

With "The Good Pulitzer Earth" being made into both a movie and a play (which means six imitations in each field if it proves successful) to say nothing of Mrs. Pearl Buck's going right ahead and bringing descendants of old Wang into the publishing world, just as if there were plenty of food to go around, it looks as if we were in for a good, old-fashioned Chinese winter.

Before the thing has gone too far (which it will), let us see just how far it can go. EDITOR'S NOTE: Owing to the subsequent failure of the play and the postponement of the movie until next year, it went no further than the following parody.

IT WAS the birthday of Whang the Gong. Whang the Gong was the son of Whang the Old Man, and the brother of Whang the Rich and of Auld Whang Syne. He was very poor and had only the tops of old Chinese wives to eat, but in his soul he was very proud and in his heart he knew that he was the son of old Whang Lung who had won the Pulitzer Prize for the Hop-Sing-and-Jump.

Now Whang the Gong, although he was known far and wide among the local missionaries as a heathen, had read enough of the Gospels to know the value of short words and the effectiveness of the use of the word "and." And so Whang the Gong spoke, and it was good. Good for fifty cents a word.

Now Whang the Gong awoke on the morning of his birthday, and opened one eye, and it was not good, so he shut it again. And he opened the other eye, and it was worse than the first. So the young man shook his head wilfully and said, "I will open no more eyes until the harvest comes." Now the harvest was full six months away, which gave the young man a hell of a lot of leeway, and he rolled over again and slept.

But Rum Blossom, the wife of Whang the Gong, did not sleep.

At four in the morning, before even the kine had begun to low or the water to run in the tub, Rum Blossom had rubbed her small hand over her small eyes, and it was not good. It was lousy. She arose, then, and went into the pump-house.

"Excuse," she said to nobody in particular, as nobody in particular was listening to her words, "excuse—I am going to have a baby." So she went into the pump-house, and, while the waffles were cooking, she had a baby, and it was a man. Which was pretty good, when you consider that it was born between waffles.

Now the winter wore on, and it was still the birthday of Whang the Gong, for Whang the Gong liked birthdays, for birthdays are holidays and holidays are good. And Rum Blossom, his wife, came to him and said, lowering her eyes as she pulled the stump of an old tree and threw it into the wood-box, "I am going to have another baby." And Whang the Gong said, "That is up to you." And he rolled over and shut another eye, which was his third, kept especially for shutting. So Rum Blossom went into the library and had another baby. And it was a woman, or slave, baby, which, in China, is not so hot.

"I will scream your shame to the whole village," said Whang the Gong when he had heard of the incident. "Yesterday you had a man child, which was good. Today you have a girl, which is bitterness upon my head and the taste of aloes in my mouth." And he repeated it over and over, such being the biblical style, "I will tell the village—I will tell the village." And Rum Blossom, his wife said, "All right. Go ahead and tell the village. Only get up out of bed, at any rate. And get your old man up out of bed, too. I am sick of seeing him around, doing nothing."

And Whang the Gong got up out of his bed, and got his old man up out of his bed, all of which made but little difference.

He went without reply then to the wall and felt for the roughness which was the mark of his clothes closet, and he removed the clod of earth which fastened it. "I will have my cutaway," he said, and went then back to bed. And Rum Blossom his wife came to him and said,

"I will get you your cutaway just as soon as I have had a child," and going into the clothes closet, she had a child and came out with the cutaway. "Here," she said, "is your cutaway. Take it and like it." And Whang the Gong took it, and liked it, for it was a good cutaway.

It seemed as though once the gods turn against a man they will not consider him again. The rains, which should have come in the early summer, withheld themselves until the fifteenth of October, which was the date for Rum Blossom to have another baby.

And Whang the Gong said to Whang Lung, the old man his father, "How come? We have no rain." And Whang the Old Man said, "True, you have no rain. But you have babies galore. One may not ask everything."

And Whang the Gong was stumped. "A baby is but a baby," he said in confusion. "But rain is rain." All of which made no sense, but sounded good.

But the Old Man would hear none of his son's sophistry, and mouthed his gums, which were of tutti-frutti, and rolled in the grass, only there was no grass and so the Old Man rolled in the stones and bruised himself quite badly. But all this meant nothing to Whang the Gong, for three moons had passed since he had eaten nothing but spinach and his eyes were on those of Lettuce, the Coat-Room Girl.

There was a day when Whang the Gong awoke and saw his wife, Rum Blossom, pacing up and down the room, but, as the room was only three paces long, the effect was unimpressive.

"Another baby, I suppose?" said Whang the Gong, shutting both eyes.

"Not so that you could notice it," replied his wife, in extremest pique. "I'm through." And there was that in her pique which allowed no comeback, and Whang the Gong knew that she was indeed through, which was O.K. with him.

And when pay-day came, Whang the Gong arose and put on his finest silken suit with an extra pair of pants and married Lettuce the Coat Room Girl, making two wives for Whang the Gong, one, Rum Blossom, to keep the books, and one, Lettuce the Coat Room Girl, to be the mother of his children. Which made it very simple, so simple that everyone watching smiled.

Saturday's Smells

NEVER, even in my best form, what you would call a "drone" or "worker" at heart, I have been having a particularly tough time of it lately just sitting at my desk.

Specialists and psychoanalysts from all over the world have been working on my case, and it was only yesterday that I myself was able to give them the key to my inability to work. It is my new pipe tobacco. It smells like Saturday, and consequently puts me in a chronic holiday mood.

This may take a little explaining. The main thesis on which I am going to build my case is that, when you were a child, certain days had their individual smells, and that these smells, when experienced today, take you back to your state of mind when you experienced them in childhood. Do I make myself clear, or must I say that all over again?

Sunday smells were, of course, the most distinctive, and, when they assail me today, I become restless and depressed and want to go to sea. In my section of the country, the first Sunday smell was of the fish-balls for breakfast. This was not so depressing, as fish-balls were good, and anyway, Sunday didn't begin to get you down until later in the day.

Then came, in slow succession, the musty draughts of the Sunday-school vestry, laden with the week's dust on the maps of Palestine and the hymnals, and freshened that morning only by the smell of black silk dresses sprinkled with lavender and the starch from little girls' petticoats and sashes. Then the return to the home, where fish-cakes had given way to fricasseeing chicken and boiling onions, which, in turn, gave way to the aroma of the paternal cigar as you started out on that Sunday afternoon walk, during which you passed all the familiar spots where you had been playing only the day before with the gang, now desolate and small-looking in the pall of Sunday.

But, sure as the smells of Sunday were, those of Saturday were none the less distinctive and a great deal more cheery. In our house we began getting whiffs of Saturday as early as Friday evening, when the bread was "set" on the kitchen table and the beans put to soak nearby. The smell of the cold bread-dough when the napkins were lifted from the pans always meant "no school tomorrow," and was a preliminary to the "no school today" smells of Saturday, which are at the basis of my present trouble.

On Saturday morning early these "no school today" smells began to permeate the kitchen, and, as the kitchen was the sole port of entry and exit during the morning's play outside, they became inextricably mixed up with not only cooking, but "duck-on-the-rock," "Indian guide" and that informal scrimmaging which boys indulge in in back yards, which goes by the name of either "football" or "baseball" according to the season of the year.

In New England, of course, the *leit motif* among the Saturday smells was the one of beans baking, but the bread and pies ran it a close second. A good cake in the oven could hold its own, too. Then, along about eleven-thirty the Saturday noon dinner began to loom up, being more plebeian than the Sunday noon dinner, it usually took the combined form of cabbage, turnips, beets and corned beef, all working together in one pot, with the potatoes, to make what is known as the "New England boiled dinner." That put a stop to any other smells that thought they were something earlier in the morning.

On the outside, Saturday morning contributed the smell of burning leaves, and of shingles on the new house that was always being built in the neighborhood; and, although sounds do not come into our lecture today, there was the sound of carpenters hammering, and the re-echoing beat of rugs being dusted, which became almost smells in their affinity to them.

Now, here is the point about my pipe tobacco. A month or so ago

I tried out a new blend, which, I discovered only yesterday, smells exactly like beans in an oven. So, when I settle down to a morning's work and light my pipe, I am gradually overcome with the delicious feeling that there is "no school today," and that I really ought to be outdoors playing.

So, without knowing why, I have been leaving my work and getting out my skates and yielding to the Saturday spirit. The only trouble has been that, under this subtle influence, every day has been Saturday, because every day has smelled like Saturday.

I don't suppose that the tradesmen to whom I owe money will think much of this explanation, but it satisfies me and the psychoanalysts perfectly. And, as yet, I have made no move to buy a less insidious-smelling pipe tobacco.

Route Nationale 14

COME with me and we will motor through Sunny France, from the tippity-tip of Cherbourg to the top-*tip*pity-tip of Cap d'Antibes! Or come with me and we will go over to Dinty Moore's on Forty-sixth Street for some spareribs and sauerkraut. Anyway, we'll do *some*thing!

If it's motoring through France we're going, we shall have to get started earlier. We shall also have to have a motor. Perhaps we had better decide right now on Dinty Moore's.

To motor pleasantly from Cherbourg to Antibes, it is preferable to use one's own car, as in a rented French limousine the driver's mustache is always too big and too black. There really isn't much worry involved in taking your own car, unless you happen to be watching while they are lowering it down from the ship to the tender. Furthermore, in your own car, you don't care so much what the children do to the back seat.

THE ARRIVAL

On arriving at the port of Cherbourg you are met on the tender by a representative of the A.A.A. who will tell you that your license plates have just barely not arrived yet, but that they will be in tomorrow *très de bonne heure* (along about noon). So this means spending the first night of your motoring trip in Cherbourg (Grand Hotel du Casino, or behind the barrels on the new pier). Anywhere you stay, you get to know Cherbourg.

While roaming the streets of this quaint old seaport town (Napoleon said of it: "*J'avais résolu de rénouveller à Cherbourg les merveilles de l'Egypte,*" but he didn't quite make it, doubtless due to the lack of Egyptians), one can see much that is of interest—to the Cherbourgians. One may also *be* seen and pointed out as a native by the boat-train passengers as they roll slowly through the Main Street. ("Look, Harry," they say, "at those picturesque old natives! Don't those people *ever* bathe, do you suppose?") One can also get a line on the boat-train passengers themselves from the outside. They don't shape up so hot, either (Beauty note: Every woman looking out at the windows of the incoming boat train has just been freshly lip sticked in preparation for embarkation.)

A good place to spend the evening while waiting in Cherbourg is not the Café de Paris across the bridge. It isn't much fun in the Grand Hotel du Casino, either. But you are all excitement at the prospect of your early start in the morning, so it's early to bed, after a chat with the quaint old negro concierge from Philadelphia, Pa.

At seven o'clock you are up and ready, with everything strapped on the car and the children buried in the back seat under the extra hampers and coats. (One child is buried so deeply that he is a great big boy by the time he is remembered and dug out.) The maps are spread open and a schedule arranged which calls for lunch at Lisieux. (Hotel France et Espagne. Bad Martinis.) A light rain is falling.

At the *mairie* it will be found that the license plates have not yet come, and eighteen shoulders will be shrugged. The car will then be driven back to the hotel (Grand Hotel du Casino, 100 fr.) and a more thorough tour made of

CHERBOURG (¼ kms.). A quaint seaport town, of which Napoleon once said: "*J'avais résolu de rénouveller à Cherbourg les merveilles de l'Egypte.*" It was his intention to revive in Cherbourg the marvels of Egypt, is the way it looks. You may see a statue of Napoleon in the public square across the bridge. On the other hand, you may not. You may also see Pauline Frederick in *The Woman Thou Gavest Me,* the film for which was found in an old bureau drawer by the exhibitor. Then there is always the Café de Paris. And the Grand Hotel du Casino.

The license plates not having come at fifteen o'clock, it is decided to spend the night in

CHERBOURG (¼ kms.). A quaint seaport town which Napoleon once designated as the place where he was to revive the marvels of Egypt. To this end he appointed Vauban, the great engineer, to construct fortifications and plan a harbor which should be impregnable. (You learn a little more each day you stay in Cherbourg. By the time I left I was being groomed as Opposition candidate for Mayor. I was letter-perfect in the opposition, but my age was against me.)

During the second evening in Cherbourg, after seeing that everything is going all right at the Café de Paris, you can read up on the rules of the road, some of the most readable being:

1. In France one keeps to the right, except when skidding.

2. Danger signals along the road are represented by black triangles with little pictures on them. Be careful not to become so interested in looking at the pictures that you forget the danger. A picture of two little hills side by side (these French!) means *cassis*, or a gully across the road (Cassis, in vermouth form, also makes a nice gully across the road if taken in sufficient quantities). A cute little gate means a *passage à niveau gardé* or protected level crossing. An even cuter choo-choo (if you are traveling with children), with smoke and everything, means an unprotected level crossing. This is the one you mustn't get too fascinated by.

3. The way to say "dust clip of front hub" is *"ressort cache poussière de moyeu avant,"* something you really don't have to learn as you can always point. In case you end up in Holland the way to say it is *"Sluitveerje der smeer-opening,"* which is just plain silly.

4. Gasoline is sold by the *bidon*. Be careful about this.

5. An automobile tourist arriving in France on March first for a four months' visit will take out a *laissez-passer* for thirty days. This immediately puts the tourist under suspicion in the eyes of all officials and sometimes ends in his incarceration.

By this time it is bedtime, as you have to make an early start in the morning. There are very tall hat-racks in each bedroom of the

Grand Hotel du Casino, from which you may hang yourself if you have to stay a third day in Cherbourg.

Up at seven, in a light rain. A chat with the colored concierge from Philadelphia, one last look around at the Café de Paris, a visit to Napoleon's monument to make sure what it was he hoped to make out of Cherbourg, and, at eleven o'clock sharp a trip to the *mairie* where there is tremendous excitement owing to the arrival of the license plates. By this time you have made such friends with every one in the place, including the Mayor, that it costs you three hundred francs in tips. The adjusting of the plates, the signing of the Peace Treaty, the shaking hands and the shaking-down, take an hour and a half, so it is decided to have lunch at the

GRAND HOTEL DU CASINO (35 fr.). A quaint old hostelry situated hard by the *quai* overlooking the harbor fortifications built for Napoleon by Vauban, the great engineer.

THE START

Leaving Cherbourg, believe it or not, we ascend a gentle grade along winding roads through picturesque Normandy (light rain). The excitement of actually riding in a moving automobile proves too much for the children and a stop has to be made just this side of

BAYEUX, famous for its tapestry and cathedral, neither of which we see. The excitement of passing through a French town other than Cherbourg is too much for the children and another stop has to be made just the other side of

BAYEUX, famous for its tapestry and cathedral, although there was a perfectly good hotel (Hotel de Luxembourg) on the way through. At this point it is discovered that the "funnies," bought in an American newspaper the day before in Cherbourg, have been packed in a suitcase on the trunk rack, necessitating taking the car apart to get them. From here on the children are engrossed in reading American "funnies," which gives us quite a stretch without a stop to

CAEN (pronounced "Kong"), famous as being the first train-stop from Cherbourg to Paris, where most American tourists think they are in Cayenne.

Engrossed in reading American "funnies"

Stop for the night at LISIEUX (scheduled for lunch the day before). Hotel France et Espagne. (Bad Martinis.) The residents of Lisieux sleep all day in order to be abroad all night under the windows of the Hotel France et Espagne (under the window of Room 34 in particular), where they walk up and down in an especially whittled type of sabot, pinching children to make them cry. Some also carry small horns or attach even smaller ones to bicycles, thereby effecting a squeak in synchronization with the bicycle wheels. This causes the fox terriers (an exceptionally repulsive breed, fat and soiled) to bark, which, in turn, causes the children to cry.

Up at four (bad Martinis) and on the road at five-thirty, passing through such interesting towns as Évreux, Mantes, Flins, and St. Germain-en-Laye, none of which are seen owing to the entire family catching up on last night's sleep.

We are awakened by the sound of heavy traffic and, on inquiring where we are, are told that we are in Paris (Porte Maillot).

Here ends the first stage of our automobile tour from Cherbourg to Antibes. The stay in Paris is regulated by the length of time it takes to recover the use of our limbs and have the *ressort cache poussière de moyeu avant* fixed. The number of remaining checks in the A. B. A. book has also something to do with it.

CONTINUATION OF TOUR

(Paris to Antibes)

The P.L.M. train (*Wagon Lits*) leaves Paris (Gare de Lyons) at 19:40, arriving at Cannes at 11:02 the next day. Fifteen minutes motor trip to Cap d'Antibes.

Naming Our Flowers

I WONDER how many of us who pretend to love the flowers really know how they got their names. I do not mean their Latin names, because nobody knows where they got those, not even the people who named them. Somebody was just in a silly mood, that was all.

But, for instance, how did the "double-gaited wertroot" come to be called that, instead of "Winkle Peter-in-Bed"? What is there in the history of "Walmsley's cowlick" that makes it necessary to call it "Walmsley's cowlick"? Wouldn't it be fascinating to know the ins and outs of flower nomenclature? Perhaps "fascinating" is too strong a word. Let us rather say "awful."

There is a legend concerning the "Crazy Kitty, or MacNerty's fields-awash" which more or less clears up the mystery of its name. It seems that the flower was originally known as "sauerkraut," because it grew to just the height of a pig's knuckle. Near a certain field in which it grew in abundance lived an old witch who was known to her intimates as "Crazy Kitty," because her name was Kitty and she was as crazy as a coot. There can be no doubt as to how Crazy Kitty got *her* name.

It seems that this old woman had a particular dislike for the flower called "sauerkraut" and used to say that if the darned thing came up next Spring as abundantly as it had in the past she would move from the neighborhood. She said this every Spring.

It was this particular dislike of Crazy Kitty's for the charming flower that caused the boys of the town to call it after her, and when she learned that her name had been applied to her pet aversion she went through the streets one night and set fire to every house, practically wiping out the community. And so the flower came to be known as "Crazy Kitty" the world over in her honor. Just why it is also sometimes called "MacNerty's fields-awash" has never been cleared up.

It has always been considered a delicate compliment to name a new and lovely flower after the wife, mother or sweetheart of the originator, which accounts for some otherwise unaccountable names, such as the "Mrs. Sam Cyzcyzocyz rose," "the Assistant Secretary of Public Works Lilian D. Wratch begonia" and "the Emma Grobdigger Naumglatz primrose." It was in honor of five little girls that the "Lapino Country Day School Basketball Team knee-action violet" became known as such.

We have only scratched the surface of the study of flowers' names, and it ought to heal right over, if we take care of it. My own method of designation is to point to the flower that strikes my fancy and say, "Give me a dozen of those yellow ones."

Johnny-on-the-Spot

IF YOU want to get a good perspective on history in the making, just skim through a collection of news photographs which have been snapped at those very moments when cataclysmic events were taking place throughout the world. In almost every picture you can discover one guy in a derby hat who is looking in exactly the opposite direction from the excitement, totally oblivious to the fact that the world is shaking beneath his feet. That would be me, or at any rate, my agent in that particular part of the world in which the event is taking place.

I have not seen an actual photograph of the shooting of the Austrian Archduke at Serajevo, but I would be willing to bet, if one is in existence, that you could find, somewhere off in the right foreground, a man in a Serbian derby looking anxiously up the street for a trolley car. And probably right up in the foreground a youth smiling and waving into the camera.

Revolutionary disturbances are particularly subject to this blasé treatment on the part of bystanders. Photographs which have come up from Cuba lately, and even those of the wildest days in Russia during the Reign of Terror—photographs taken at the risk of the lives of the photographers themselves—all show, somewhere in their composition, an area of complete calm in which at least one man is looking at his watch or picking his teeth.

In one which I have before me from Havana we see crowds of people fleeing before machine-gun bullets, soldiers dashing hither and yon with uplifted sabres, puffs of smoke stippling the background, and down in one corner, by a news kiosk, a man in his shirt-sleeves looking up at a clock.

And I shall probably be wearing a derby

At any rate, there'll be one guy who knows what time the trouble started—provided he knew that it *had* started.

Are these men in derby hats really men of iron, who take revolutions and assassinations in their stride as all part of the day's work, or are they hard of hearing, or near-sighted, or, possibly, are they just men who go through life missing things?

I like to think of them as in the third category, for I know that if I were on the spot during any important historical event I would not know about it until I read the papers the next day. I am unobservant to the point of being what scientists might call "half-witted." It isn't that I don't see things, but that I don't register them. This is what makes it so difficult for me in traffic.

I could have worked in a shop in the Place de la Bastille, or have sold papers across from the Old State House in Boston, or have been an usher in Ford's Theatre in Washington, and yet would probably have noticed nothing of the events for which those spots are famous. I possibly might have been aware of a slight commotion and, if I had worked in Ford's Theatre, wondered why the curtain was rung down so early; but, on going home, I would have been pretty sure to report a routine evening to the family. "They didn't finish *Our American Cousin* tonight," I might have said. "Some trouble with the lights, I guess."

All this makes for a calm, well-ordered existence, with practically no nerve strain. Those men in derbies and I, provided we do not get hit by stray bullets, ought to live to a ripe old age if we take any kind of care of our kidneys at all. Dynasties may fall, cities may collapse, and the world be brought down about our ears, but, unless something hits us squarely in the back, we are sitting pretty.

I do rather dread the day, however, when I look at a photograph of the focal point of the World Revolution and see myself smirking into the camera with my back to the fighting. And the worst of it will be that I shall probably be wearing a derby.

Down with Pigeons

ST. FRANCIS OF ASSISI (unless I am getting him mixed up with St. Simeon Stylites, which might be very easy to do as both their names begin with "St.") was very fond of birds, and often had his picture taken with them sitting on his shoulders and pecking at his wrists. That was all right, if St. Francis liked it. We all have our likes and dislikes, and I have more of a feeling for dogs. However, I am not *against* birds as a class. I am just against pigeons.

I do not consider pigeons birds, in the first place. They are more in the nature of people; people who mooch. Probably my feeling about pigeons arises from the fact that all my life I have lived in rooms where pigeons came rumbling in and out of my window. I myself must have a certain morbid fascination for pigeons, because they follow me about so much—and with evident ill-will. I am firmly convinced that they are trying to haunt me.

Although I live in the middle of a very large city (well, to show you how large it is—it is the largest in the world) I am awakened every morning by a low gargling sound which turns out to be the result of one, or two, or three pigeons walking in at my window and sneering at me. Granted that I am a fit subject for sneering as I lie there, possibly with one shoe on or an unattractive expression on my face, but there is something more than just a passing criticism in these birds making remarks about me. They have some ugly scheme on foot against me, and I know it. Sooner or later it will come out, and then I can sue.

This thing has been going on ever since I was in college. In our college everybody was very proud of the pigeons. Anyone walking across the Yard (Campus to you, please) was beset by large birds who insisted on climbing up his waistcoat and looking about in his wallet for nuts or raisins or whatever it is you feed pigeons (bichloride would be my suggestion, but let it pass).

God knows that I was decent enough to them in my undergraduate days. I let them walk up and down my back and I tried to be as nice as I could without actually letting them see that I was not so crazy about it. I even gave them chestnuts, chestnuts which I wanted myself. I now regret my generosity, for good chestnuts are hard to get these days.

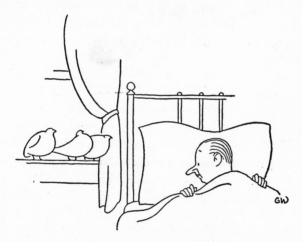

Pigeons walking in at my window and sneering at me

But somehow the word got around in pigeon circles that Benchley was antipigeon. They began pestering me. I would go to bed at night, tired from overstudy, and at six-thirty in the morning the Big Parade would begin. The line of march was as follows: Light on Benchley's window sill, march once in through the open window, going "Grumble-grumble-grumble" in a sinister tone. Then out and stand on the sill, urging other pigeons to come in and take a crack at it.

There is very little fun in waking up with a headache and hearing an ominous murmuring noise, with just the suggestion of a passing shadow moving across your window sill. No man should be asked to submit to this *all* his life.

I once went to Venice (Italy), and there, with the rest of the tourists, stood in awe in the center of St. Mark's Piazza, gazing at the stately portals of the church and at the lovely green drinks served at Florian's for those who don't want to look at the church all of the time.

It is an age-old custom for tourists to feed corn to the pigeons and then for the pigeons to crawl all over the tourists. This has been going on without interruption ever since Americans discovered Venice. So far as the records show, no pigeon has ever failed a tourist—and no tourist has ever failed a pigeon. It is a very pretty relationship.

In my case, however, it was different. In the first place, the St. Mark's pigeons, having received word from the American chapter of their lodge, began flying at me in such numbers and with such force as actually to endanger my life. They came in great droves, all flying low and hard, just barely skimming my hat and whirring in an ugly fashion with some idea of intimidating me. But by that time I was not to be intimidated, and, although I ducked very low and lost my hat several times, I did not give in. I even bought some corn from one of the vendors and held it out in my hand, albeit with bad grace. But, for the first time in centuries, no pigeon fell for the corn gag. I stood alone in the middle of St. Mark's Square, holding out my hand dripping with kernels of golden corn, and was openly and deliberately snubbed. One or two of the creatures walked up to within about ten feet of me and gave me a nasty look, but not one gave my corn a tumble. So I decided the hell with them and ate the corn myself.

Now this sort of thing must be the result of a very definite boycott, or, in its more aggressive stage, an anti-Benchley campaign. Left to myself, I would have only the very friendliest feelings for pigeons (it is too late now, but I might once have been won over). But having been put on my mettle, there is nothing that I can do now but fight back. Whatever I may be, I am not yellow.

I tried to be as nice as I could

Here is my plan. I know that I am alone in this fight, for most people like pigeons, or, at any rate, are not antagonized by them. But single-handed I will take up the cudgels, and I hope that, when they grow up, my boys will carry on the battle on every cornice and every campus in the land.

Whenever I meet a pigeon, whether it be on my own window sill or walking across a public park, I will stop still and place my hands on my hips and wait. If the pigeon wants to make the first move and attack me, I will definitely strike back, even to the extent of hitting it with my open palm and knocking it senseless (not a very difficult feat, I should think, as they seem to have very little sense).

If they prefer to fight it out by innuendo and sneering, I will fight it out by innuendo and sneering. I have worked up a noise which I can make in my throat which is just as unpleasant sounding as theirs. I will even take advantage of my God-given power of speech and will say, "Well, what do you want to make of it, you waddling, cooing so-and-sos?" I will glare at them just as they glare at me, and if they come within reach of my foot, so help me, St. Francis, I will kick at them. *And* the next pigeon that strolls in across my window ledge when I am just awakening, I will catch with an especially prepared trap and will drag into my room, there to punch the living daylights out of him.

I know that this sounds very cruel and very much as if I were an animal hater. As a matter of fact, I am such a friend of animals in general that I am practically penniless. I have been known to take in dogs who were obviously impostors and put them through college. I am a sucker for kittens, even though I know that one day they will grow into cats who will betray and traduce me. I have even been known to pat a tiger cub, which accounts for my writing this article with my left hand.

But as far as pigeons go, I am through. It is a war to the death, and I have a horrible feeling that the pigeons are going to win.

Contributors to this Issue

UNFORTUNATELY the current issue of our magazine has had to be abandoned because of low visibility and an epidemic of printers' nausea, but we felt that our readers would still want to know a little something of the private lives of our contributors. At any rate, here we go:

ELWOOD M. CRINGE, who contributed the article *Is Europe?* is a graduate of Moffard College and, since graduation, has specialized in high tension rope. He is thirty-two years old, wears a collar, and his hobbies are golf, bobbing for apples, and junket.

HAL GARMISCH, author of *How It Feels to Be Underslung*, writes: "I am young, good-looking and would like to meet a girl about my own age who likes to run. I have no hobbies, but I am crazy about kitties."

MEDFORD LAZENBY probably knows more about people, as such, than anyone in the country, unless it is people themselves. He has been all over the world in a balloon-rigged ketch and has a fascinating story to tell. *China Through a Strainer*, in this issue, is not it.

ELIZABETH FEDELLER, after graduation from Ruby College for Near-Sighted Girls, had a good time for herself among the deserted towns of Montana and writes of her experiences in a style which has been compared unfavorably with that of Ernest Hemingway. She is rather unattractive looking.

On our request for information, GIRLIE TENNAFLY wrote us that he is unable to furnish any, owing to a short memory. He contributed the article on *Flanges: Open and Shut*, which is not appearing in this issue.

We will let ESTHER RUBRIC tell about herself: "Strange as it may seem," writes Miss Rubric, "I am not a 'high-brow,' although I write on what are known as 'high-brow' subjects. I am really quite a good sport, and love to play tennis (or 'play at' tennis, as I call it), and am always ready for a good romp. My mother and father were missionaries in Boston, and I was brought up in a strictly family way. We children used to be thought strange by all the other 'kids' in Boston because my brothers had beards and I fell down a lot. But, as far as I can see, we all grew up to be respectable citizens, in a pig's eye. When your magazine accepted my article on *How to Decorate a Mergenthaler Linotype Machine*, I was in the 'seventh heaven.' I copied it, word for word, from Kipling."

DARG GAMM is too well-known to our readers to call for an introduction. He is now at work on his next-but-one novel and is in hiding with the Class of 1915 of Zanzer College, who are preparing for their twentieth reunion in June.

We couldn't get IRVIN S. COBB or CLARENCE BUDINGTON KELLAND to answer our request for manuscripts.

No Pullmans, Please!

I SUPPOSE that it is just looking for trouble on my part, but what are they going to do with all the old Pullman cars when the streamliners come into general use? I hope that they don't try to palm one of them off on me.

I simply couldn't take care of an old Pullman. I haven't got the space, in the first place. It's all I can do to find room for my big bag after I have unpacked it. Imagine trying to crowd a Pullman in, too!

Neither have I the inclination. I see no reason why I should be made to take over something that I really don't want, do you? And yet I have a horrible premonition that some day soon they are going to drag around a car named "Gleeber's Falls" or "Angostura" and ask me to give it a home.

The first time I read about the advent of the new type of sleeping car, I said, quick as a flash, "Here it comes! I get the old ones!" They've got to do *some*thing with all those "Laburnums" and "Latvias." And I always seem to get things like that. "Give it to old Bob," people say, when they are tearing down their houses. "It will be just right for his room!"

I am to blame, in a way, for a long time ago I set out to furnish a room in a sort of knick-knack fashion. I even invited contributions from my friends. But what I meant was contributions that I could use. I didn't mean that I was starting a whaling museum or that I planned to build more rooms. I had more or less in mind a mid-Victorian study of the "what-not" variety. Well, I got my "what-nots."

It began with little articles to line up on top of a bookcase, miniature geese, little men with baskets, shells with eggs in them and broken stags. I also was not averse to hanging oddments on the walls. My friends entered into the spirit of this admirably. Every one had fun but the lady who dusted.

Then people began looking around town for heavier gifts. It got to be a game. Trucks began arriving with old busts of Sir Walter Scott, four-foot statues of men whose shirtfronts lit up when attached to an electric connection, stuffed owls and fox terriers that had lain too long at the taxidermist's. This phase ended with the gift of a small two-headed calf in a moderate state of preservation.

From then on the slogan became "Send it to Benchley!" Wrecking concerns were pressed into service, and chipped cornices from the old Post Office, detached flights of stairs, hitching posts and railings began pouring in. Every day was like Christmas in Pompeii. The overflow went into the bedroom and I started sleeping under an old spinet, covered over with a set of bead curtains which had been brought to me from a bordello in Marseille.

The friendly mood in which the game started changed gradually to one of persecution. The idea began to embarrass me and to make it impossible for me to move about. On several occasions it became a matter for the police, and once the Missing Persons Bureau took a hand in it and searched my room for a runaway college girl. They found nothing, however, but three Chinese laborers who had been smuggled into the country and delivered to my place in a caterer's wagon.

So perhaps I have a right to be worried about those out-of-date Pullmans. I have had stranger things foisted on me. I think that this time I will put my foot down. At the first sign of a Pullman being brought up the stairs I will bolt the door, leaving my friends to their own devices with it. I don't want any more truck in this room, much less a full-blown Pullman, and, ungracious as it may seem, I don't intend to have it.

Mysteries from the Sky

I THINK that I am violating no confidence when I say that Nature holds many mysteries which we humans have not fathomed as yet. Some of them may not even be worth fathoming.

What, for instance, do we know of the many strange things which fall from the sky? I don't mean old overshoes and snaffle-bits, which everybody knows about, but those large masses of nergium and philutium which are always dropping out of nowhere onto Kansas and Oklahoma.

They have never been actually identified as nergium and philutium, because I made those names up, but they certainly are some form of calci-colocate ($Cb_2Ci_2M_3$) or Sneeden's Disease. When subjected to a white heat this substance explodes with a loud bang (Ba_2Ng_2) and is never seen or heard of again. And see if I care!

The most famous deposit of this kind occurred near Dormant, Kansas, in 1846. Following a heavy thunderstorm during the night workers in the fields were more surprised than pleased to find that a whole new State had been added to the Union right on top of their wheat, apparently having dropped from the sky. This made it necessary to elect two more Senators to go to Congress and to have one more State fair each year. All this resulted in the Civil War.

The so-called "rain of frogs" in North Dakota in 1859 was another mix-up. Enoch Kaffer, a farmer, was walking along the road near Oyster Bed one day when he was hit on the head by a falling frog. On looking up to see where it had come from, he was hit over the eye with another frog. Deciding that it was time to get out of there, he started to run, but soon found himself pelted on all sides by a rain of frogs, all in an ugly humor.

On reaching home Kaffer told his experience to his wife, who divorced him. That she had a certain amount of right on her side was shown by subsequent investigations which disclosed no sign of any frogs or even frog footprints in the neighborhood of where he had been. Kaffer himself, however, stoutly maintained his innocence and finally went insane.

Another somewhat similar case is recorded in what was then Indian Territory. An Indian by the name of Ferguson was missing from his home for two days, and on finally returning said that he had been delayed by being hit by a falling meteorite which had come flaming through the sky at him as he was crossing a field.

As proof of his story he displayed an ugly cut across the bridge of his nose and a black eye. There was also a cigarette burn on the forefinger and a corresponding one on the middle finger of his right hand. The odd part about this incident is that the next day an enormous meteorite was discovered half-buried in the field he had crossed, where it is to be seen to this day. The Indian, however, disappeared.

These are only a few of the mysteries which Nature has up her sleeve to drop down on us if we get fresh and try to stand up straight. In the face of them we ought either to be very humble or else get good and sore.

Isn't It Remarkable?

ON A recent page of colored reproductions of tomb-paintings and assorted excavations from holes in ancient Egypt there appears a picture of a goose with the following rather condescending caption:

Remarkably Accurate and Artistic Painting of a Goose from Pharaoh Akhenaten's Palace, Drawn 3300 Years Ago.

What I want to know is—why the "remarkable"? Why is it any more remarkable that someone drew a goose accurately 3300 years ago than that someone should do it today? Why should we be surprised that the people who built the Pyramids could also draw a goose so that it looked like a goose?

As a matter of fact, the goose in this particular picture looks more like a goose than that of many a modern master. Just what we think we are, in this age of bad drawing, to call an Egyptian painting "remarkably accurate and artistic" I don't know, but we have got to get over this feeling that anything that was done correctly in 1000 B. C. was a phenomenon. I say that we have got to get over it, but I don't know how.

People managed to drag along in ancient Egypt, from all that we can gather. They may not have known about chocolate malted milk and opera hats, but, what with one thing and another, they got by. And, presumably, every once in a while somebody felt like drawing a goose. And why not? Is there something exclusively twentieth-century about the art of goose-drawing?

We are constantly being surprised that people did things well before we were born. We are constantly remarking on the fact that things are done well by people other than ourselves. "The Japanese are a remarkable little people," we say, as if we were doing them

a favor. "He is an Arab, but you ought to hear him play the zither."
Why "but"?

Another thing, possibly not exactly in this connection, but in line
with our amazement at obvious things. People are always saying,
"My grandfather is eighty-two and interested in everything. Reads
the paper every day and follows everything."

Why shouldn't he be interested in everything at eighty-two?
Why shouldn't he be *especially* interested in everything at eighty-
two? What is there so remarkable about his reading the paper every
day and being conversant on all topics? If he isn't interested in
everything at eighty-two when is he going to be? (I seem to be
asking an awful lot of questions. Don't bother answering them,
please.)

It is probably this naïve surprise at things that keeps us going.
If we took it for granted that the ancient Egyptians could draw a
goose accurately, or that Eskimos could sing bass, or that Grandpa
should be interested in everything at eighty-two, there wouldn't
be anything for us to hang our own superiority on.

And if we couldn't find something to hang our own superiority
on we should be sunk. We should be just like the ancient Egyptians,
or the Eskimos, or Grandpa.

Do Dreams Go by Opposites?

TWO or three fishermen have written in asking this department if it believes that dreams go by opposites. I am still trying to tie up their question in some way with fishing, but I can't quite figure it out. I don't even know that they were fishermen.

However, I think that it is safe to say that dreams *do* go by opposites; otherwise, how do you explain the steamboat?

I have a record of a dream in my files which ought to put an end to any doubt on the matter. It was a dream reported to our Dream Clinic by a man who has since settled down and become the father of a family, and, therefore, does not want his name used. (He isn't ashamed of the dream, but the family didn't pan out very well.)

According to this man (and there is no reason to doubt his word), he had been worried about business matters for several days preceding the dream, and had decided to just get into bed and pull the covers up around his head. This was around noon.

He had no intention of going to sleep, but, what with one thing and another, he dozed off, and before he could stop himself was dreaming at a great rate. In his dream he was in a large, brilliantly lighted public dining-room with all his clothes on. This, in itself, marks the dream as unusual. He not only had his clothes on, but he was *not* running for a train. This, he thought, was funny, but paid little attention to it at the time.

It seemed to him that he sat fully clothed in this public dining-room, not running for a train—in fact, not doing anything at all for quite a long time, although probably it was for the fraction of a second, really. Then he woke up in a cold sweat. He was so unnerved by this dream that he took off all his clothes, *went* to a public dining-room and *ran* for a train, which was just at that moment leaving the cloak room. He missed it.

Now, here was a dream which worked out in exactly the opposite fashion in his waking experience. This we will call Case A. The man's name will be furnished on request. It was George A. Lomasney.

Case B is almost as strange and equally impressive in proving that dreams go by opposites. A woman was the dreamer in this case (though, aren't we all?) and she is very anxious to give her name, and to waltz with someone, if possible.

In her dream she was in a greenhouse full of exotic plants, which was on a sort of funicular, running up and down the side of a mountain. The mountain was just a shade narrower than the greenhouse, so the ends of the greenhouse jutted out on either side, making it difficult for automobile traffic, which was very heavy at this point, to pass.

In the greenhouse with the woman was a deaf elk which had got in somehow through a hole in the screen. The elk couldn't hear a word that the woman was saying, so she just went on with her tapestry-weaving, as she had to have the job finished before the greenhouse got to the top of the mountain on its 11 o'clock trip. (That is, 11 o'clock from the foot of East Fourteenth street, where it started.)

Now, the amazing thing about all this was that exactly the opposite thing happened to the woman the very next day. She was *not* in a funicular greenhouse; she did *not* see a deaf elk, and she knew nothing about tapestry-weaving.

Laugh that off, Mr. Scientist!

News from Home

SOMETIME, maybe sooner than I think, I am going to stop writing little pieces for the newspapers and retire to my llama farm in Peru. I dread it, in a way, because I was once badly chased by a llama. At any rate, that was my story at the time.

Aside from this dread of llamas, and a slight vagueness concerning the location of Peru, I am going to resent getting out of touch with the Homeland. I am going to want to subscribe to newspapers from the States, if only to keep an eye on the "Help Wanted" ads. I don't even know whether there is any money in llamas or not.

And here comes the sad part. After years of scanning newspapers for strange items on which to vent my wrath I have incapacitated myself for regular newspaper reading. I see nothing on the printed page but what might be called the *curiosa*. The long stories, concerning international financial scandals and State Department crises, escape me. I am a slave to the oddments in the news. What am I going to do when I get to Peru and just want to glance over a newspaper to see what the home folks are doing?

Suppose, for example, I had been in Peru today, and coming in from a llama-inventory had been greeted by my hibisca boy with the news that a bundle of papers had arrived from the States. I had settled myself, with a glass of llamanade, for a quiet evening with the latest dispatches from New York, Chicago and the Pacific Coast. I might even have a native girl to strum a guitar for me as I read.

What am I able to discover? What are the only items in today's news that catch my eye?

(A) Zebe, the infant African zebra born in the Fleishacker Zoo in San Francisco, is a "100-striper." Ordinary zebras have but 90 to 95 discernible stripes from nose to tail-tip, but Zebe has 100.

I had settled myself for a quiet evening with the latest dispatches

(*B*) John H. Happel, on the witness stand in Los Angeles for killing his wife last November, said, "She was too fresh, and I just taught her a lesson."

(*C*) Herman Strutter, of Perry, N. Y., says that a beaver gnawed off his wooden leg while he was asleep, and shows teeth-marks to doubters.

(*D*) Fire Chief John T. Oliver, of the Marblehead (Mass.), Fire Department, resigned from service because he cannot get his 150 call-firemen to attend fires. They take Sundays and holidays off without notifying him, and he cannot fine them the customary $1.00 in such cases, as they are Civil Service employes and are immune from such fines.

(*E*) Japanese fishermen train cormorants to work for them. The birds dive for fish and catch them at the rate of 100 per hour, bring them to the boat and deliver them, frequently under protest, to their trainers.

(*F*) People in Binghamton, N. Y., looked out of their windows and found the ground covered with snowballs, rolling along without visible means of propulsion, and increasing in size as they rolled. The Weather Bureau explained that this was a phenomenon, rare in the East, resulting from a peculiar combination of soft, wet snow, a high wind and a temperature of about 36 degrees.

What kind of news is that for a homesick man to read in a batch of papers fresh off the boat? And yet they are the only items that caught my eye in the day's dispatches. I have been trafficking so long in this type of stuff that I can see nothing else.

I sometimes wonder if it has all been worth while. I sometimes even wonder if I shall ever go to Peru.

The Children's Hour

I DON'T want to be an alarmist, but I think that the Younger Generation is up to something. I think that there is a plot on foot.

I base my apprehension on nothing more definite than the fact that they are always coming in and going out of the house, without any apparent reason. When they are indoors, they sit for a while without doing anything much. Then they suddenly decide to go out again for a while. Then they come in again. In and out—in and out.

Of course, this applies only to Saturdays and vacation time. I don't know what they do at school but presumably they stay put. They can't just wander in and out of classrooms and school buildings as they do at home.

This foot-loose tendency is most noticeable during spring and summer vacations. Let us say that two or three of them leave the house right after breakfast. In answer to the question: "Where are you going this morning?" they say, "Oh, just around."

In half an hour they are back, with possibly three others. They don't talk. They just come in. Sometimes they sit down in various attitudes of abandon. Sometimes they walk slowly around the room. Sometimes they just stand and lean against the wall. Then, after perhaps five minutes of this, they start outdoors again in a body.

This goes on all day. Each time they return, they have two or three new ones with them, but there seems to be no reason why fresh members have come. They don't act as if it made any difference to them *where* they were. They do not even appear to enjoy each other's company very much. They are very quiet about it all, except for slamming the screen door. It is ominous.

All that I can figure out is that they are plotting a revolution. When they go out, I think that they work secretly on laying cement foundations for gun-bases, or even lay mines. Then they come indoors to look around and see if the old folks have begun to suspect anything yet. Assuring themselves that all is well, some-one gives the signal and they are off again to their plotting.

I don't think that anyone but mothers and fathers of adolescent families will know what I mean, but I have spoken to several parents about it and they have all noticed the same thing. There is a restlessness abroad among the Young Folk, but it is a quiet, shambling sort of restlessness which presages a sudden bugle call some day, at which they will all spring into action.

All that I ask is that they let me in on their plans. It would help if they were noisier about the thing and did a little yelling now and then. It's this constant coming in and going out of the house like slippered Moslems fomenting a revolt that gets me down.

All I hope is that they start something—anything—before I am too old to run.

Back to Mozart

SOME time ago, in this space, I attempted to cheer up others, who felt Life closing in on them with nothing accomplished, by writing that Napoleon never saw a steamboat until he was fifty-eight and that Mozart never wrote a bar of music until he was ninety.

A very pleasant lady correspondent has written in to ask me if there has not been some mistake. She has always understood, she says, that Mozart died at the age of thirty-five and that he began to compose at the age of four.

I don't believe that we can be thinking of the same Mozart. The Mozart that I meant was Arthur Mozart, who lived at 138th street until he died, in 1926, at the age of ninety-three.

This Mozart that I referred to was a journeyman whistler, who went about from place to place, giving bird calls and just plain whistles. He was a short, dark man, with a mustache in which everyone claimed he carried a bird. After his death this was proven to be a canard. (This is not a pun on the French word for "duck." He didn't carry a duck there, either.)

Up until the age of ninety, however, Arthur had never composed anything for himself to whistle, always relying on the well-known bird calls and popular airs of the day. That is, they were popular until Arthur gave them a workout.

But just before his ninetieth birthday, the Mozarts got together and decided that "Grampa Arthur," as they called him, ought to unbelt with a little something for posterity. So they gave him a pitch-pipe, and stood around waiting for him to swallow it.

But, instead of swallowing it, Mozart went into the next room and worked up a fairly hot number for woodwinds and brasses, called *Opus No. 1*, because it was such hard work. It was a steal from Debussy, but the cadenzas were Mozart's. He also went into the coda right after the first six bars.

This Arthur Mozart is the one I had reference to in my article. The Mozart that my correspondent refers to was evidently a prodigy of some sort, if he composed at the age of four. He also must have worked on one of the night-club pianos like Harry Richman's. Maybe it was Harry Richman!

All this shows what comes of not giving initials when you mention a name in print. But how was I to know that there were two Mozarts who were composers?

Spy Scares

WHENEVER you read about the unearthing of a big international spy ring in some European country, you may be pretty sure that the government of that country has been naughty and is trying to give the people something else to think about for a minute or two.

"O-o-oh! Look over there!" the government is saying. "See dat dreat bid spy!" And, while the public is looking, it tries to cram a bunch of incriminating letters and contracts down the drain pipe. It's an old gag, but a good one.

Of course, every government has spies in every other country, and every other country knows about them. It is merely a form of international courtesy, like exchange professors. So long as the spies don't actually block traffic or blow up the newer buildings, they can snap their cameras and rattle their blueprints to their hearts' content. In fact, they give a rather nice cosmopolitan air to the streets.

Now, if a government can get out of a jam simply by crying "Spy-ring! Spy-ring!" why can't individuals work the same strategy? There must be some spies in your own neighborhood that you could use in a pinch.

Let us say that you are due home for dinner at seven. What with one thing and that other thing, you are delayed until possibly one-thirty in the morning, just too late for the roast lamb. You don't want any dessert.

"What did you think we were having tonight—a watch night service?" says the Little Woman, barely opening her mouth to say it.

Don't you say a word. Just look serious.

"I suppose they were rebuilding the office and you got walled up in the masonry," she continues. "You were lucky to get out at all, I suppose."

Now is the time. "This is not the occasion for flippancy," you say. "Our country, your country and my country, is in peril."

This is a new one, and it has her stopped for a minute.

"What do you know about your friend Mrs. Geefer?" you continue, taking out your notebook and pencil.

"I know that she thinks that a two-spades bid means that she is to pass," comes the answer, without thinking. Then the eyes narrow. "What's this Mrs. Geefer element being injected into the conversation? What has she got to do with a half-past-one dinner?"

"Mrs. Geefer is right now being kept under surveillance as a member of an international spy ring. She, and a man named Wilcensic, are agents for the Soviet government."

"What did they do—make you head of the Secret Service? Is that what kept you so late?"

"We won't discuss my part in this affair. I am under sealed orders. The question is—do you care enough about your country's welfare to co-operate in tracking down this spy ring?"

"You can go out into the kitchen and track down a coffee ring if you want something to eat; that's what *you* can track down. Or did they have food, too, at that brewers' track meet you were at?"

Things can go on like this until breakfast time or you can go out and make believe round up Mrs. Geefer yourself for your country. But the chances are that you will get nowhere with your spy scare. You have to have a bigger territory to work in.

That's one of the advantages of being a government instead of just a private liar.

Artist's Model Succumbs!

A STRANGE case has just come to light involving an artist's model in London, who, to date, has not been able to drive one man mad. She hasn't been able even to drive one man to drink. The police are working on it now.

Dorine LaBoeuf was the only daughter of a poor laborer, and was born in a thatched hut, or hutched thatch, in Normandy. Or hatched thutch.

She was noted for her beauty, even in those days—which will give you some idea. Later she married and settled down in Lyons and never went to London at all. So, you will see, we have started off with the wrong girl. She has nothing to do with the story at all, and I don't know what I was thinking of.

The girl *I* mean was born in Kansas City, but was fatter than Dorine LaBoeuf as a child. She was so fat that they despaired of her life at one time, but when she got to London (*how* she got to London is another story—and a better one) she calmed down a little and got a job as an artist's model. She posed for automobile accessories and moccasins.

Now, everyone knows that an artist's model is quite likely to drive men mad, and end up as a dope feind. (*i* before *e*, except after *c*.) This girl, in spite of her great beauty and collection of time-tables, couldn't even manage to end up as a dope fiend. (The proofreader caught it this time.)

I hope I'm not boring you.

She posed and she posed and she posed, but nobody ever even threatened to kill *her*, much less himself. It was the slowest year for suicides that London had had since Chelsea became the Greenwich Village of America.

We are now getting around slowly to the unpleasant fact that this girl was not so hot-looking. *She* thought she was, and the man at the desk thought she was fair (that's the way he phrased it: "She's fair"), but that was where it ended.

I don't know why I'm telling you all this, except that you asked me to tell you the story of the London model who didn't drive men mad. You don't remember that, do you? I suppose that next you'll be saying that you aren't even reading this.

Well, all fooling aside now! This girl is actually in London at this minute, and I can prove it. And do you know who she is? She is the wife of a very prominent man, who offered me a great deal of money (three dollars) if I would keep it out of the papers.

But once a newspaperman, always a newspaperman, and a good "story" (newspaper jargon for "cub") is more important than all the money in the world. That's why newspapermen are so poorly paid.

Ladies Wild

IN THE exclusive set (no diphtheria cases allowed) in which I travel, I am known as a heel in the matter of parlor games. I will drink with them, wrassle with them and, now and again, leer at the ladies, but when they bring out the bundles of pencils and the pads of paper and start putting down all the things they can think of beginning with "W," or enumerating each other's bad qualities on a scale of 100 (no hard-feeling results, mind you—just life-long enmity), I tip-toe noisily out of the room and say, "The hell with you."

For this reason, I am not usually included in any little games that may be planned in advance. If they foresee an evening of "Consequences" coming over them, they whisper "Get Benchley out of the house. Get him a horse to ride, or some beads to string—anything to get him out of the way." For, I forgot to tell you, not only am I a non-participant in parlor games, but I am a militant non-participant. I heckle from the sidelines. I throw stones and spit at the players. Hence the nickname "Sweet Old Bob," or sometimes just the initials.

One night last summer, I detected, from the general stir among the ladies and more effete gents, that I was being eased out of the house. This meant that the gaming was about to begin. But instead of the usual clatter of pencils among the *croupiers*, I saw someone sneaking in with a tray of poker chips. They almost had me out the door when I discovered what was up.

"Well, so long, Bob," they said. "Good bowling to you."

"What's this?" I came back into the room. "Are those poker chips?"

"Sure, they're poker chips. It's all right to play poker, isn't it? The reform administration's gone out."

I assumed a hurt air. In fact, I didn't have to assume it. I was hurt.

"I don't suppose I'm good enough to play poker with you," I said. "All I'm good enough for is to furnish the liquor and the dancing girls."

"Why, we thought you didn't like games. You always act like such a goddamned heel whenever a game is suggested."

"My dear people," I said, trying to be calm, "there are games and games. 'Twenty Questions' is one game, if you will, but poker—why, poker is a man's game. It's my dish. I'm an old newspaperman, you know. Poker is the breath of life to a newspaperman." (As a matter of fact, I never played poker once when I was on a newspaper, and was never allowed to do more than kibitz at the Thanatopsis games of Broun, Adams, Kaufman, and that bunch, but poker is still my favorite game in a small way, or at least it *was*.)

Then there was a great scrambling to get me a chair, and sell me chips. "Old Bob's going to play!" was the cry. "Old Bob likes poker!" People came in from the next room to see what the commotion was, and one woman said that, if I was going to play, she had a headache. (I had ruined a game of "Who Am I?" for her once by blowing out a fuse from the coat-closet.)

As for me, I acted the part to the hilt. I took off my coat, unbuttoned my vest so that just the watch-chain connected it, lighted my pipe, and kept my hat on the back of my head.

"This is the real poker costume," I said. "The way we used to play it down on the old Trib. There ought to be a City News ticker over in the corner to make it seem like home."

"I'm afraid he's going to be too good for us," said one of the more timid ladies. "We play for very small stakes, you know."

"The money doesn't matter," I laughed. "It's the game. And anyway," I added modestly, "I haven't played for a long time. You'll probably take me good." (I wish now that I had made book on that prediction.)

It was to be Dealer's Choice, which should have given me a tip-off right there, with three women at the table, one the dealer.

"This is the real poker costume," I said

"This," she announced, looking up into space as if for inspiration, "is going to be 'Hay Fever.'"

"I beg pardon," I said, leaning forward.

"'Hay Fever,'" explained one of the men. "The girls like it. One card up, two down, the last two up. One-eyed Jacks, sevens, and nines wild. High-low."

"I thought this was going to be poker," I said.

"From then on you play it just like regular poker," said the dealer.

From then on! My God! Just like regular poker!

Having established myself as an old poker-fan, I didn't want to break down and cry at the very start, so I played the hand through. I say I "played" it. I sat looking at my cards, peeking now and then just to throw a bluff that I knew what I was doing. One-eyed Jacks, sevens, and nines wild, I kept saying that to myself, and puffing very hard at my pipe. After a minute of owlish deliberation, I folded.

The next hand was to be "Whistle Up Your Windpipe," another one which the girls had introduced into the group and which the men, weak-kneed sissies that they were, had allowed to become regulation. This was seven-card stud, first and last cards up, deuces, treys, and red-haired Queens wild, high-low-and-medium. I figured out that I had a very nice straight, bet it as I would have bet a straight in the old days, and was beaten to eleven dollars and sixty cents by a royal straight flush. Amid general laughter, I was told that an ordinary straight in these games is worth no more than a pair of sixes in regular poker. A royal straight flush usually wins. Well, it usually won in the old days, too.

By the time the deal came to me, my pipe had gone out and I had taken my hat off. Between clenched teeth I announced, "And this, my frands, is going to be something *you* may not have heard of. This is going to be *old-fashioned draw-poker*, with *nothing* wild." The women had to have it explained to them, and remarked that they didn't see much fun in that. However, the hand was played. Nobody had anything (in comparison to what they had been having in the boom days), and nobody bet. The hand was over in a minute and a half, amid terrific silence.

That was the chief horror of this epidemic of "Whistle Up Your Windpipe," "Beezy-Weezy," and "Mice Afloat." It made old-fashioned stud seem tame, even to me. Every time it came to me, I elected the old game, just out of spite, but nobody's heart was in it. I became the spoil-sport of the party again, and once or twice I caught them trying to slip the deal past me, as if by mistake. Even a round of jackpots netted nothing in the way of excitement, and even when I won one on a full house, there was no savour to the victory, as I had to explain to the women what a full house was. They thought that I was making up my own rules. Nothing as small as a full house had ever been seen in that game.

The Big Newspaper Man was taken for exactly sixty-one dollars and eight cents when the game broke up at four A.M. Two of the women were the big winners. They had finally got it down to a game where everything was wild but the black nines, and everyone was trying for "low."

From now on I not only walk out on "Twenty Questions" and "Who Am I?" but, when there are ladies present (God *bless* them!), I walk out on poker. And a fine state of affairs it is when an old newspaperman has to walk out on poker!

Cocktail Hour

IT IS all very well for New York and other large cities to go cosmopolitan in their new-found freedom, and to sit at sidewalk cafes in the springtime, sipping their *apéritifs* and *demi-blondes*. That was to be expected with Repeal.

But I must, merely as a passer-by, ask ladies who run tea-rooms not to put signs reading "Cocktail Hour" in the .windows of their tea-shops at two o'clock in the afternoon. Two P.M. is *not* "cocktail hour," no matter how you look at it. The very suggestion is terrifying.

How would you like to be walking along a perfectly normal street, with the hot sun beating down on your new straw hat and a rather heavy corned-beef-hash-with-poached-egg from luncheon keeping step with you, and suddenly to look up and see, pasted on the window of a tea-shop, a sign reading "Cocktail Hour"? I am just putting the question to you as man to man.

If two P.M. is "cocktail hour" in a tea-shop, what do you suppose four-thirty P.M. is? No wonder those shops close early. By nine they would be a shambles.

Do you suppose that the habitues of these otherwise respectable places begin looking at their watches along about one-thirty, just as they are finishing lunch, and say to each other, "Almost cocktail time at the tea-room!" making a little ceremony of it, the way other people do at five-thirty? It can't be very formal, with so many going right back to work afterward. Just regular business clothes, probably. There'll be only the regular bunch there. You know, the cocktail crowd!

Unless a stop is put to this strange perversion of daytime hours, we shall soon be seeing little signs pasted in the window of our favorite breakfast counter reading "Have you had your matutinal absinthe and wheat-cakes?" or "When you hear the signal, the time will be exactly ten forty-five A.M. Time for our Special Chartreuse and Brandy Whooperoo!"

If the tea-rooms conducted by ladies want to celebrate "cocktail hour" at two P.M. that is their own business, of course, but they ought not to be so doggy about it. They should quite frankly come out with signs saying "Pick-Me-Up Hour! Whisky Sours and Bismarck Herring for Receding Heads!" or "Don't try to last the afternoon out in your condition. A Silver Fizz will at least keep your hat on." Don't be so delicate in the matter. Come right out for the Hangover Trade.

But please, *please,* don't ask us older boys to look at signs reading "Cocktail Hour" just as we are going back to work from lunch. We have got men's work in the world to do.

Why We Laugh—or Do We?

(Let's Get This Thing Settled, Mr. Eastman)

IN ORDER to laugh at something, it is necessary (1) to know *what* you are laughing at, (2) to know *why* you are laughing, (3) to ask some people why *they* think you are laughing, (4) to jot down a few notes, (5) to laugh. Even then, the thing may not be cleared up for days.

All laughter is merely a compensatory reflex to take the place of sneezing. What we really want to do is sneeze, but as that is not always possible, we laugh instead. Sometimes we underestimate our powers and laugh and sneeze at the same time. This raises hell all around.

The old phrase "That is nothing to sneeze at" proves my point. What is obviously meant is "That is nothing to *laugh* at." The wonder is that nobody ever thought of this explanation of laughter before, with the evidence staring him in the face like that.*

We sneeze because we are thwarted, discouraged, or devil-may-care. Failing a sneeze, we laugh, *faute de mieux.* Analyze any funny story or comic situation at which we "laugh" and it will be seen that this theory is correct. Incidentally, by the time you have the "humor" analyzed, it will be found that the necessity for laughing has been relieved.

Let us take the well-known joke about the man who put the horse

---

* Schwanzleben, in his work *Humor After Death,* hits on this point indirectly when he says, "All laughter is a muscular rigidity spasmodically relieved by involuntary twitching. It can be induced by the application of electricity as well as by a so-called 'joke.'"

in the bathroom.* Here we have a perfect example of the thought-sneeze process, or, if you will, the sneeze-thought process. The man, obviously an introvert, was motivated by a will-to-dominate-the-bathroom, combined with a desire to be superior to the other boarders. The humor of the situation may *seem* to us to lie in the tag line "I want to be able to say, 'Yes, I know,'" but we laugh at the joke *subconsciously* long before this line comes in. In fact, what we are really laughing (or sneezing) at is the idea of someone's telling us a joke that we have heard before.

Let us suppose that the story was reversed, and that a *horse* had put a *man* into the bathroom. Then our laughter would have been induced by the idea of a landlady's asking a horse a question and the horse's answering—an entirely different form of joke.

The man would then have been left in the bathroom with nothing to do with the story. Likewise, if the man had put the *landlady* into the bathroom, the *horse* would obviously have been *hors de combat* (still another form of joke, playing on the similarity in sound between the word "horse" and the French word "hors," meaning "out of." Give up?).

Any joke, besides making us want to sneeze, must have five cardinal points, and we must check up on these first before giving in:

(1) The joke must be in a language we can understand.

(2) It must be spoken loudly enough for us to hear it, or printed clearly enough for us to read it.

(3) It must be about *something*. You can't just say, "Here's a good joke" and let it go at that. (You *can*, but don't wait for the laugh.)

(4) It must deal with either frustration or accomplishment, inferiority or superiority, sense or nonsense, pleasantness or un-

---

* A man who lived in a boarding house brought a horse home with him one night, led it upstairs, and shut it in the bathroom. The landlady, aroused by the commotion, protested, pointed to the broken balustrade, the torn stair carpet, and the obvious maladjustment of the whole thing, and asked the man, confidentially, just why he had seen fit to shut a horse in the common bathroom. To which the man replied, "In the morning, the boarders, one by one, will go into the bathroom, and will come rushing out, exclaiming, 'There's a *horse* in the bathroom!' I want to be able to say, 'Yes, I know.'"

pleasantness, or, at any rate, with some emotion that can be analyzed, otherwise how do we know when to laugh?

(5) It must begin with the letter "W."*

Now, let us see just how our joke about the horse in the bathroom fulfills these specifications. Using the *Gestalt*, or Rotary-Fric-
tional, method of taking the skin off a joke, we can best illustrate by
making a diagram of it. We have seen that every joke must be in a
language that we can understand and spoken (or written) so clearly
that we can hear it (or see it). Otherwise we have this:

FIG. 1.

Joke which we cannot hear, see, or understand
the words of

You will see in Figure 2 that we go upstairs with the man and the
horse as far as the bathroom. Here we become conscious that it is not
a *true* story, something we may have suspected all along but didn't
want to say anything about. This sudden revelation of *absurdity*

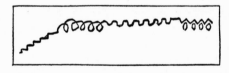

FIG. 2.

The horse-in-bathroom story under ideal conditions

(from the Latin *ab* and *surdus*, meaning "out of deafness") is represented in the diagram by an old-fashioned whirl.

* Gunfy, in his *Laughter Considered as a Joint Disease*, holds that the letter
"W" is not essential to the beginning of a joke, so long as it comes in somewhere before the joke is over. However, tests made on five hundred subjects
in the Harvard School of Applied Laughter, using the Mergenthaler Laugh
Detector, have shown that, unless a joke begins with the letter "W," the
laughter is forced, almost unpleasant at times.

Following the shock of realization that the story is not real, we progress in the diagram to the point where the landlady protests. Here we come to an actual *fact*, or factual *act*. Any landlady in her right mind *would* protest against a horse's being shut in her bathroom. So we have, in the diagram, a return to normal ratiocination, or Crowther's Disease, represented by the wavy line. (Whoo-hoo!)

From then on, it is anybody's joke. The whole thing becomes just ludicrous. This we can show in the diagram by the egg-and-dart design, making it clear that something has definitely gone askew. Personally, I think that what the man *meant* to say was "That's no horse—that's my wife," but that he was inhibited. (Some of these jokes even *I* can't seem to get through my head.)*

---

* A. E. Bassinette, in his pamphlet *What Is Humor—A Joke?*, claims to have discovered a small tropical fly which causes laughter. This fly, according to this authority, was carried from Central America back to Spain by Columbus's men, and spread from there to the rest of Europe, returning to America, on a visit, in 1667, on a man named George Altschuh.

Weather Records

WHATEVER else this year of grace goes down for in the history books, it certainly has gone hog-wild on weather records.

You couldn't walk around the weather bureau for the broken heat and cold records. Sometimes they even broke a record for medium temperature just to keep the ball rolling.

Of course, when you come to think of it, it isn't so much of a stunt to break a weather record. When you really come to think of it, you might go crazy trying not to break one. The wonder is that a record isn't broken every day. (Meteorological note: As a matter of fact, one is broken every day, if you know where to look.)

In the first place, there are 1,460 major records each year, all aching to be broken. There is a heat, cold, rain-precipitation and snowfall record for each day in the year. Then there are the number of years the weather bureau has been keeping records, and the number of weather bureaus—Give up?

There is always a slightly cocky note in the weather bureau's announcement that "yesterday was the hottest May 27th since 1899, on which date the thermometer registered 91 degrees." On reading it you fall over forward in a belated sunstroke.

But they don't say anything about the fact that on May 26th of last year the temperature may have been 92 degrees. They don't say "yesterday was the hottest May 27th since May 26, 1933." Oh, no! They've got to have that record, sleazy as it is.

Why not get right down to really unimportant details and say "3 P.M. yesterday was the hottest overcast 3 P.M. on a May 27th to fall on a Sunday since 1887," or "more snow was tracked into the vestibule of the Weather Bureau yesterday between 9 A.M. and noon than on any previous day in its fifty years of existence." Statements like this would lend variety to weather reports, besides building up the supply of record-breaking days.

It would also be fun for the citizenry itself to send in little personal weather record-breakers, for publication just underneath the official statement:

"At 11:30 last night all heat records for the guest room of Mrs. Albert J. Arnkle at Bellclapper, Long Island, were broken when the thermometer registered a flat 96. The highest previous mark set by this guest room was 94 on the night of July 4, 1911. By an odd coincidence, Mr. George Losh was the guest occupying the room on both nights, so he can vouch for the figures being accurate."

"Yesterday, besides being the hottest Sunday since Friday, June 16th, 1929, found Mr. Larz Swamberg, of 486 Oakroot St., in the oddest assortment of clothing since he last wore diapers on June 11, 1890. He appeared at 10 A.M. wearing a Swiss Alpine coat of some crash material, pyjama pants and a pair of felt slippers. Later in the day he substituted a sleeveless jersey for the crash coat and replaced the slippers with a pair of rope *espadrilles*. At 4 P.M., when the thermometer reached its peak, Mr. Swamberg also established an all-time record for the household by discarding everything but a Panama hat and sitting in the bathtub. Mr. Swamberg feels the heat."

There is no reason why the Weather Bureau should get all the credit for record-breaking weather. We can all do our part.

Home Made Jokes

IN MILWAUKEE last month a man died laughing over one of his own jokes. That's what makes it so tough for us outsiders. We have to fight home competition.

Just get a calm, unpartisan angle on the joke that the man died laughing over. A friend of his, at dinner, said,

"I once shot a rabbit weighing thirty-five pounds."

And the victim-to-be came back with "And I once shot one three pounds heavier." At which crack he laughed so hard that he slipped off his chair to the floor, dead.

Now, what can you do about that, if your job is supposedly to make people laugh? Of course, there is *nothing* to do about the originator of the joke now. That has all been taken care of. But how is one to get a line on what will knock people off their chairs with laughter and what won't?

We might as well face the fact that the whole conversation was pretty comical at that, and that the poor man's return shot was a gem. A rabbit weighing thirty-five pounds has a Gargantuan touch to it, but to have it topped by one weighing thirty-eight pounds (only thirty-eight, mind you! Rabelais would have had it weigh two tons), this is a bit of understatement in exaggeration that marks the deceased as a genius.

But how can one start a conversation in which the other fellow says that he shot a thirty-five-pound rabbit? Things like this can happen only around a dinner table and probably only in Milwaukee.

The only flaw in the make-up of the man who came through with the thirty-eight-pound rabbit was that he laughed at his own joke.

If he had given it with a dead pan he would be alive today and would have been visiting me in New York at my expense.

Of course, he would have had to bring his thirty-five-pound rabbit man along as a stooge, but I'll bet that, between the two of them, I could have got three more subjects for this department.

Men of Harlech!

IT IS too late to do anything about it now, but I sometimes wish that my paternal ancestors had not been Welsh. I can't seem to get the hang of Welsh songs.

In certain moods I love to lapse
into song, loud and fairly clear

In certain moods, I love to lapse into song, loud and fairly clear (clear enough, I am told), and, under such conditions, it is more fitting if one can sing the songs of one's own race. It makes it easier to get to crying.

But I don't know any Welsh songs, and even if I did, I couldn't sing them. We never spoke Welsh at home for some reason, possibly because my maternal stock was Scotch-Irish. We compromised on a rather flat New England dialect, containing practically no romantic implications, and I have inherited no folk-songs from that quarter either.

The Welsh are great singers, I am told, which makes it all the more tantalizing. It would be nice if I could, when the lust for singing comes over me, settle back and go into a Welsh miners' chorus, so that people would nudge each other and whisper, "His people were Welsh, you know. It's practically a folk-song with him!" That's the way to sing, my lads! Sing the songs that are in your blood!

But what am I to do about Welsh songs? Mr. J. B. Morton, in the *London Express*, has reconstructed, or improvised, a Welsh song for us, which will give you some idea of what I am up against in my sentimental, nostalgic moments. I quote from memory and, therefore, I am afraid, sketchily:

WELSH SONG

Wirion digon gul noch noch
With a hey down derry and a ddwpllwdpoch
Ei gsith och deb nam rydidd gam
With a hey derry di-do caethion pam.
Llewsithery fwll ned dinam cnu
Gwerthyr yw brenin myy fansth
Sing hey for the nhaith meddyn ddica gstrth.

(*Note to linotyper:* I'm terribly sorry about putting you to all that trouble. As a matter of fact I left out one line just to make it a little easier for you and, as a result, shall probably be deluged with letters from angry Welshmen. *R. B.*)

But you see how I am fixed when it comes time to lapse into songs of the Home Land. I don't even know any Ulster songs. So the result is that when I feel a spell of loud singing coming on I go German, and no one is more surprised than the Germans.

So far as I know, and so far as anyone can tell who has heard me sing German, I have not a drop of German blood in me. But in a rather pathetic attempt to find some *Heimat* songs that I can sing I give myself, body and soul, to the Rhineland, although, to be

It would be nice if I could go into a Welsh miners'
chorus

specific, I am more inclined toward Austria as my adopted song-country. Austria or Bavaria. I think that really I am more Bavarian than anything when I get to singing.

This sort of thing could make for internationalism, if carried far enough, so I will say no more about it. But the whole thing could have been avoided if the Welsh had written songs that I could sing.

Summer Shirtings

I HOPE that I give no offense in saying that I am not partial to Summer. I perspire on the back of my head, do not shape up well in sports clothes and have hay fever. I also hate Daylight Saving.

But there is one relief that Summer brings which is a boon to me personally. It gives me a three months' respite in my struggle with dress shirts, a struggle of such intensity and long duration that I have been asked to write it up under STRUGGLES for the next edition of the *Encyclopedia Britannica*.

For I am what is known as a "bender" in the dress shirt circles. This corresponds to a "bleeder" in the medical world. One touch, or even so much as one step forward, and my shirt front bends. By the end of an evening I am lucky if it is still buttoned and covering any portion of my chest.

I see all the other boys with their shirt fronts in immaculate flatness after an evening of wrestling, and I sometimes go into a corner and cry softly to myself at my affliction. I have asked my friends what kind of shirt they wear and how they put it on. I have even borrowed theirs for a tryout and induced them to help me into it. And in three minutes it looked like the surface of the Merrimac River when the ice is breaking up.

I hope that nobody, on reading this, will try to recommend for me. I am past experimentation, I have tried shirts that you get into from behind, like an old-fashioned Stevens-Duryea. I have tried shirts that went on over my head (naturally, after I had got my hair brushed), and I once got caught in one of them, like a rat in a trap, and had to have it cut away from my head. I have tried shirts that button like a coat, and shirts that come already

I sometimes go into a corner and cry

buttoned which were laid on me, like armor plate on a battleship, with rivets. They all bend in from three to six minutes.

I have even had shirts made for me with tails so long that I could gather them around my ankles and use them for socks. French shirts, in particular, are built on the "funny-suit" principle, and can be used as an aviator's flying rig if necessary. (I hate to think of an occasion on which it would be necessary, however.)

The only difference that I have noticed in any of them is that, in addition to billowing, some of them have too short bosoms, so that they don't meet my waistcoat. This gives an ignorant appearance, as well as an untidy one.

In the Winter I spend most of an evening trying to pull my coat together over my shirt front until the bending has reached a point too near my neck to be hidden. In the Summer I can wear a good, roomy double-breasted coat which buttons well over the wound, or, still better, I can don a soft shirt and be my old self again.

Hail, Summer! Hail, soft dress shirts.

Word Torture

IN HIS column a short time ago Mr. O. O. McIntyre asked who could tell, without looking it up, the present tense of the verb of which "wrought" is the past participle. That was, let us say, of a Thursday. Today my last fingernail went.

At first I thought that it was so easy that I passed it by. But, somewhere in the back of that shaggy-maned head of mine, a mischievous little voice said, "All right—what is it?"

"What is what?" I asked, stalling.

"You know very well what the question was. What is the present tense of the verb from which the word 'wrought' comes?"

I started out with a rush. "I *wright*," I fairly screamed. Then, a little lower, "I wrught." Then, very low, "I wrouft." Then silence.

From that day until now I have been muttering to myself, "I wright—I wraft—I wronjst. You wruft—he wragst—we wrinjsen." I'll be darned if I'll look it up, and it looks now as if I'll be incarcerated before I get it.

People hear me murmuring and ask me what I am saying.

"I wrujhst," is all that I can say in reply.

"I know," they say, "but what were you *saying* just now?"

"I wringst."

This gets me nowhere.

While I am working on it, however, and just before the boys come to get me to take me to the laughing academy, I will ask Mr. McIntyre if he can help me out on something that has almost the same possibilities for brain seepage. And no fair looking *this* up, either.

What is a man who lives in Flanders and speaks Flemish? A

292

Flem? A Flan? A Floom? (This is a lot easier than "wrought," but it may take attention away from me while I am writhing on the floor.) And, when you think you have got it the easy way, remember there is another name for him, too, one that rhymes with "balloon." I finally looked that one up.

At present I'm working on "wrought."

"I Know of It"

THERE are various forms of the disease, the victim of which is unable to say "No." Some of these forms are more serious than others, and often lead to electrocution or marriage.

But the least excusable of the lot is the inability to say an outright "No" when someone, in the course of a narrative, asks if you know So-and-so, or are acquainted with such-and-such a town. You may have never heard of So-and-so, or of such-and-such a town, but, rather than sound abrupt, or a spoil-sport, you murmur weakly, "I know *of* him," or "I know where it *is*."

This gets you nowhere. It may make you a little easier to talk to for the moment, but sooner or later you will pay.

"No-phobia" reaches its height of futility when someone is giving you directions as to how to reach some place that you really want to reach (I am taking it for granted that others suffer from the same disease as mine).

I ask, "Just how do I get to your place?"

"Well, you know Beeker Drive?"

"Sure." (I do know Beeker Drive, but from there on the directions mean nothing to me.)

"Well, you go up Beeker until you come to Cranshaw. You know Cranshaw, don't you?"

"Oh, sure!" (I can always ask someone.)

"Well, you turn right on Cranshaw and go along until you come to that old cider mill on the right—for about a—oh, a mile and a——"

"Oh, sure, I know about where it is." (If I can't tell an old cider mill when I see one, I am pretty dumb. As it turns out, I'm pretty dumb.)

"Well, you turn right just beyond that until you come to Crawsfoot River Road—you know that, don't you?"

"I know *of* it, yes." (By this time I have decided not even to listen any more. But I still keep nodding, "Yes . . . sure . . .")

The result is, I spend the night crashing up and down the wrong streets and am known as a boor who never arrives on time. And all because I didn't have the guts to say, "I haven't the slightest idea what you are talking about."

The other night I overheard what might be the last word in polite evasion of ignorance. A patrician-looking dame, obviously slumming at a night club, was listening to a story being told by her escort, obviously *not* slumming.

In the line of his narrative, he asked, casually, "You know that old brewery that used to be at the corner of First Ave. and 51st St.?"

And the lady, not wishing to commit herself too much to a shady past and yet not wishing to hold up the story, replied, "I know *of* it."

Possibly that is one reason why some of us are so weak. We don't want to hold up the story.

The Card

FAR be it from me to criticize another man's idea of a good time, unless he lurches into me bodily or sets my coat on fire, but I have often pondered, in an uncritical way, on the possible excitement to be derived from a man's putting on a woman's hat for comedy purposes.

I don't mean a female impersonator in the theatre. I once dressed up as a woman in a college show and had a simply *marvelous* time.

I mean those ordinary brokers and engineers—and writers—who, in the middle of a party at someone's house, or at a table in a night club, are suddenly seized with a protean urge to appear in a woman's hat.

This particular form of transvestitism has nothing to do with effemination. The hat-wearers are usually rather burly he-men, given to golf and Scotch-and-sodas, who, twenty years ago, sneered audibly at wrist watches for men. They are almost always 100 per cent male, sometimes even 108 per cent.

Neither is it entirely a form of exhibitionism. The first big laugh that they get from the ladies when they appear in female headgear may be gratifying, but I have seen them when it almost looked as if they didn't care whether they were seen or not. At a certain stage of elation, they just have to put on a woman's hat, that's all.

Nothing is more dispiriting than to see a man who, at the peak of his romp, has adorned himself with a green hat with a feather in it, and then, as his lift has worn off, has forgotten to take it from his head. He wanders about gloomily, or broods in a corner, wishing he were at home and in bed, oblivious of the fact that the sordid remnant of his masquerade is still perched jauntily over

*At a certain stage of elation, they just have to put on a
woman's hat*

one ear. It is enough to make one swear off drinking forever just to see him.

The other night at one of our more cosmopolitan night clubs a young man sat at a table next to me regaling the ladies of his party with snatches of song and fragments of reminiscence. To cap his efforts he seized his partner's hat, set it smartly over his right eyebrow, and was rewarded with a salvo of applause.

Then the girls came on for the floor show. They were in the customary state of *déshabille* and the young man was ecstatic. "Oh, boy!" he announced. "This is what I've been waiting for!" And he beat on his plate with the little hammer provided for the purpose.

My own attention being temporarily diverted from him, it was some minutes before I looked back to see how he was taking the bacchanal. He was asleep, with the hat still on and his hammer clutched tightly in his chubby fist.

But it was the sleep of a man whose work had been well done. He had put on a woman's hat at some point in the evening.

How Long Can You Live?

READING insurance tables of longevity is not only depressing but confusing. One hardly knows how to make one's plans for the future.

As I understand it, the following are some of the signs by which you can tell whether you are designed for a ripe old age or a quick getaway into the Land of Nod:

If you are taller on one side than the other, and twenty pounds overweight at the age of 45, with a tendency to tip over backward, you will probably not live past 60.

If you are short, fat, 79 years old and irascible to strangers, you can't possibly make 65.

If you are a poet and fat, you have an independent income and should get along great. (Chatterton was an exception to this, although he was not fat and did not have an independent income—unless he was holding out.)

If you are engaged in an occupation which keeps you outdoors, like snake-whip cracking, are taller than the average (6 ft. 9 in.) you should live to a ripe old age, unless you don't hold the snake-whip far enough away from your body.

People whose grandparents were all long-lived and lived with the family, shoot each other before they are 40.

If you have long legs, but short ankles, are over 45 and overweight, but do not seem to let it make any difference in your mode of living, you will probably keep on living until you say, "When."

If you are three feet tall and 20 pounds overweight (30 pounds gross) and bite at people's shins as they pass by, it doesn't make any difference how long you live, you'll never be President.

The best way to be, in order to live to be 100 (for some reason it is taken for granted that you *want* to live to be 100—doubtless something the insurance companies thought up by themselves) is to be about 6 feet tall, to weigh around 175 pounds, avoid diabetes and starches, live out-of-doors (going indoors at night after you have reached 80) and keep your parents and grandparents alive at the point of a pistol, if necessary.

Another good way is to forget about it.

My Face

MERELY as an observer of natural phenomena, I am fascinated by my own personal appearance. This does not mean that I am *pleased* with it, mind you, or that I can even tolerate it. I simply have a morbid interest in it.

Each day I look like someone, or some*thing*, different. I never know what it is going to be until I steal a look in the glass. (Oh, I don't suppose you really could call it stealing. It belongs to me, after all.)

One day I look like Wimpy, the hamburger fancier in the Popeye the Sailor saga. Another day it may be Wallace Beery. And a third day, if I have let my mustache get out of hand, it is Bairnsfather's Old Bill. And not until I peek do I know what the show is going to be.

Some mornings, if I look in the mirror soon enough after getting out of bed, there is no resemblance to any character at all, either in or out of fiction, and I turn quickly to look behind me, convinced that a stranger has spent the night with me and is peering over my shoulder in a sinister fashion, merely to frighten me. On such occasions, the shock of finding that I am actually possessor of the face in the mirror is sufficient to send me scurrying back to bed, completely unnerved.

All this is, of course, very depressing, and I often give off a low moan at the sight of the new day's metamorphosis, but I can't seem to resist the temptation to learn the worst. I even go out of my way to look at myself in store-window mirrors, just to see how long it will take me to recognize myself. If I happen to have on a new hat, or am walking with a limp, I sometimes pass

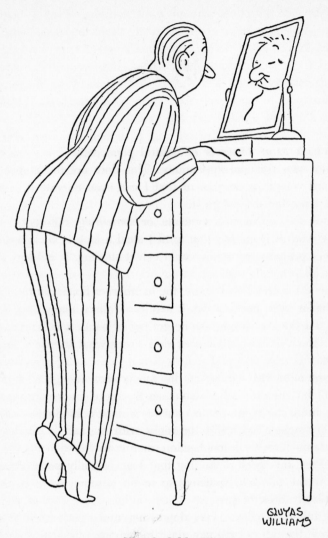

One day I look like Wimpy

right by my reflection without even nodding. Then I begin to think: "You must have given off *some* visual impression into that mirror. You're not a disembodied spirit yet—I hope."

And I go back and look again, and, sure enough, the strange-looking man I thought was walking just ahead of me in the reflection turns out to have been my own image all the time. It makes a fellow stop and think, I can tell you.

This almost masochistic craving to offend my own aesthetic sense by looking at myself and wincing also comes out when snapshots or class photographs are being passed around. The minute someone brings the envelope containing the week's grist of vacation prints from the drug-store developing plant, I can hardly wait to get my hands on them. I try to dissemble my eagerness to examine those in which I myself figure, but there is a greedy look in my eye which must give me away.

The snapshots in which I do not appear are so much dross in my eyes, but I pretend that I am equally interested in them all.

"This is very good of Joe," I say, with a hollow ring to my voice, sneaking a look at the next print to see if I am in it.

Ah! Here, at last, is one in which I show up nicely. By "nicely" I mean "clearly." Try as I will to pass it by casually, my eyes rivet themselves on that corner of the group in which I am standing. And then, when the others have left the room, I surreptitiously go through the nevelope again, just to gaze my fill on the slightly macabre sight of Myself as others see me.

In some pictures I look even worse than I had imagined. On what I call my "good days," I string along pretty close to form. But day in and day out, in mirror or in photograph, there is always that slight shock of surprise which, although unpleasant, lends a tang to the adventure of peeking. I never can quite make it seem possible that this is really Poor Little Me, the Little Me I know so well and yet who frightens me so when face to face.

My only hope is that, in this constant metamorphosis which seems to be going on, a winning number may come up sometime, if only for a day. Just what the final outcome will be, it is hard to predict. I may settle down to a constant, plodding replica of Man-Mountain Dean in my old age, or change my style completely and end up as a series of Bulgarian peasant types. I may just grow old along with Wimpy.

But whatever is in store for me, I shall watch the daily modulations with an impersonal fascination not unmixed with awe at Mother Nature's gift for caricature, and will take the bitter with the sweet and keep a stiff upper lip.

As a matter of fact, my upper lip is pretty fascinating by itself, in a bizarre sort of way.

Easy Tests

ONE of the measures suggested to aid in the reduction of the number of automobile accidents is the prohibition of gasoline sales to intoxicated drivers. Another good way would be the prohibition of liquor sales to intoxicated drivers.

The trouble with the gas prohibition is that the gas-station man is to be the judge of who is intoxicated and who isn't. Short of marrying the driver, how is he going to tell?

How is he going to spot one of those dignified drunks, who pull themselves up to their full height and scowl just before they fall over on their faces? And what about the frolicsome teetotaler who is merely full of animal spirits? (Maybe he shouldn't be sold gas anyway.)

For the aid of the gas-station boys we might list a few infallible symptoms of intoxication in drivers:

1. When the driver is sitting with his back against the instrument board and his feet on the driver's seat.

2. When the person sitting next to the driver gets out at the gas station and says he thinks he'll take a bus the rest of the way.

3. When the people in the back seat are crouched down on the floor with their arms over their heads.

4. When the driver points to the gas-tank and says, "A pound of liver, please."

5. When the driver is in fancy dress with a paper whistle in his mouth which he is blowing constantly.

6. If the driver insists that the gas-station man take the driver's seat while he (the driver), fills the tank, first exchanging hats.

7. When the driver goes into the rest-room and doesn't come out.

8. When there is a clothesline full of washing draped over the radiator hood.

9. When the driver is alone and is stark naked.

10. When there is no driver at all.

Encore

NEW YORK has been in for its annual revival of Gilbert and Sullivan operas. Sometimes I'm glad when they are announced, and sometimes I'm sorry.

I am glad because I happen to like Gilbert and Sullivan. Not *all* of Gilbert and Sullivan, but enough to rate as a fan. And I am sorry because most Gilbert and Sullivan audiences drive me crazy.

A real Gilbert and Sullivan audience has much to recommend it. It is made up of obviously nice people, most of them past middle-age, and many of them unaccustomed to going to the theatre in these days when going to the theatre is such a gamble. They would rather stay at home, and you have a feeling that staying at home with them would be no hardship. They look like people who would talk well at their own dinner-table, and are the only group of theatre-goers who look as if they hadn't put on evening clothes just to go to the theatre. They may not be the latest thing in dinner-clothes, but you have a feeling that these people would have had them on anyway, theatre or no theatre.

But there their attractiveness ceases. Possibly because they do *not* go to the theatre regularly, or possibly because they are just thoughtless (people who dress for dinner at home *can* be thoughtless, too), they do not realize that the fact that they have loved "Dear Little Buttercup" all their lives does not warrant them keeping it being repeated ten times by their applause. A lot of other people are sick of "Dear Little Buttercup," if only because they have heard it in the Civic Center so many times sung by the real-estate agent's wife. Neither does it warrant their humming it to each other, half a beat ahead of the singer.

Furthermore, a great many of the lines in Gilbert's dialogue are *not* funny now, especially after one has heard them for forty years straight. They couldn't be funny to anyone who did not know, and feel strongly about, the topics of the day in which they were written. And yet, to hear your G. & S. fans laugh, you would think that they came like a bolt from the blue and hit the nail right on the head. I am afraid that a lot of these nice people are pretending just a teeny-weeny bit.

But take *Iolanthe!* There's a Gilbert and Sullivan opera that I could hear over and over again three times in the same evening! And don't think I let them get away with a couple of encores to each song, either.

Hey, Waiter!

MR. PETERS usually had his lunch sent in to his office, since it consisted of a glass of milk and perhaps a wisp of chicken. It seemed hardly worth while to check one's coat and hat at a restaurant for just that, to say nothing of unfolding a napkin and telling a waiter about it. And besides, Mr. Peters was still a little self-conscious in restaurants. Something left over from his boyhood still haunted him with the feeling that he had got into the wrong dining room. For, in spite of his long list of murder victims, Mr. Peters was at heart a timid and retiring citizen.

On certain occasions, however, he had to go out to lunch, as, for instance, when some out-of-town representative wanted to talk business. Out-of-town representatives can always talk business better when munching on a roll, and tablecloths are notoriously better scratch pads than office stationery, possibly because they cannot be saved and held against the scratcher. So on this particular day (you have no reason to know on *what* particular day yet, but you will have in just a minute) Mr. Peters found himself headed for the Belvidere grill with Mr. Hertz of the Oldtown Drop Forge and Tool Company, to settle several unimportant things over a curry of lamb.

Mr. Hertz was no stranger to Mr. Peters, but he was not what you would call a "crony." He was a rather disagreeable man, who always wore a stiff white shirt and a bow tie with a batwing collar, having decided early in his business career that an important man should dress in an important manner. In fact, his dress was one of the few ways that Mr. Hertz had of showing that he was an important man. His dress and his attitude toward underlings. In his attitude toward underlings he acted as Mussolini looks. (Come to think of it, when Mussolini is not dressed up as a *carabinieri* or a *bersaglieri* he also seems to be wearing a stiff white shirt and a bat-wing collar. This is probably just a coincidence.)

As they checked their hats and coats, Mr. Hertz began his campaign to show the employees of the establishment that he was not going to be imposed upon.

"Hang that coat somewhere where you can find it, now," he said to the girl. "I don't want to have to stand around all night waiting when I come out." And then he added to Mr. Peters, "You have to watch these girls. They're a dumb bunch."

The girl, who was a friend of Mr. Peters, said she would do her best to put the coat where she could remember it. Mr. Peters slipped her a wink and a quarter in advance. It wouldn't be such a great loss, he thought to himself, if Mr. Hertz *did* lose that coat. It was like something you take along on a camping trip in case the nights get cold.

The head waiter, who was also a friend of Mr. Peters, led them to a table by the window, usually considered a choice location by those who like to see what they are eating, especially if it is blue-fish. But Mr. Hertz took it as a personal affront.

"What are you trying to do—freeze us to death?" he growled at the head waiter.

His tone implied that the man was a member of a gang in conspiracy to get this guy Hertz at any cost. He even went to the window and examined the casing.

"There's a draft here that would blow you out of your chair," he said. "Give us another table!"

"I thought—" began the head waiter.

"Never mind what *you* thought," snapped Mr. Hertz. "It's what *I* think. I'm paying for this lunch."

And he picked out a table that pleased him better and sat down. It happened to be a table whose occupants had just left.

"And get some of this stuff cleared off, too," he said, adding sarcastically, "unless you are just being paid to wear a dress suit in the daytime."

Mr. Peters laughed apologetically, trying to make the head

waiter think that Mr. Hertz was just an old joker. The head waiter laughed, too, but without spirit. Mr. Hertz didn't laugh at all.

"These captains think they own the world," he said to Mr. Peters. "They'd kill you if they could." And Mr. Peters thought that maybe it wasn't a bad idea.

"Now let's see," muttered Mr. Hertz, picking up the menu and turning to the waiter who stood by, "what's here that's fit to eat? Anything?"

"The chicken hash is very nice today, sir," said the waiter.

"You *would* suggest that," snapped Mr. Hertz. "I never sat down at a table that the waiter didn't try to make me take the chicken hash. What do you get, a rakeoff on all the chicken hash you sell?"

The waiter smiled uneasily.

"Good *night!*" said Mr. Hertz. "What a layout! Why don't you have something that people can eat once in a while? What's that you've got on your shirt front? That looks good."

The waiter looked in embarrassed fashion at his shirt front, but couldn't think up a good answer. There was a spot there, but he didn't know what it was. So he said nothing.

"A surly boy, eh?" said Mr. Hertz. "Well, that takes a quarter off your tip." And then, with a knowing nod to Mr. Peters, "*That's* the only language these wops understand."

"Eric is a Swede, aren't you, Eric?" asked Mr. Peters with forced geniality, trying to get the conversation out of its nasty tone.

"Swedes are the worst of all," said Mr. Hertz. "Well, Swede, have you got any mussels?"

"Not this time of year," said the waiter. "The clams are very good, sir."

"O, not this time of year eh? Well, that's the first time I ever knew that mussels had to have a certain time of year. What do they do, just come out in the summer? Why don't you just say that you haven't got 'em? Nobody asked you their habits."

"I'll have some chicken hash," put in Mr. Peters. He really didn't want it, but he wanted to do something to discredit Mr. Hertz.

"Well, you're easier than I am," said Mr. Hertz. "I can't eat any of this truck on here. Broil me a small steak and make it snappy.

And have it well done on the edges, too. Don't bring it to me half cooked."

"Any potatoes, sir?" asked the waiter, in evident relief that the first stage of the ordeal was over.

"I *said* potatoes! Are you deaf? *Hashed in cream potatoes!* Do you want me to write it out for you? And some new peas, too, if you think you can remember all that."

The waiter disappeared, perspiring from every pore.

"These waiters give me a pain in the eye," said Mr. Hertz. "They never listen and then when they get out in the kitchen they match to see what they'll bring you. In my traveling around the country I've found that the only way is to treat 'em rough if you want to get any service at all."

"That's one way," replied Mr. Peters, snapping a piece of roll at the saltcellar.

Mr. Hertz drew out of his pocket a neat packet of letters, from which he extracted one. It proved to be something written in connection with the Oldtown Drop Forge and Tool Company, and it interested Mr. Peters only slightly more than it would interest you if I were to tell you about it. Mr. Peters would not have been interested in the private correspondence of Lucretia Borgia if offered to him by Mr. Hertz. In fact, Mr. Hertz was in a precarious position, if he only knew it.

A detailed résumé of this document consumed perhaps four minutes, at the end of which Mr. Hertz looked around the room and then banged heavily on the table, frightening Mr. Peters out of his rather sinister musings and attracting the attention of the head waiter.

"Come here!" he shouted.

The head waiter came over.

"What are they doing—fishing for that food out in the river? We've been waiting half an hour."

"I'm sorry, sir," said the head waiter. "You ordered something that took a little extra time to prepare. I'll see where it is."

"Extra time! How long does it take you to put a steak on the fire and broil it? It's been three-quarters of an hour now. I could slap a cow to death and get a steak out of it in the time you've taken."

Unfortunately, the waiter put in an appearance at this moment, bearing Mr. Peters' chicken hash.

"Well, here you are!" snarled Mr. Hertz. "What do you do out there in the kitchen—play chess?"

"I'm sorry, sir," said the waiter. "Your steak took a few minutes—"

"*You're* sorry? What do you think *I* am? I'm *hungry!* My God, I've seen rotten service in my time, but never anything that could beat this. Where's my steak?"

"I'm getting it right now, sir," said the waiter.

Mr. Hertz's voice was now raised to a pitch in which most men speak over a long distance telephone.

"Where's the manager?" he bellowed. "I've stood all of this I'm going to!" And he pushed his chair back like a man about to go and look for a manager.

Now, as any friend of Mr. Peters knows, there is one thing which upsets him probably more than anything else, and that is to be made conspicuous in a public place. And Mr. Hertz was rapidly attaining a conspicuousness usually reserved for men with sidewalk fits. As he turned to project his venom more fully on the members of the restaurant staff, Mr. Peters reached over and dropped something in his glass. And Mr. Hertz, to refresh himself after his tirade, immediately obliged by drinking it.

The waiter came rushing up with the steak, but Mr. Peters was alone at the table.

"The gentleman has left the room, Eric," he said. "I don't think he'll be back for his steak. I'll take the check—and here's something for yourself." And, taking one more bite of his chicken hash, Mr. Peters put his napkin on the table and walked out.

As he passed through the anteroom he sensed a commotion in the gentlemen's lavatory, but, as two hospital attendants seemed to be headed in that direction, he decided to go back to his office.

"You can give Mr. Hertz's overcoat to some good horse," he said to the coatroom girl as he passed. "He won't need it where he's going."

Sporting Life in America

TURKISH BATHING

ONE of the more violent forms of exercise indulged in by Americans today is Turkish-bath sitting. This invigorating activity has almost entirely replaced the old-fashioned tree chopping and hay pitching which used to work our fathers up into such a rosy glow and sometimes land them in an early grave. Turkish-bath sitting has the advantage of not only making you perspire freely, but of giving you a chance to get your newspaper read while perspiring. And you can catch cold just as easily after a Turkish bath as you ever could after pitching hay. Easier.

A man seldom thinks of taking Turkish baths until it is too late. It is usually at that time of life when little diamonds of white shirt have begun peeping out between the buttons of his vest, or when those advertisements showing men with a large sector of abdomen disappearing under the influence of a rubber belt have begun to exert a strange fascination for him. Then he remembers about Turkish baths. Or when he wakes up some morning with his head at the foot of the bed and the lights all going and the windows shut. Then, somewhere in the recesses of what used to be his mind, there struggles a puny thought vaguely connected with steam rooms and massage.

"That might do me some good," he thinks, and promptly faints. In both of these cases he is anywhere from one day to one year too late.

However, he takes a chance. He totters to the nearest emporium which features pore-opening devices, checks his watch and what is left of his money, and allows a man to pull off his shoes. Just

314

in time he remembers that he has on the lavender running drawers which someone once sent him as a joke, and quickly dismisses the attendant, finishing disrobing by himself and hiding the lavender running drawers under his coat as he hangs them up. Not that he cares what the attendant thinks, but you know how those guys talk.

Then, coyly wrapping a towel about himself, he patters out into the hot room. A hot room in a Turkish bath is one of the places where American civilization appears at its worst. One wonders, on glancing about at the specimens of manhood reclining on divans or breathing moistly under sheets, if perhaps it wouldn't be better for Nature to send down a cataclysmic earthquake and begin all over again with a new race. It is slightly comforting in a way, however, because no matter how far along you have allowed your figure to get, there are always at least half a dozen figures on view which make yours look like that of a discobolus.

I can imagine no lower point of self-esteem than to find yourself one day the worst-looking exhibit in a Turkish bath. They should keep a pistol handy for just such cases. And you might shoot a couple of others while you are at it. It would save them all that bother of lacing up their shoes again.

In the hot room there isn't much to do. You can read a newspaper, but in a couple of minutes it gets a little soggy and flops over on your face, besides becoming so hot that turning over a page is something of an adventure. If, by any chance, you allow an edge of it to rest on an exposed bit of your anatomy, it isn't a quarter of a second before you have tossed it to the floor and given up reading. Then comes the period of cogitation.

As you sit waiting for your heart to stop beating entirely, you wonder if, after all, this was the thing to do. It occurs to you that a good brisk walk in the open air would have done almost the same thing for you, with the added advantage of respiration. People must die in hot rooms, and you wonder how they would identify you if you were quietly to smother.

The towel around your waist would do no good, as they are

all alike. You regret that you were never tattooed with a ship flying your name and address from the masthead. The only way for them to tell who you were would be for them to wait until everybody else had gone home and find the locker with your clothes in it. Then they would find those lavender drawers. So you decide to brave it out and not to die.

Conversation with your oven mates is no fun either. If you open your mouth you get it full of hot air and you are having trouble enough as it is keeping body and soul together. In the second place, you know that you look too silly to have your ideas carry any weight.

I remember once sitting on a sheet-covered steamer chair with my head swathed in a cold towel to keep my hair from catching on fire and thinking that there was something vaguely familiar about the small patch of face which was peering at me from under a similar turban across the room. As the owner of the face got up to go into the next torture chamber I recognized him as an English captain whom I had last seen in the impressive uniform of those Guards who sport a red coat, black trousers, and an enormous fur busby with a gold strap under the chin. I at once hopped to my feet, and, clutching my towel about me with one hand, extended my other to him.

"Well, fancy seeing you here!" was about all that seemed suitable to say. So we both said it. Then we stood, perspiring freely from under our head cloths, while he told me that he was in New York on some military mission, that the King and Queen were both well, and that England was counting a great deal on the coming Naval Conference to establish an entente with America.

In my turn, I told him that I was sure that America hoped for the same thing and that, to my way of thinking, the only impediments to the success of the conference would be the attitude of France and Italy. He agreed in impeccable English, and said that he had some inside information which he wished that he might divulge, but that, all things considered—

And then, as my mind began to stray ever so slightly, the idea of this gentleman in a sheet and a head towel having any secrets from *any*one struck me as a little humorous. To make things worse, a picture came to my mind's eye of how he would look if he had that busby on right now, with the gold strap under his chin, and I gave up my end of the conversation.

He must have, at the same time, caught a picture of me standing behind a none-too-generous towel, giving it as my opinion that France and Italy were the chief obstacles to international accord in naval matters, for he stood slightly at attention and, bowing formally, said, "Well, I'll be toddling along. See you again, I hope." There was an embarrassed shaking of hands and more formal bowing and he went his way, while I went out and flung myself into the pool.

There is one feature of Turkish bathing which I have not had much experience in, and that is the massage. Being by nature very ticklish, I usually succeed in evading the masseur who follows me about suggesting salt rubs, alcohol slaps, and the other forms of violence. I tell him that I am in a hurry and that I really shouldn't have come at all. He chases me from one room to another, assuring me that it won't take long. Then I plead with him that I have got a bad knee and am afraid of its flying out again. This just spurs him on, because bad knees are his dish.

Once in a while I slip on the wet tiles and he gets me, but I prove to be such a bad patient, once he has me down on the slab, that he passes the whole thing up and gives that irritating slap which means, in the language of the masseur, "All right! Get up— if you can."

Once, while I had my back turned, he played a powerful stream from two high-powered hydraulic hoses on me from clear across the room, which threw me against the wall and dazed me so that I went back into the hot room again instead of getting dressed. I would rather that the masseurs let me alone when I am in a Turkish bath. *I* know what I want better than they do.

As a matter of fact, I don't know why I go to a Turkish bath at all. I emerge into the fresh air outside looking as if I had been boiled with cabbage for five hours, with puffy, bloodshot eyes, waving hair, and the beginnings of a head cold. It is all I can do to get back to my room and go to bed, where I sleep heavily for eleven hours.

And invariably, on weighing myself, I find that I have gained slightly under a pound.

However, it is a part of the American sporting code and we red-blooded one-hundred percenters must carry on the tradition.

Why I Am Pale

ONE of the reasons (in case you give a darn) for that unreason-
able pallor of mine in mid-Summer, is that I can seem to find no
comfortable position in which to lie in the sun. A couple of
minutes on my elbows, a couple of minutes on my back, and then
the cramping sets in and I have to scramble to my feet. And you
can't get very tanned in four minutes.

I see other people, especially women (who must be made of
rubber), taking books to the beach or up on the roof for a whole
day of lolling about in the sun in various attitudes of relaxation,
hardly moving from one position over a period of hours. I have
even tried it myself.

But after arranging myself in what I take, for the moment, to be
a comfortable posture, with vast areas of my skin exposed to the
actinic rays and the book in a shadow so that I do not blind myself,
I find that my elbows are beginning to dig their way into the sand,
or that they are acquiring "sheet-burns" from the mattress; that the
small of my back is sinking in as far as my abdomen will allow, and
that both knees are bending backward, with considerable tugging
at the ligaments.

This is obviously not the way for me to lie. So I roll over on my
back, holding the book up in the air between my eyes and the sun.
I am not even deluding myself by this maneuver. I know that it
won't work for long. So, as soon as paralysis of the arms sets in, I
drop the book on my chest (without having read more than three
consecutive words), thinking that perhaps I may catch a little doze.

But sun shining on closed eyelids (on *my* closed eyelids) soon in-
duces large purple azaleas whirling against a yellow background,

Often I have to be assisted to my feet.

and the sand at the back of my neck starts crawling. (I can be stark naked and still have something at the back of my neck for sand to get in under.) So it is a matter of perhaps a minute and a half before I am over on my stomach again with a grunt, this time with the sand in my lips.

There are several positions in which I may arrange my arms, all of them wrong. Under my head, to keep the sand or mattress out of my mouth; down straight at my sides, or stretched out like a cross; no matter which, they soon develop unmistakable symptoms of arthritis and have to be shifted, also with grunting.

Lying on one hip, with one elbow supporting the head, is no better, as both joints soon start swelling and aching, with every indication of becoming infected, and often I have to be assisted to my feet from this position.

Once on my feet, I try to bask standing up in various postures, but this results only in a sunburn on the top of my forehead and the entire surface of my nose, with occasional painful blisters on the tops of my shoulders. So gradually, trying to look as if I were just ambling aimlessly about, I edge my way toward the clubhouse, where a good comfortable chair and a long, cooling drink soon put an end to all this monkey-business.

I am afraid that I am more the pale type, and should definitely give up trying to look rugged.

Whoa!

PAUL REVERE leaped into his saddle.

"Through every Middlesex village and farm, Bess, old girl!" he whispered in his mare's ear, and they were off.

And, as he rode, the dauntless patriot saw as in a vision (in fact, it *was* a vision) the future of the land to which he was bringing freedom.

He saw a hundred and ten million people, the men in derbies, the women in felt hats with little bows on the top. He saw them pushing one another in and out of trolley-cars on their way to and from work, adding up figures incorrectly all morning and subtracting them incorrectly all afternoon, with time out at 12:30 for frosted chocolates and pimento cheese sandwiches. He saw fifty million of them trying to prevent the other sixty million from doing what they wanted to do, and the sixty million trying to prevent the fifty million from doing what *they* wanted to do. He saw them all paying taxes to a few hundred of their number for running the government very badly. He saw ten million thin children working and ten thousand fat children playing in the warm sands. And now and again he saw five million youths, cheered on by a hundred million elders with fallen arches, marching out to give their arms and legs and lives for Something to Be Determined Later. And over all he saw the Stars and Stripes fluttering in the artificial breeze of an electric fan operated behind the scenes.

So tugging at the reins he yelled, "Whoa, Bess! We're going back to the stable."

NOTE: This piece was first published in 1924, when derision was not confused with disloyalty.

The Menace of Buttered Toast

Maybe I am a fool, but I want to go in for bulb culture. Oh, I know there is no money in it! I know that I shall just get attached to the bulbs when I shall have to give them away to somebody who wants to grow crocuses or tulips or something, and there I shall be, alone in that great, big, lonely old house that my grandfather, the Duke, left me.

This will mean, naturally, that I shall have to give up writing for a living. This God-given talent which I have must be tossed aside like an old mistress (or is it "mattress"?) and my whole energy must be devoted to the creation and nurture of little bulbs which someday will grow into great, big, ugly crocuses, defacing beautiful green lawns all over the country. But I feel the call, and what else is there to do?

Now, since I am resolved to abandon the belles-lettres, the only decent thing is to pass on the secret of word magic to someone else. Having held the reading public spellbound for years with my witchery, I must disclose its secret in order that some poor sucker may take it up and carry on the torch, bringing cheer to the sick and infirm and evasive notes to Brooks Brothers and the Westchester Light and Power Company. I have therefore decided to set down here the magic formula, by means of which I have kept the wolf from getting upstairs into the bedrooms. Here is a sample of a typical Benchley piece:

PERSONALLY, if you ask me (and, so far as I have heard, nobody has asked me yet, but I shall go right ahead just the same) I feel that we, as a nation (and when I say "as a nation" I mean "as a nation") eat too much buttered toast.

Buttered toast is all right, provided neither of my little boys butters it (my two little boys seem to have an idea that butter grows on trees, when everybody knows that it is cut in great sheets by a butter-cutter [butter-cutter, butter-cutter, where have you been?] whence it is shipped to the stamping-room where it is stamped by large blonde ladies with their favorite initials and done up in bundles of twenty-five to be sent to the Tissue Paper Department for wrapping), but I *do* think, and I am sure that *you* would think so, too, if you gave the thing a minute's thought, that there is such a thing as overdoing buttered toast.

In the first place, you order breakfast. (By ordering breakfast, I mean that you get up out of bed, go into the kitchen in your bathrobe, cut three slices of whatever happens to be in the bread box [usually cake], toast it, and butter it yourself.) The words "buttered toast" come naturally in any breakfast order. "Orange juice, two four-minute eggs, *buttered toast*, and coffee." Buttered toast and coffee must be spoken together, otherwise you will hear from the State Department.

Here is where we make our big mistake. If, for once (or even twice), we could say "coffee" without adding "buttered toast," it wouldn't be so bad, but, as my old friend, President James Buchanan, used to say (he was President more as a favor to Mrs. Buchanan than anything else), "You can't eat your cake and eat it too."

It being Christmas Eve (or isn't it? I am all mixed up), we ought not to be very hard on buttered toast, because it was on a Christmas Eve that buttered toast was invented. There were six of us (five counting the Captain) all seated around an old stove (the stove was only eleven years old, but that seemed old in those days, and I guess that it *is* old for a stove), when up spoke Baby Puggy, the daughter of the termagant.

"What's all this?" said Baby Puggy. (All *what* never seemed to occur to her to explain, and if she was satisfied, what the hell are you kicking about?)

"I am in no state to bandy legs about," replied her uncle, who, up to this time, had entirely monopolized the conversation.

"I am getting awfully sick of this sort of thing," said Old Doctor Dalyrimple (they called Dr. Dalyrimple "old" because he was 107, and a very good reason, too, for calling him old), "and I have a good mind to go home and go to bed."

"You are in bed, but you're not at home," piped up little Primrose, a frightful child. "They gave your bed at home away to the Salvation Army."

"It serves them right—I mean the Salvation Army," said Old Doctor Meesky (who had changed his name from Dalyrimple to Meesky since we last saw him). And there, so far as anybody can tell, ends the story of Little Red Mother Hubbard, and, I can almost hear you say, "Who cares?"

But about buttered toast. (Not that I care about buttered toast, and not that I think you care.) If we are to have buttered toast brought to us on our breakfast trays (or is it "drays"?) I would suggest the following ways to get around the unbearable boredom of the thing:

1. Have the Football Rules Committee decree that no buttered toast shall be dunked in coffee which does not fill at least one-half (¾) the cup. This will do away with fumbling.

2. Nobody connected with the theatre, either in a managerial capacity (this includes calling "half-hour" and holding up the left leg of the tenor's trousers while he is stepping into the right leg) or as an actor (God knows what this includes) shall sell tickets to any performance for more than $11.50 over and above the box office price—or, at any rate, shall not boast about it.

3. My two small boys shall not throw paper aeroplanes so that they hit Daddy any nearer his eye than his temple.

4. I forget what this rule is.

5. I remember this, but wish I hadn't.

6. Nobody named "Cheeky" shall be allowed to compete.

This, I think, will fix matters up. And if you find that your buttered toast has become soggy after having lain under a small china Taj Mahal with a hole in the top (maybe the *real* Taj Mahal has a hole in the top, for all I know. It ought to have, to let all those people in and out) then just send for the Captain (you remember the Captain!) and tell your troubles to him (song cue: "Tell Your Troubles to the Captain. He Will Weather or Not").

But I *do* think that something has got to be done about buttered toast. I am not one to cavil (cavil me back to Old Virginny) but I do think, if you ask me (and I don't remember anyone's asking me [oh, I guess I said that in the beginning of this article. Sorry!]) But I do think, personally, that—where was I?

Do I Hear Twenty Thousand?

The scene is in the "Three Æons for Lunch" Club, made up of the shades of those authors who have "done something" while on earth. Shades of advertising men are admitted because advertising is really a form of belles-lettres and, besides, they keep a club going. SHELLEY, SWIFT, TENNYSON, POPE, POE *and others are lounging about the library table preparatory to going in to lunch.*

SHELLEY *picks up a copy of the February issue of* Book News *from the Earth and thumbs its pages over with a badly assumed nonchalance.*

SHELLEY

Ho-hum! I wonder what the news is from the old book-mart.

SWIFT

If you're looking for the article on the Jerome Kern book auction, it's on page 45. Congratulations.

SHELLEY

(*blushing furiously*)

Jerome Kern book auction? Has there been a—oh, yes, you mean the auction of Jerome Kern's library.

(*Turns unerringly to page 45.*)

SWIFT

Don't be naïve. You read all about it yesterday at that very table. You even copied out the various prices the books brought.

SHELLEY

(*trying to read article as if for first time*)

Honestly, Dean, I wasn't reading—that was this article on Richard Halliburton I was reading—well, I'll be darned—honestly, Dean, this is the first time I knew about this—

POE

What's all the blushing about?

(*to the steward*)

Another round of the same, Waters.

TENNYSON

Not for me, Edgar, thanks. Not in the middle of the day.

POE

Another round of the same, Waters. . . . Come on, Bysshe, what's in the magazine you want us to know about?

SWIFT

Oh, they had an auction in New York of Jerome Kern's library and Bysshe was in the Big Money. . . . $68,000, wasn't it, Bysshie?

SHELLEY

Well, that's what it seems to say here. I don't understand it.

(*Puts magazine down where it can easily be reached by the others.*)

POE

(*picking it up*)

What else was sold?

SWIFT

Oh, you didn't come off so badly, Eddie. An old letter of yours about Mrs. Browning was in the money, too.

POE

My God! Nineteen thousand five hundred! Say, that's not so bad, is it—for a letter, I mean?

SWIFT

Not so *bad!* It's *perfect!* You never earned nineteen thousand five hundred in your whole life. I almost tied you, though. Some sucker paid seventeen thousand for a first edition of *Gulliver*.

TENNYSON

(*yawning slightly*)
May I take a look at that, please?

SHELLEY

Your *Maud* drew down something like nine thousand.

SWIFT

I thought you hadn't read the article, Bysshe.

SHELLEY

I just saw that item—it was right there under mine.

TENNYSON

(*reading*)
Oh, well, it was just a portion of the manuscript—probably a couple of stanzas. Anyway, I don't like the idea of auctioning off things like that. It sort of takes some of the beauty away.

SWIFT

What beauty is that?

TENNYSON

You wouldn't understand, Swift.

LAMB

I think Alfy is right. It rather cheapens the thing to have a lot of Americans and things bidding for one's work.

POE

Well, a lot of Americans and things fell pretty heavily for some old hack-work of yours, Charlie. You ran second to Bysshe with a neat $48,000.

LAMB

Who—me? Who—I? Forty-eight thousand? For what?

POE

For a mess of stuff you did for *Hone's Weekly*, it says here.

LAMB

Well, I'll be darned. Why, I dashed that off in about an hour a week. Was always late with my copy, too. Hone used to get crazy.

POE

He'd be crazier if he knew that it was worth forty-eight grand now.

SWIFT

You weren't such a big money-maker as a subject, though, Charlie. That thing Bill Wordsworth did about you after you died got only a measly twenty-five hundred.

LAMB

You mean *Ode to the Memory of Charles Lamb?*

SWIFT

Look—he remembers the title!

LAMB

I never cared very much about that myself. It didn't seem to me that Bill did all he might have done with the material.

WORDSWORTH
(*putting down his newspaper*)
No? Well, I did all I felt like doing. I had to have something in

for the Christmas number and that was all I could think of. They already had a poem scheduled on Milton, which was what I wanted to do.

LAMB

I would say that a poem by you on Milton would be worth about seven dollars now—on the original papyrus.

WORDSWORTH
(*going back to his newspaper*)
Yeah?

SHELLEY

I'm surprised to see that the original manuscript of Keats's "I stood tip-toe upon a little hill" got only $17,000.
(*As the others are talking,* SHELLEY *repeats, a bit louder.*)
I'm surprised to see that the original manuscript of Keats's "I stood tip-toe" got only $17,000.

SWIFT

I heard you the first time, Bysshe. You're surprised that Keats's "I stood tip-toe" got only $17,000.

SHELLEY

Yes. I always rather liked that. Nothing wonderful, of course, but, if my stuff got $68,000, I should think that Keatsie's would get more than $17,000.

SWIFT

That was just a few lines of Keats, Bysshe, and stuck into an ordinary edition of his works. Yours was the whole, uncut volume of *Queen Mab*—a very fine thing purely from the book-making standpoint, I daresay. Anything that's uncut always gets more money.

POE

By the way, whoever owned that originally didn't think a hell of a lot of it, did he? Not to cut the leaves, I mean.

SHELLEY

It was probably one of those copies the publishers sent me for gifts which I never gave away.

SWIFT

Any time *you* ever gave away a book.

SHELLEY

(*ignoring him*)

Say, what do you know about this! It says that *Queen Mab* got the highest price ever paid for a book at an auction. That doesn't seem believable, does it? I mean, *Queen Mab* wasn't my best, by a long shot.

SWIFT

The Gutenberg Bible got more.

SHELLEY

Yes, but I mean literature.

SWIFT

Oh, the Gutenberg Bible was just a stunt of typesetting, I suppose?

SHELLEY

You know very well what I mean, Dean. I think the Bible is a fine book, a great book, but, after all, the big price that it brought was, in a way, due partly to the fact that Gutenberg set it up. You know that.

POE

I've been adding it up, boys, and right here in this room there is represented about $160,000. What about another round?

TENNYSON

Not for me, thanks. Not in the middle of the day.

POE

Well, $160,000 is a lot of money. We can't let it pass un-
noticed . . . Waters! Another round of the same.

WATERS

Yes, sir. . . .
 (*aside to* POE)
Was that last round yours, Mr. Poe?

POE

 (*looking in his wallet*)
Why, er—sure! Sure thing! Just put it on my account, Waters.

WATERS

 (*aside to* POE)
You're posted, Mr. Poe. I'm sorry.

POE

By George, that's right. Well-er— Never mind, then, Waters,
Er— Dean, you don't happen to have—er—

SWIFT

Awfully sorry, old boy. You couldn't have struck me at a worse
time—just charge it to me, Waters—oh, that's right—I forgot. *I'm*
posted right now.
 (LAMB *and* WORDSWORTH, *sensing trouble, have slipped
 quietly away to lunch.*)

SHELLEY

I really ought to pay for the whole thing, you know, winning all
that money. Next time, I shall insist.
 (*A new member who has been looking at the magazines all
 during the conversation approaches the group.*)

NEW MEMBER

I hope you'll pardon me, gentlemen, but I couldn't help over-hearing. I hope you'll allow me to pay for the drinks today. My manuscripts wouldn't bring much in the open market right now, but they didn't do so badly in the original sale . . . Waters, will you please bring another round for us all and charge the whole thing to me—Mr. Hopwood, you know. Mr. Avery Hopwood.

WATERS

Yes, sir. Thank you, Mr. Hopwood.

(*The drinks are brought and the gentlemen carry them in to lunch with them.*)

SHELLEY

(*exiting with the rest*)

I really don't understand it, though, for *Queen Mab* was never one of my favorites.